THE MATCH KING

THE MATCH
KING

IVAR KREUGER, THE FINANCIAL
GENIUS BEHIND A CENTURY OF
WALL STREET SCANDALS

FRANK PARTNOY

PublicAffairs
New York

For Dad

PublicAffairs books are available at special discounts
for bulk purchases in the U.S. by corporations, institutions,
and other organizations. For more information, please contact
the Special Markets Department at the Perseus Books Group,
2300 Chestnut Street, Suite 200, Philadelphia, PA 19103,
call (800) 810-4145, ext. 5000, or e-mail special.markets@perseusbooks.com.

Designed by MacGuru Ltd.
Text set in Sabon MT Pro

A CIP Catalog record for this book is available from the Library of Congress
ISBN: 978-1-58648-743-0

First Edition

10 9 8 7 6 5 4 3 2 1

CONTENTS

"He must surely have been the best-liked crook that ever lived"
Frederic Whyte

"Boiler-room operators, peddlers of stocks in the imaginary Canadian mines, mutual-fund managers whose genius and imagination are unconstrained by integrity, as well as less exotic larcenists, should read about Kreuger. He was the Leonardo of their craft"
John Kenneth Galbraith

"Everything in life is founded on confidence"
Ivar Kreuger

PREFACE

By Thursday, October 24, every market in the world was in freefall: mortgages, stocks, bonds, and even derivatives that were supposed to act as insurance against losses. For most investors, it had been the worst week of the worst month of the worst year in financial history. Housing prices plunged. Lenders froze. Foreign markets crashed. By the time the closing bell rang at the New York Stock Exchange, many nest eggs were empty shells.

Officials at the Exchange announced that the markets would not reopen until Monday. Given the ferocious selling that afternoon, everyone needed some time to calm down. A record number of shares had traded on Thursday, and the market overall was down nearly 20 percent for the month. Prominent bankers and regulators scheduled closed-door meetings to discuss how they might stem the panic.

That evening, one of the world's wealthiest men stood at a precipice. He had been at the center of a seven-year stock market boom, and had pioneered many of the complex new instruments that had come to dominate modern finance. His securities were among the most widely held in the world, and, incredibly, even as the markets collapsed, investments in his companies were holding firm.

As this remarkable man surveyed the turmoil, he worried that investors might lose faith in him, just as they had turned on other companies. The markets were volatile, and when people abandoned an investment, they did so in herds. Voracious short sellers bet against securities, vaporizing their value within days, or even minutes, as bad news spread to worse. One day a firm was a healthy household name, known and respected throughout the world. The next day that firm teetered on the edge of bankruptcy and disrepute. The victims of the crisis already included several prominent institutions.

This was not a time to disappoint anyone. Yet during the next few days, this man would be at risk of disappointing everyone, including his closest advisors. For the first time, his accountants and investment bankers were seriously questioning some of his transactions. They especially wanted to know about the debts of some secret subsidiaries he had incorporated in Luxembourg. These debts, known as "off balance sheet obligations," didn't appear in any of his companies' financial statements, and his advisors wanted proof that there was money to repay them.

The man insisted there was no reason to worry. He promised that during the next few days he would close his biggest deal yet, a massive loan to a government that was hungry for cash. The markets would be closed Friday, and he was scheduled to meet with this country's finance minister on Saturday morning, to finalize the terms of the loan. This deal, he assured them, would erase any doubt about his finances. It would be front-page news in *The New York Times* and the *Wall Street Journal*. The editors at *Time* already were planning to put his face on their upcoming cover and to run a feature story about how he continued to defy the deepening financial crisis.

But in order for his plans to work, the man had to take one massive risk. Given the panic, he could not raise all of the cash needed to fund the loan right away. Instead, he would have to promise to cover the loan himself. Until the markets recovered, his entire fortune would be staked on that one foreign government loan. It was a stunning and unprecedented idea, but he was prepared personally to guarantee one of the largest loans in history.

On the Monday after he signed the loan, in October 1929, the markets crushed his hopes with the largest collapse in financial history, the events that people called the "Great Crash." Instead of soaring, as he had hoped and imagined, stocks fell by 25 percent in two days – days that came to be known as Black Monday and Tuesday.

This man became the symbol of the 1920s excesses. The congressional investigation into his companies led to the securities laws that govern today's markets. His colleagues and advisors were publicly humiliated. His once-prestigious investment bank fell into disgrace and then dissolved in bankruptcy. Regulators, who had welcomed the man as a financial savior of investors and a high priest of business, suddenly claimed he had been the world's greatest swindler.

Today, the need to understand this man's rise and fall is greater than ever. Financial markets leave most of us mystified and helpless. We have so many questions. Where should we put our money? Which investments are safe? Should we trust our brokers? Will the institutions we work for or invest in suddenly implode, like Bear Stearns or Enron or Lehman Brothers or Bernard L. Madoff Securities? When will the next crisis hit, and who will it hurt?

Most people cannot spot financial crises in advance. We buy just before the collapse, when in retrospect we realize that we should have sold. Then we sell at the bottom, when we should have bought. At the same time, we are spellbound by the people who outsmart the markets – Warren Buffett, George Soros, and the hundreds of hedge fund managers who somehow pocket nine- and ten-figure bonuses, even during times of panic and crisis.

What do they see that we do not? One view is that they understand the complexities of modern finance, including the $600 trillion derivatives market, which average investors cannot hope to penetrate. Indeed, the sharp contrast between bewildered masses and financial élite might seem unprecedented today. Even the language of modern finance sounds new: swaps, off balance sheet liabilities, offshore subsidiaries, complex corporate voting structures, hybrid securities, credit default swaps, and collateralized debt obligations.

But in truth not so much of this is new, and the new part is not why the savviest people make so much money. Warren Buffett and George Soros eschew derivatives. Hedge fund managers bet against the Wall Street banks that develop complex products. The best investors – today and yesterday – make money not because they understand abstruse mathematical models, but because they have a deep intuition about the timing and machinations of financial markets. Markets have been complex for a long time, and their ebbs and flows always have depended, not only on intricate disclosures about assets and liabilities, but also on human psychology. That has not changed since the 1920s.

The man whose life forms the basis of this book was a master of investor psychology, and his various schemes – legitimate and not – captured the imagination of shareholders in the 1920s in the same way dot.com internet ventures, auction rate securities, analyst stock tips, and derivatives backed by subprime mortgages have recently. We tend to think of these kinds of investments as scandalous because ultimately they caused so many people to lose money. But each of them also enriched those who understood what the schemes were designed to do, as well as the investors who knew when to buy and when to sell.

For better and worse, this man is the father of today's financial markets. Hedge fund managers and investment bankers employ many of the same techniques he invented. Major companies use the tools he pioneered. America's securities laws were a direct response to his spectacular collapse. He was, in many ways, the original Bernie Madoff.

Modern business leaders follow his footsteps and missteps. The chief executive officer today is an essentially political position, which requires men and women to assume public postures that often conflict with their true personalities. Many corporate executives who confront this tension become infected with hubris, as this man did. Like him, they come to believe they can overcome any skepticism and dig out of any financial hole, no matter how deep. Given the complexity of accounting, they, and their employees, manage reported earnings in a way that diverges from reality. Securities analysts and journalists entice them to repeat optimism so frequently that they come to believe it, just as he did. Some corporate officers become mentally unstable as the pressure mounts, especially at times of calamity. Many have unhappy endings.

Even the 2008 financial crisis followed a trail that was strikingly similar to this man's path: start with massive undisclosed risks on Wall Street; magnify those risks with excess leverage; pyramid that leverage with complex new financial instruments few people understand; pay bankers and accountants small fortunes to look the other way; and then watch helplessly as prices plunge and investors realize their savings are built on sand. The names and details change, but the cycles of mania, panic, and crash do not. Financial history repeats, and our rollercoaster markets trace directly back to one man.

By the end of his story, in 1932, he was on the front page of newspapers and magazines almost every day. His story was the subject of bestselling books and popular film. He was the most eligible bachelor in the world and the most sought after economic and political counselor. He was as comfortable advising President Herbert Hoover as he was dancing with Greta Garbo. He was as influential in art and architecture as he was in industry.

Yet memories of this man have faded, even more than the blue telex printing on the thousands of cables he sent from luxury liners and five-star hotels as he moved among offices in New York and throughout Europe. Many of those telegrams, along with decades of personal letters and financial statements, have sat virtually unexamined for years in a castle in Vadstena, Sweden. When I first saw the collection there, I was overwhelmed. Piled end to end, these documents would stretch for miles.

For the past six years, I have researched this man, and his doings and misdoings. This book distills the elements of his story that I have found most relevant to investing and business today. It also paints a picture of an extraordinary human being, a man who deserves to be known as more than "the best-liked crook that ever lived," as British writer Frederic Whyte put it. My hope here is to resurrect him for anyone who is interested in markets, or who worries that, left unattended, even the most compelling stories in the cycle of history can disappear.

This is the story of Ivar Kreuger.

1

COMING TO AMERICA

On a promising fall day in 1922, 42-year-old Ivar Kreuger boarded *Berengaria*, the German luxury liner, at Southampton.[1] He wore a charcoal suit, as he typically did in public, and carried his favorite hat, a gray Homburg with a black stripe. Photographs from the time show a man constantly in shadow, with a sharp nose and small eyes, deep-set and dark.[2] His receding hair was closely cropped and combed back to expose a smooth, prominent forehead. If Ivar had been chomping a cigar, a passenger might have mistaken him for a slimmed-down Al Capone.

Few of the Americans returning from travel in Europe recognized Ivar at this point – in 1922, he was not yet a household name – but everyone would have seen him hasten aboard at the last minute. He rushed through the reception line, carrying an elegant cane and a dispatch case stuffed with papers. Once aboard, he scanned the crowd, headed for the largest group of unattached women he could find, and introduced himself with a bow.

When he opened his mouth to speak, it was clear that this was no mere mafia don. He spoke in beautifully constructed paragraphs, the sentences forming patterns like the parallel zigzags and hooks embroidered in the medieval Viking tapestries that had become so popular in his native Sweden.[3] Did they know *Berengaria* was christened after the wife of Richard the Lionheart? Ivar's eyes twinkled as he remarked that the name was apt, was it not?

He turned from group to group, working the crowd, posing questions like an inquisitive teenage boy, and then answering himself with the sagacity and life experience of a man twice his age. Would this trip be safe? Of course. *Berengaria* was 5,000 tons heavier than *Titanic*, with a stronger, safer hull, and redesigned bulkheads that were high and watertight.[4] New maritime rules, enacted after *Titanic* sank a decade earlier, mandated that every cruise ship carry stacks of lifeboats. Wireless communications were now flawless. It was unimaginable that a ship, particularly one from the Cunard Line, could be stranded at sea without radio contact.

What about the first-class cabins? Ah yes, they were stunning, all 714 of them, resembling rooms in a fine German home, with covered verandahs stocked with live greenery. Those three towering funnels? Surprisingly, one was a dummy, just for show, or, as Ivar might have preferred to put it, for "aesthetic balance." The clean air on deck? The ship's two working funnels were technological marvels. Did they know *Berengaria* was the first luxury liner to burn oil instead of coal?

Although Ivar dominated every conversation, he did so with a modest, almost self-deprecating air. He seemed apologetic, even embarrassed, that he knew all these things. As he moved among the passengers, he left them feeling that they, not he, had been asking all the questions. Even as Ivar held forth, they wanted him to say more, not less.

Ivar interlaced snippets about art, architecture, film, and travel, and criss-crossed topics from the Dutch masters to Dreiser to winter gardens to the stunning teenage actress he had just discovered in Stockholm. When the Vikings stitched together strips of cloth, they built a continuous dramatic arc, from the top left of a tapestry to the bottom right. When Ivar began weaving a story, he created a similar effect. A listener had no choice but to follow him to the end.

Whatever the topic, though, Ivar always returned to business. He might quote a stanza of poetry or an excerpt from a political speech, in one of five languages he spoke fluently, but invariably he would next mention how it brought to mind a passage from a quarterly corporate report he recently had read, or an announcement by a leading firm. The thread of his argument would be surprisingly continuous, and it would become apparent that Ivar had been moving the conversation toward that business item from the beginning.

Even more striking than Ivar's flowing prose was his gaze. When he locked into one of the passengers, everyone else melted away. Even the strongest personalities were mesmerized by the fix of his stare. As one of Ivar's closest colleagues put it,

There was an odd air of greatness about Ivar. I think he could get people to do anything. They fell for him, they couldn't resist his peculiar charm and magnetism. Above all, there was a look about him that made a difference. I saw J. P. Morgan's eyes many times in New York. They were like fire coals. But Ivar's eyes were not like that. They had another quality. Though small and narrow, they seemed capable, if he desired, of looking right through you.[5]

What the passengers aboard *Berengaria* did not know was that Ivar spent hours every day just preparing to talk. When Ivar knew he would be meeting a new group of people, he planned the first impression he hoped to make in advance: whom to meet first, which nuggets of information to drop, and where to move next. He always formed an exit plan. As *Berengaria* slid out to sea, Ivar could tell that this first impression had been a good one. Now, it was time to slip away, to let their views of him set, like a carefully baked soufflé. He excused himself, bowed again, and rushed to the ship's communications room. That concluded his opening act.

What kind of man, the passengers must have wondered, couldn't wait to finish a glass of champagne? Who couldn't even pause to take a breath before dashing off to send a cable from the ship's radio shack? This tornado of a man hadn't even told them his name.

About an hour after *Berengaria* left Southampton, a passenger headed to send a cable, and was surprised to see that the man who had rushed on board earlier was still there. The wireless officer politely turned that passenger away from the door, repeating the precise words Ivar had insisted he say: "I'm sorry, but Mr Ivar Kreuger has engaged the wires for his exclusive use."[6] Ivar had given the officer an absurdly large gratuity so he could have the room to himself. This was Act Two of his planned entrance.

Word spread among the passengers about Mr Ivar Kreuger, exactly as he had intended, and others stopped by for a glimpse of this mysterious man. Through the small window they could watch Ivar send message after message, his shadowed eyes flicking across columns of numbers on the papers he had packed in his dispatch case. The wireless's new multiplexing technique, pioneered by the Radio Corporation of America, had the capacity to allow up to eight passengers to send cables at once. Yet Ivar monopolized the lines.

Ivar remained in the radio shack until the passengers finally tired of dropping by to see if he was still there sending cables. According to later reports, probably exaggerated, he sent messages continuously for twenty-four hours. In any event, he stayed long enough to create the impression he wanted. In the dénouement, Ivar slipped away to his first-class cabin, exhausted but satisfied.

Fortunately, Ivar's associates had laid out his state room just as he had instructed. The room was fragrant with the precise arrangements of fresh flowers Ivar preferred, including apple blossoms and pink roses from one of his pergolas in Stockholm. Everything was in order. In the morning, while Ivar slept, a few of his men would answer any questions the passengers might have. And now that Ivar had left the radio shack, the ship's wireless finally was available. The passengers aboard *Berengaria* could spread the news about the remarkable man who was coming to New York.

Ivar was sailing to America for one simple reason: that's where the money was. After a brief recession, a post-war boom had ignited the Roaring Twenties, and by 1922 the country was awash in cash. Investor mania had reached even middle-class families, who were spending record amounts on a range of new luxuries: not only shares and bonds, but radios, Mah Jong sets, movie tickets, and, of course, alcohol and cigarettes. The streets of American cities were jammed with new cars – Lexingtons, Maxwells, Briscoes, and Templars, along with Buicks, Dodges, and Fords – and the wealthiest families were buying vacation homes in Miami and California, and sailing to and from Europe on elegant passenger liners.

Optimism and affluence washed through the American economy, as investors began playing the stock market, many for the first time. The buzz inside smoky jazz clubs and behind the curtained grilles of speakeasies was as often about Anaconda or General Motors as it was about the new Atlantic City beauty pageant. At the New York Stock Exchange, where a seat cost more than $100,000 – a hundred times the average annual income – brokers traded shares of the most prestigious companies, such as American Telephone and General Electric.

Just outside the Stock Exchange, at the so-called "Curb Market," boys with telephones attached to their heads swung down from windows to relay buy and sell orders to the brokers trading stocks, rain or shine, on the curb of Broad Street below. A British journalist who had just arrived in New York wrote that "you could talk about Prohibition, or Hemingway, or air conditioning, or music, or horses, but in the end you had to talk about the stock market, and that was when the conversation became serious."[7]

A new business-friendly Treasury Secretary, Andrew Mellon, who had resigned from fifty-one corporate directorships to join President Warren G.

Harding's cabinet, pledged to reduce corporate taxes.[8] The Federal Reserve lowered interest rates, to spur lending and investment. The Stock Exchange, a private corporation, imposed few rules on investing, and there were no federal laws restricting the purchase or sale of securities. In these laissez-faire markets, investors were free to go wild.

And wild they went. The hottest two emerging industries were cars and radio. Annual car sales had doubled from two years earlier, and there were now more than 15 million cars on the road. Manufacturers introduced faster, safer, and cheaper models every year, and the only asset people wanted more than cars were securities issued by car companies. Anyone who bought shares of General Motors or Fisher Body or Yellow Cab expected to double or triple their money after just a few years.

Shareholders of the Radio Corporation of America, known as RCA, did even better. RCA enjoyed a wireless communications monopoly, thanks to Navy Secretary Franklin D. Roosevelt, who had engineered a "marriage of convenience" among the government, General Electric, and Westinghouse, which manufactured wireless devices.[9] RCA's superheterodyne receiver became the dominant technology. When Ivar or other passengers sent messages from *Berengaria*, they used a new RCA transmitter.

As recently as 1920, only about 5,000 families had owned in-home radio sets, and RCA's share price was around a dollar then.[10] At that time, radio wasn't doing much better than other businesses suffering through the post-war recession. Then WBAY, a pioneering New York radio station, sold the first-ever advertising spot, a pitch for apartments in Jackson Heights – and the world changed overnight. Radio stations popped up in every major city, and radio sales soared, to $60 million in 1922. RCA's share price flew even higher than its sales. Anyone who held RCA shares during the 1920s earned an average annual return of 60 percent. All of that gain was from share price appreciation, not any periodic payments from the company. RCA did not even pay a dividend.

A few naysayers argued that shares of General Motors and RCA were over-valued, because actual profits were slim. Shares represented a claim to future dividend payments, so share prices should reflect the value of expected future dividends. The pessimists noted that RCA didn't pay a dividend, and claimed it never would, because it didn't make any money. Their point was simple: no profits, no dividends, no value. Without dividends, the share price couldn't keep going up.

But these shares were a bet on tomorrow, not today. If people thought the share price of General Motors would rise in the future, no one could prove them wrong now. And even though RCA didn't pay a dividend or earn much actual profit, the people who bet on that company were winners, year after year. RCA's share price rose because investors believed RCA eventually would make money and pay dividends. It was hard to argue with expectations, well grounded or not. The skeptics who bet against RCA were stepping in front of a speeding train.

American consumers and investors were in a buying mood. Ivar wanted – and needed – their dollars, and he had a plan to get them. By 1922, he had mastered the complexities of modern finance, and had created a web of related corporations and new financial instruments spanning the globe. But Ivar wasn't trying to sell anything complex. At least not at first. This time, his pitch involved a basic and essential product everyone used and could understand, something even more straightforward and common than cars or radio. That product was the safety match.

At the time matches were a staple, something the typical American needed almost as much as food, clothing, and shelter. People used matches to light kerosene lamps, gas heaters, stoves, and, of course, tobacco. When the sun set, they struck matches to light fires for cooking, candles for reading, and cigarettes for smoking. Everyone carried matches; everyone used them; everyone bought them.

Ivar told the story of the safety match to anyone who would listen. A German chemist had invented phosphorous matches in 1832, but the German matches had been too dangerous, both because the yellow phosphorous necessary to light the match was poisonous, and because the Germans had put the phosphorous in the match head, which was prone to light accidentally. The Swedes took the German invention and captured the market by emphasizing safety, simplicity, and innovation.

First, the Swedes developed a safer red phosphorous. Then they moved the phosphorous to a striking surface on the match box. Boxes were labeled "safety matches" and were printed with the slogan "Will Only Light on the Box." They were an instant hit. By 1922, Sweden was the leading exporter of matches, and Swedish Match Corporation made two-thirds of all matches used in the world.[11] Matches were Sweden's pride, and its most important export.

In the heady US markets, safety matches were the ideal new investment, and Ivar Kreuger was the perfect messenger. Matches, like cars and radio, were tangible products. They used new technology, and could be exported throughout the world. Antitrust regulators had declared monopolies illegal at home, but, by investing in Swedish Match, Americans could earn profits from a monopoly abroad. Ivar's sales pitch was compelling. An investor who heard him talk about Swedish Match for more than a few minutes invariably would pull out a checkbook.

Nearly every passenger on *Berengaria* used Swedish matches, and many would have heard of Swedish Match Corporation. By the time Ivar's henchmen briefed the passengers, they also would have known that Ivar controlled Swedish Match, and that his grand postwar plans were to establish a global match monopoly. By all appearances, he was well on the way.

In retrospect, it was surprising that Ivar had ended up in the match business in Sweden. As a child, he had watched his father, Ernst August, a fifth generation Swede, work in the small factory their ancestors had built near Kalmar, a city in the southeast, overlooking the Baltic Sea. Ernst August was a handsome man, with strong chiseled cheekbones and a high forehead. He was conservative and trustworthy, but he was not the family's leading mind. Ivar found his father's job as a factory manager uninspiring. Given the advances in technology, anyone could supervise the mechanized splint sorting, leveling, dipping, and packing of matches.

It was even more surprising that Ivar would return home. He had been the black sheep of a family dominated by his big-boned Scandinavian mother and his five blonde, fair-skinned sisters. His mother, Jenny, was as wild as Ernst August was stable. She had been born in Dutch South Africa, where her father had hurried in search of riches in the mines, just as the "forty-niners" were rushing for gold in America. There were hints of her family's history of mental illness in her sharp eyes, which darted in as many directions as her corkscrewed hair. Jenny's multicolored, multilayered outfits, and her elaborate bracelets and combinations of long necklaces and thick chokers, were a sharp contrast to Ernst August's simple dark suits and bowties.[12]

Jenny found it difficult to relate to her quiet, poker-faced boy, just as he found it difficult to relate to her. She was embarrassed when he repeated Sunday sermons verbatim or recited the scientific names of plants. He sat quietly, playing games in his head and planning his escape, while his mother and sisters frolicked in the family's middle-class flat in Kalmar and up and down East Sea Street. Ivar spent hours alone at nearby Kalmar Slott, the massive twelfth-century castle perched above the Baltic, where he saw the abandoned turrets as both an inspiration and a warning that even the strongest defenses ultimately could crumble. When his brother, Torsten, was born, Ivar shared the schemes he had concocted at Kalmar Slott, and kept secret from his mother: to stage a coup at the local school, to escape to Stockholm and then America, and to become a world leader and a wealthy businessman.

After Ivar left Kalmar and graduated from engineering school in Stockholm, his rise was surprisingly fast: he worked construction jobs throughout America and Mexico, formed a construction partnership in London, and then expanded into other industries, including film, real estate, and telecommunications. By the time of the world war, he was a millionaire and an industry leader. When he saw that his family's match business was struggling, he decided to return home, not just to help his family but also to exploit the enormous opportunity in matches.

While the factories of Europe worked overnight to produce war materials, Ivar quietly purchased match factories throughout Sweden.[13] He was a pioneer of vertical integration, buying timber tracts and chemical factories to secure the raw materials needed to make matches. Finally, he merged the leading Swedish competitors to form Swedish Match, a single dominant business with initial capital of about $10 million. Ivar owned half of Swedish Match, held all of the senior executive positions, and controlled the company's board.

Ivar was attracted to the match business, not for what it was, but for what it might become. In 1922 the industry was highly competitive. Profit margins were narrow. Swedish Match manufactured 20 billion boxes of matches per year, but its profits per box ranged from just a few cents down to a fraction of a penny.

Ivar's plan was to limit competition and increase profits by securing a monopoly on match sales throughout the world, mimicking the nineteenth-century oil, sugar, and steel trusts. Then, Swedish Match could raise prices without losing sales. According to Ivar's plan, now that the world war was over, he would make a fortune from the peace.

Swedish Match Corporation was just one part of Ivar's empire. He controlled ten other businesses through his public "holding" company, Kreuger & Toll, another Swedish corporation. In addition to its stake in Swedish Match, Kreuger & Toll also invested in banking, real estate, and the film industry. Ivar formed separate real estate companies to hold his properties,[14] and he used separate subsidiaries for each business, in order to avoid registration fees applicable to larger companies.[15]

One of his property holdings was Kvasten 6 Biblioteksgatan, where the well-known Stockholm cinema Röda Kvarn was located.[16] This purchase led Ivar to become involved in the film industry, and to meet prominent directors and actors, include a leading director in Sweden, Mauritz Stiller. Ivar formed Svenska Filmindustri, a company that dominated Swedish cinema and brought him great pleasure, though little money. SF, as the company was known, was at the center of the golden age of Swedish film, and made critically acclaimed movies based on novels by the country's leading writers. SF had an agreement to produce five novels by Selma Lagerlöf, who had won the Nobel Prize in 1909.[17] Unfortunately, the films were expensive and generated better reviews than revenue. In 1922, he restructured his film business and took losses of 80 percent.[18]

But the financial difficulties of film were the exception for Ivar, and his other companies rolled on. Overall, Ivar's network of separately managed subsidiaries was incredibly profitable. Investors in Kreuger & Toll consistently made double-digit returns and Ivar had increased his holding company's dividend to a whopping 25 percent of "par value," the initial capital Ivar had raised. No American company came close to that.

Ivar controlled his holding company with a tight grip. Its board of directors was Ivar, Ivar's father, Ivar's partner Paul Toll, and two of Ivar's closest colleagues. As one of those colleagues later explained, annual meetings were perfunctory. Ivar would walk in briskly and deliver a quick monologue:

> Good morning, gentlemen. Will the secretary please read the minutes? It has been decided to increase the capital of Kreuger & Toll by twelve million kronor by issuing new shares at a rate of two hundred and forty percent of par. Do I hear any objections? Thank you, gentlemen. Good morning.[19]

Kreuger & Toll's annual financial statements contained no explanation as to how the company had made so much money. One of the largest profit entries was labeled simply "profits from other investments." Ivar's earlier investors, from outside America, hadn't seemed to mind the vagueness. Why worry about such details when the company paid a 25 percent cash dividend? Their investment would be returned in four years. And, on top of dividends, investors in Kreuger & Toll also made money as the value of their investments rose. Ivar already had made his investors quite wealthy. They saw no reason to ask probing questions about what Ivar's "profit from other investments" might be.

Before 1922, Ivar had raised most of his capital in Europe, particularly from Swedish banks. As Ivar watched the Americans enter a period of buying mania, he saw a new source of funds. Ivar had studied financial history and was aware of infamous periods of mania and later panic, such as the South Sea Bubble of 1720 and the infamous rise and collapse of Dutch tulip bulb trading in 1637.[20] In those cases, men became rich as they rode the wave of investors speculating on risky ventures. Ivar knew the timing was crucial; American optimism would not persist forever. When investors were manic, they would purchase just about anything. But during the panic that inevitably followed mania, the opposite was true: no one would buy. Anyone who bought into the South Sea Company or Dutch tulip bulbs, but held the investment for too long, lost everything when panic hit. It was important to strike, and then exit, early.

Anyone who remained skeptical about Ivar's businesses could look to the consistent track record of Kreuger & Toll, the parent company of Swedish Match, from as far back as 1907, when Ivar and Paul Toll formed the firm to do construction projects in Europe. Now Ivar's companies were poised to outperform even shares of RCA and General Motors. When investors learned about the dividends Kreuger & Toll had been paying, they simply went mad. These people were willing to buy shares of companies that, like RCA, did not pay any dividend. What would they think of a reputable company that paid 25 *percent* a year? Plus a sizeable gain on the value of their investment? It was enough to make even the most conservative investors lose their minds.

As Ivar knew, the number of conservative investors in the United States – the people who might question how his companies could pay such large dividends – was dwindling. Instead, stock buying and selling was dominated by exuberant day traders, people who bought and sold shares of risky companies throughout the day, often holding positions for just a few minutes.[21] There was no securities regulator governing these people or the brokers who sold them shares. Nor were there government laws or warnings about rapid trading in and out of stocks. As a result, there were more day traders per capita during the early 1920s than at any other time in history.

Scattered throughout major cities were scores of unregulated "bucket shops," shady brokerage firms that encouraged aggressive trading, charged high fees, and sold highly volatile investments that seemed too good to be true, and often were. There were no actual "buckets" at these shops. The term derived from British beer swillers, who walked from pub to pub in London's

East End, filled a bucket at each one, and then carried the dregs back to their own small stores, where they offered the dubious brew along with even more dubious wagers on stocks and commodities. A patron might overpay for the beer, but his real losses came from bets on future grain prices.[22]

The American version of bucket shops offered margin loans instead of second-hand alcohol. Day traders could borrow as much as 99 cents per dollar invested. Trading on razor-thin margin was intoxicating, but risky, especially if the shop operator could manipulate the prices of stocks, as they often could and did. If you put up $1,000 to buy $100,000 worth of stock, a decline of just 1 percent would wipe out your position.

Most people who bought from bucket shop operators lost money, but that didn't stop them, and it certainly didn't stop the bucket shops. Human beings inevitably overestimated the probability of success. Too many young men thought they could become the next Babe Ruth; too many young women sought to become Mary Pickford. Four of five people believed they were of above average skill when driving a car. A majority of people said they could outsmart the stock market, or win money gambling. As stock trading became more popular during the early 1920s, so did this kind of cognitive error, and the widespread passion about markets led investors to focus on winners more than losers, like the gambler who vividly remembers cashing a winning ticket from a particular race at the horse track, but conveniently forgets that she lost money overall.

At the time, even the hardest skeptics were drawn to widely publicized tales of successful trading schemes, which dominated print advertising and radio info-mercials. Americans have always wanted to believe rags-to-riches stories are true, and the more they heard about young men from poor backgrounds who made implausible fortunes, the more they believed those stories could be theirs.

One widely publicized tale, which Ivar and the other passengers aboard *Berengaria* certainly would have known, was about Jesse Livermore, whom many regarded as the greatest market speculator of all time.[23] Livermore reflected the burgeoning optimism of investors, and the 1920s were his heyday, the time when he went from being rich to being absurdly rich. The *Saturday Evening Post* serialized his biography, and a million readers followed his story. Livermore confirmed the quintessentially American belief that an average person can beat the market.

As the story went, young Jesse Livermore left his family's small Massachusetts farm for a job posting stock quotes at brokerage firm Paine Webber in

Boston. In his spare time, he devised a set of trading rules for the most volatile shares bought and sold by the devious bucket shop dealers. By outsmarting them, and by trading on inside information, he turned $5 into $1,000 by the age of fifteen. He made his first million soon after that.

When the bucket shops finally banned Livermore, he switched to trading shares of leading companies on the New York Stock Exchange, where he made still more millions. He bought several mansions, a fleet of limousines, and a steel-hulled yacht, which he sailed to Europe. He became an instant hero to many investors. His stories were so popular that Edwin Lefèvre, the author of the articles in the *Saturday Evening Post*, assembled them into a bestselling book, *Reminiscences of a Stock Operator*.[24] During the years after the book's publication, Livermore lost the entire $100 million he had made betting on the markets, and then shot himself with a .32 caliber Colt automatic pistol.

Another example of the irrational exuberance of the era was Charles Ponzi, who had a similar tale, and a similarly unhappy ending.[25] Ponzi also was from a poor family, and he skipped school to work odd jobs for more than a decade, including a stint at a bank where he was fired for forging checks. After he served a prison term for the check forgeries, Ponzi worked a temporary job as a messenger at J. P. Poole, a Boston import/export broker, and he discovered that the value of so-called "postal reply coupons" – slips of paper that substituted for foreign stamps – had been set at fixed exchange rates in 1919, and not adjusted since then. Meanwhile, the value of several European currencies, particularly the Spanish peseta, had plummeted. Because the value of the postal reply coupon had not been adjusted since then, Ponzi thought he could buy coupons in Spain at a discount and then sell them in America at a profit.

There was only one catch: the entire supply of postal reply coupons was small, less than $1 million. Even if Ponzi could buy every coupon issued in Spain and take them all home, there wasn't that much money to be made. Moreover, travel was expensive, and he wasn't the only person who knew about the scheme. Still, Ponzi thought it was worth trying to raise money based on the idea.[26]

Ponzi placed some magazine advertisements stating that he could double an investor's money within six months by purchasing postal reply coupons outside the United States and then redeeming them at home for a higher price. Much to his surprise, 40,000 people sent him money. He distributed some of this money as "profits" to the earliest investors, who then spread word about their newfound fortunes. Others heard the news and bought in. And so on. Investors from California to Maine sent him more than $15 million. He had to hire sixteen clerks just to collect and deposit the cash.

Ponzi's scheme didn't last long. A journalist exposed him after just a few months by pointing out that Ponzi could not possibly have bought enough postal reply coupons to sustain the profits he advertised – there simply weren't sufficient coupons in the world. When investors who weren't at the top of the pyramid learned about these limitations, they tried to bail out. Unfortunately, they were too late. Their money was gone.

Ponzi didn't invent the idea of a financial pyramid where a few early investors (at the top) receive payments from many later investors (at the bottom). And he certainly wasn't alone: during the early 1920s, hundreds of promoters marketed investment pyramids in commodities, real estate, and diet supplements.

Indeed, what was remarkable about this scheme wasn't Ponzi. It was his victims. If people really would believe that a 34-year-old ex-bank clerk who had just served three years in prison for check kiting was capable of doubling their money in six months by exchanging millions of 10 cent postal coupons from Europe – well, if they would believe that, then they would believe anything.

That meant they were ready for Ivar Kreuger.

Americans who were excited by stories of Livermore and Ponzi were enthralled by Ivar. He wowed the passengers on *Berengaria* with dramatic tales of his various construction projects: from his exploits in Johannesburg while building the Carlton Hotel to his twelve-year odyssey putting up the Stockholm City Hall with nearly 8 million bricks. Architects already were calling Stockholm City Hall the most beautiful building in Scandinavia, and its stunning room, the "Blue Hall," was soon to house a 10,270-pipe organ and host the Nobel Prize ceremonial dinner.

Unlike Livermore and Ponzi, Ivar seemed destined to have a happy ending. He generated increasing profits for his investors, year after year. Kreuger & Toll was composed of legitimate businesses. It produced and sold tangible assets. As the company's most recent annual report circulated among the passengers, the excitement on board rose like the frenzy of a bucket shop. The report was simple, just a few lines. It noted Kreuger & Toll's link to Swedish Match and its 25 percent dividend, but said little about where that money came from. Over half of the company's profits were listed simply as "earnings from various transactions."

These passengers didn't need any financial detail from Ivar. A reliable 25 percent dividend was impressive enough. Ivar himself seemed trustworthy, and made dozens of new friends during the journey. He danced with the women, and smoked cigars with the men. He delighted everyone with stories of the up-and-coming actresses working for his film production company. Ivar seemed the sort of person who would take care of you, no matter what happened. By the time the ship docked in New York, the passengers were practically begging to give him their money.

As they disembarked, Ivar performed the final act of this trip. On shore, when a journalist who had heard about his arrival took out a pipe and asked for a match, Ivar pretended to fumble through his pockets looking for, but not finding, one of the billions of Swedish safety matches his factories had produced that year. The journalist bought the charming, and disarming, story, and the front-page headline the following morning was: "The Match King Who Does Not Carry a Match!"[27]

2

GETTING TO LEE HIGG

Donald Durant read the news of Ivar Kreuger's arrival on *Berengaria* in his office at Lee Higginson & Co. in New York. In the early 1920s, Lee Higginson was one of the most prestigious and profitable banks in the world – just behind J. P. Morgan but ahead of Goldman Sachs and Lehman Brothers. The firm's roots were in Boston, not New York, yet even as America's financial business shifted from State Street to Wall Street during the early twentieth century, Lee Higginson remained one of a handful of global "money banks."

A native New Yorker, Durant had worked his way up from nothing at the firm, starting as a stock boy in the Manhattan branch office eighteen years earlier. Durant had been promoted faster than anyone in the firm's seven-decade history. While Ivar was building Kreuger & Toll from an empty shell into a hugely profitable European firm, Durant was helping develop Lee Higginson's New York office into the new engine that would drive the venerable bank into the future.

Durant looked nothing like the typical banking partner of the era. Most bankers were exactly what paintings from the time suggested: old, fat, and bald (or balding) with unfathomably beefy moustaches. Durant was just thirty-four years old, a generation younger than most Lee Higginson partners, and eight years younger than Ivar.[1] Durant was trim and athletic, his thick hair slicked back to reveal a handsome forehead, high cheekbones, a clean-cut face, and a charming smile. He looked more like Fred Astaire than a banker.

Lee Higginson's stodgy partners were drawn to Durant's handsome charm, wit, and New York street smarts. Like Ivar, Durant was comfortable playing a range of roles. He had served in the infantry during the world war, and his devotion to the sea suited the Boston sailing crowd. Durant had earned the designation "master mariner," and he navigated the politics of Lee Higginson as easily as he sailed through Boston harbor. He developed relationships with clients during trips to the coast of Maine on a Marconi-rigged 50-foot yawl called *Sequoia*.[2] Durant sailed his own ship. And he looked fabulous doing it.

Durant devoured the details of Ivar's trip to America. His sources told him that Kreuger & Toll and Swedish Match were two of the hottest companies outside the United States. His colleagues in London reported that Ivar already had made them a fortune on a highly unusual and complex swap transaction that even the sharpest investment bankers there could not understand. Ivar had opened an account with Higginson & Co., the British branch of Lee Higginson, and then offered a deal that, stripped to its essentials, involved Ivar selling shares worth 30 pounds to the London bankers, but charging them just 20 pounds. At its core, this swap guaranteed a profit of 10 pounds per share for Higginson & Co. Ivar said he would debit the 10 pound difference to one of his personal accounts, and he explained a number of complicated aspects of that debit. The British bankers lost interest in the murky details after they heard "riskless profit of ten pounds."[3]

The Higginson & Co. deal was baffling. Even if Ivar could control the market, so that he could buy low there and sell high in London, it wasn't clear why he would give such arbitrage profits to Higginson & Co., instead of keeping them for himself. Outside the rarefied world of investment banking, this complicated transaction might have been called a bribe. But Higginson & Co. accepted it and, as Ivar had hoped, began praising him to the firm's counterparts in New York, including Donald Durant.

At the same time, Ivar asked a Swedish stockbroker named Gustav Lagerkrantz to visit Durant and to recommend, casually and unobtrusively, that Durant ask to meet with Ivar. Durant had no reason to suspect a connection. From Durant's perspective, Lagerkrantz was just another broker seeking access to one of America's top banks. Durant headed Lee Higginson's syndicate department, a group that arranged new securities issues, helped divide the securities among the top banks, and then sold the securities to investors. Lagerkrantz naturally would have wanted Lee Higginson's syndicate department to allocate its most promising investments to his Swedish clients. When Lagerkrantz happened to mention Ivar Kreuger during his meeting with Durant, it appeared to be merely an aside. Durant never imagined that Ivar had arranged it all.

Meanwhile, Lagerkrantz received side payments from Ivar. In 1922, Ivar sent Lagerkrantz "the usual sum for the month" plus an additional 2,000 dollars, which Lagerkrantz said he needed to pay rent and settle some personal matters.[4] Although these communications suggested bribery, the *quid pro quo* was more likely implicit. Lagerkrantz was a broker and Ivar had paid him large trading commissions in the past. It was only reasonable for Lagerkrantz to help Ivar, and then expect that Ivar would continue to pay large, or perhaps even larger, commissions in the future.

For Durant, news about Ivar seemed to come from every direction, just as Ivar had planned. First, Higginson's London office. Then, Lagerkrantz. Now, the media surrounding the arrival of *Berengaria*. Ivar sounded like the ideal new opportunity. He was one of Europe's brilliant industrialists. He had built a modest family match company into one of the world's largest industrial trusts. Kreuger & Toll's dividend in Sweden was 25 percent. Durant thought he could sell *that* to anyone. When he read about Ivar's arrival in New York, he eagerly requested a meeting.

Ivar responded that he was busy with other business, but would try to arrange a time. Ivar did not want to seem too enthusiastic; he had learned that playing hard to get was a promising strategy with America's élite. Just a few months earlier, Ivar had been invited to join Congressional Country Club, and when he did not respond to the invitation, the club's chairman, Admiral Cary T. Grayson, had sent a letter imploring Ivar to join: "You will recognize among the names presented here a number of your friends and associates, and we sincerely trust, Mr Kreuger, that we shall have the pleasure of having you as one of us."[5]

Ivar waited a few more days, to ensure that publicity about him had saturated Lee Higginson. Finally, he arranged to meet Durant.

Lee Higginson, or "Lee Higg" as it was popularly known, had been a dominant player in global finance since before the Civil War. John Lee and George Higginson, cousins by marriage, had formed a stock brokerage house on State Street, Boston, in 1848.[6] The partners included three generations of Harvard men, many related by Boston blue blood, and they were wary of outsiders. One Higginson complained of the "self-made man without the backing of a family to keep him straight."[7] Another remarked, "I have never met one such yet in my business life who has not sooner or later lied to me, or at least tried to cheat me."[8]

Henry Lee Higginson led the firm until his death in 1919. Henry was a prominent philanthropist – he founded the Boston Symphony Orchestra – and his advice about the banking business echoed Pierpont Morgan's famous testimony to Congress that character came before money or property. According to Henry, "The house has always tried to do its work well and to have and keep a high character. Character is the foundation stone of such a business, and once lost, is not easily regained."[9]

Following Henry's counsel, Lee Higg's partners advised the leading corporations of the day, such as American Telephone and General Electric, and the partners carefully avoided even a hint of self-interest. When James Storrow, Jr, a Harvard graduate from a prominent Boston family and a Lee Higg partner, became the lead banker and advisor to General Motors, he refused to permit the firm to own shares of the company. This policy cost Lee Higg a fortune in missed profits as General Motors shares soared in value, but it preserved the firm's venerable reputation. Storrow insisted that his partners stick "closely to the things which we are trained to analyze and know how to weigh in the balance."[10]

Lee Higg maintained its conservative culture even as it expanded to New York. Frederic W. Allen, the head of the New York office, was indistinguishable from the Boston partners, except, perhaps, that he had attended Yale, not Harvard. Allen was a physically massive and imposing presence, and he served as the distinguished leader of several philanthropic and business groups, including as head of Yale's rowing committee and a director of Chase National Bank.[11] Like the Higginsons, Allen was no self-made man.

During the world war, Frederic Allen was appointed Director of War Savings, and promoted the purchase of War Savings Certificates by Americans with a patriotic flourish. In one major speech, Allen gushed that "Every person who buys will not only help his country, but greatly benefit himself. If Benjamin Franklin, who secured no small part of his reputation as an advocate of thrift, were alive today he would be the flag bearer of this great undertaking. What he had to say about thrift over a century ago is as true today as it was then, and the war is bringing home the truth of it. War Savings Certificates are intended for everybody. They are within the reach of all."[12]

Allen advocated thrift privately as well. A few years before he died, Henry Lee Higginson wrote to Allen that "As the house grows older, I think it grows more careful."[13] Allen was proud to hear it, and absolutely agreed with the firm's conservative objective.

Still, Frederic Allen and his partners recognized that the markets were changing. Given its Boston roots, Lee Higginson lacked the national networks of Morgan or National City, a leading commercial bank. The firm needed someone to establish stronger connections, first with new companies whose securities would appeal to investors, and then throughout the United States with the investors themselves. Every American already knew Jack Morgan. They were getting to know National City's chairman, Charles Mitchell, a former electrical goods salesman, who had been encouraging his brokers with sales contests, high commissions, and motivational speeches. Lee Higginson needed someone to join this fray, and to introduce the firm's name and the companies it discovered to the public. It wouldn't hurt if this man resembled Fred Astaire.

Donald Durant understood the common person, someone élite bankers, including the Higginsons, had politely ignored for decades. Since the Civil War, bankers had focused on wealthy institutions: first the railroads, then industrial companies, and most recently foreign corporations and governments. But now that individual human beings, men and women, were rushing to buy stocks, not only from unregulated bucket shops, stock jobbers, and brokers in lower Manhattan, but also from the leading national banks, Lee Higg needed Durant to help them connect.

Recently, Durant had become popular on Wall Street and among investors. In June 1922, colleagues from other banks elected him to serve as vice-president of the Bond Club of New York,[14] a prominent group that hosted monthly lunches on Lower Broadway and an annual retreat at the Sleepy Hollow Country Club, just north of Tarrytown.[15] The charge of the Bond Club was "to maintain high standards and just principles and to promote good fellowship and intellectual intercourse among men engaged and interested in the distribution of investment services."[16] Durant also oversaw publication of the *Bawl Street Journal*, an eight-page satirical newspaper with gag articles and spoofs of bankers and, it was claimed, the largest circulation of any amateur humor publication in the world.[17] He seemed the ideal mixture of upstanding banker and regular guy.

The partners of Lee Higginson gave Durant a broad mandate: explore new markets and find unique and previously untapped investment opportunities that would seize the imaginations of new American investors. If Durant could find companies with compelling stories and appealing leaders, Lee Higginson's partners could do even more than make unimaginably large amounts of money; they could help remake the economic structure of society, democratize markets, and lift investors out of their post-war doldrums. Durant, like the investors he sought, was brimming with enthusiasm. Frederic Allen's inspirational speeches about War Savings Certificates could have applied equally to Durant: he and his firm wanted to be "within the reach of all."

It was no surprise, then, that during the summer of 1922, as Ivar was pondering his trip to New York, the men of Lee Higginson made what would turn out to be the most important decision in the firm's history. They elected Donald Durant, a self-made man, to be their newest partner.[18]

Unlike James Storrow, Jr, and the Higginson brothers, Durant hadn't attended Harvard. Unlike Allen, he hadn't attended Yale. His father hadn't been a banker. His uncles and cousins weren't bankers, either. Durant was a most unlikely addition to the prestigious Lee Higginson partnership. He didn't even have a moustache.

Now, just a few months after his election to the partnership, Donald Durant was about to meet Ivar Kreuger, another self-made man, someone who could offer Americans a truly new and exciting investment opportunity. The partners at Lee Higginson were giddy. They could not possibly have thought this meeting ultimately would lead to the destruction of their firm.

In truth, this trip on *Berengaria* was not Ivar's first attempt to profit from what he believed would be a post-war boom in America. Just three years earlier, he had set up a corporation in New York called American Kreuger & Toll, which he had hoped would attract American investors. Yet that company had failed – spectacularly so. Ivar's recent public relations blitz, and his planned performances at sea, were designed to obscure that failure, and to remarket Ivar as someone new to America.

It is worth stepping back, briefly, to see just how poorly Ivar's earlier dealings in New York had gone. If Durant had known these details, he would not have wanted to meet Ivar. But Durant did not know, and probably could not have imagined, how far Ivar had strayed from his previous focus on the production and sale of matches. Nor could Durant have guessed how poorly Ivar's negotiations with American match manufacturers already had gone, or why they had collapsed.

Ivar's first attempt to raise funds from American investors had begun in 1919. He had planned to have American Kreuger & Toll replicate his approach during the previous decade in Europe: acquire control of local match production, squelch the competition, and then raise prices. The name of his new business was apt. It was to be an American clone of Kreuger & Toll, his Swedish industrial company.

However, Ivar quickly confronted two major obstacles. First, monopolies were illegal in the United States. Unlike a few decades earlier, when industrywide trusts were essentially unregulated, prosecutors were now targeting antitrust violators. Ivar couldn't simply buy every match factory, as he had in Europe.

Second, another company, Diamond Match, already controlled much of the US production of matches. To the extent anyone was likely to achieve Ivar's plan of an American monopoly, legal or not, it was Diamond Match, not him.

If Ivar understood the magnitude of these challenges, he did not take them seriously, at least at first. Instead of setting up the business himself in New York, he had sent Anders Jordahl, a Norwegian friend who knew more about liquor than loans. Ivar and Jordahl had become close during a stint working construction in Vera Cruz, fifteen years earlier. In Mexico, they had opened a restaurant and bar, gambled on foreign exchange, and led what even single twenty-something Scandinavian men traveling abroad would have called an adventuresome social life. Jordahl had even persuaded smooth-skinned Ivar to grow a moustache, though that was short-lived.

Jordahl was great company for Ivar, but not great for Ivar's company. When Jordahl arrived in New York during winter 1919, he wrote that American Kreuger & Toll would "give Kreuger the fresh foothold he wanted in the States."[19] Of course, that foothold would be expensive. Jordahl asked Ivar to wire him 500,000 dollars to get the business started.[20]

Jordahl began burning through that cash immediately. He took the new business in unusual directions for someone who was supposed to be pursuing New York's banking élite. First, he set up a new office, not downtown where the bankers were, but in midtown near Broadway and the most popular theaters in the city. This was an odd choice for an industrial firm seeking the attention of Wall Street. Ostensibly, Jordahl chose this location because he and Ivar believed midtown would become the new financial section of the city as banks migrated north. Perhaps some clients would have found this explanation plausible.

But the real reason Jordahl selected an office near Broadway was Ivar's newfound obsession with the entertainment industry. Donald Durant had been something of a playboy in his youth, but even he would have been surprised by the amount of time Ivar was devoting to teenage actresses. Lately, Ivar had become more fixated on Swedish film projects and aspiring female models than on the American match industry.

One of Ivar's recent discoveries was a teenage hat clerk he had met while shopping at Stockholm's stylish version of Macy's, PUB, Paul U. Bergström's department store emporium on Hötorget Plaza.[21] Ivar had met many other women while shopping, one of his favorite pastimes. Yet this girl was special. She was stunningly beautiful, and nearly as charismatic as Ivar. Ivar must have seen something of his own personality in her eyes. After she showed Ivar a few Homburgs he promised her that, with his help, she would become a leading model and actress. He meant it, and she believed him. Ivar had no trouble charming her, and everything else followed smoothly.

Although Greta Gustafson was just fifteen years old when she met Ivar, they quickly became close. Ivar had grand plans for Greta. He persuaded her to take modeling and acting classes, and even paid to produce her first short film. He introduced her to his contacts in the film industry and supported her financially while she began studying at the Royal Dramatic Theater in Stockholm. From the time Jordahl left for America until Ivar's meeting with Durant, Greta would appear in three short films and two features, including one called *Peter the Tramp*, which was produced by Ivar's production company, Svenska Filmindustri.

In Manhattan, Jordahl found that, given Ivar's focus on film and theater, and the young women who went with them, an office downtown near Wall Street was not "a suitable location for our purpose."[22] Instead, Jordahl secured a one-year lease on the eleventh floor of the Guaranty Trust Building. The lease price was high for the area (roughly 4 dollars per square foot), and the brokers' promises that the building soon would be renovated were dubious. What clinched the deal for Jordahl was the location: 44th Street and Fifth Avenue, just a few blocks east of the theaters on Broadway and a short walk from many fashionable restaurants. Even if the business failed, the midtown space would be a superb bachelor pad for Jordahl, and for Ivar, who planned to spend more time in New York.

Ivar paid Jordahl a handsome salary of 12,000 dollars a year plus 7,000 for expenses – roughly the same salary as a mid-level banker or corporate lawyer. Jordahl received additional perks as well. Periodically, he would receive a notification from a bank that some obscure company he had never heard of had deposited more money in the American Kreuger & Toll account.[23]

Films did wonders for Ivar's social life, but they weren't making him any money, especially in the United States. American moviegoers were indifferent to Swedish films, and the artist then known as Greta Gustafson was not yet a star. By March 1921, Ivar's total revenue from film exports to the United States was just a quarter of a million dollars, and his costs were much higher.

After two years of losses, Ivar pressed Jordahl to find American Kreuger &

Toll some "business activity with corresponding earnings."[24] When the 1921 summer film season didn't generate any success, Ivar cabled to Jordahl that "it is extremely important that negotiations regarding Swedish films in United States are taken up immediately."[25] Ivar was concerned that his American venture was headed in the wrong financial direction. It wasn't just about the money, although that clearly was one of Ivar's concerns. Ivar knew the social status of a failing film producer would be well below that of a successful one.

It took Jordahl months, but he finally secured an agreement with the 42nd Street Theater to show one Swedish film, *Körkarlen*, over Christmas. This film was a gamble: the umlaut in the title was enough to keep most New Yorkers away, and the story was not exactly holiday fare, particularly at a time when popular films were titled *Cops* or *Robin Hood* or subtitled "A Symphony of Horror."[26] *Körkarlen* was based on a 1912 novel by Swedish author Selma Lagerlöf (that umlaut again), the first woman to win the Nobel Prize for Literature. The story tracked a legend that the last sinner to die in a calendar year would spend the following year driving a phantom chariot that took the souls of the dead. Anyone who read the book would be even less likely to see the movie. For a late December audience in Manhattan, one of the film's best features was that it was silent.

On December 22, the manager of the 42nd Street Theater abruptly backed out.[27] Jordahl frantically called on other theaters – the Republic just west of Broadway and the Central on Broadway at 47th Street – but everyone gave Jordahl what, in the entertainment industry, was known as the "run around." One theater promised the first two weeks after the New Year, but then said it could run the movie only from December 28 through January 3. Others just said no.

Ivar's American film business quickly became both a money pit and a distraction. As Jordahl burned through Ivar's cash, both men focused on movies more than matches. Meanwhile, American Kreuger & Toll's import business suffered. Although Ivar's match shipments to the United States doubled during 1921, they were still just 45,000 cases.[28] Ivar faced intense competition from Diamond Match, the leading American firm, as well as high excise taxes on imported matches, and the threat of antitrust prosecution if he tried to monopolize US production. His prospects were bleak.

Ivar decided his last chance to penetrate the American match industry was to open negotiations with W. A. Fairburn, the president of Diamond Match. Ivar sent an inquiry, and Fairburn replied that he was interested in a partnership with Swedish Match, but only with respect to Diamond's interests in Japan, South America, and Europe – not the United States. The men discussed forming a new company, but Fairburn wanted Swedish Match to take the lion's share of any debt burden.

In a letter Ivar must have found insulting, Fairburn said Swedish Match alone should guarantee the debt payments of a new company, because the mere involvement of Diamond Match would be worth at least as much as Ivar's guarantee. Fairburn wrote,

> I am inclined to the opinion that the prestige of The Diamond Match Co. in the United States, allied in the forming of the new Company, and with the reputation, influence and ability of The Diamond Match Co. behind the new International Company, will have as much influence on the sub-scribing public in this market as the guarantee of Bond interest by the Swedish Company.[29]

That was too much for Ivar. Did Fairburn have any idea who Ivar was? If Fairburn wanted to pontificate about the "prestige" of Diamond Match, he would have to deal with one of Ivar's underlings from then on. Ivar didn't want to abandon the prospect of an American match deal, but he refused to correspond directly with Fairburn.

It wasn't difficult for Ivar to choose between spending time with W. A. Fairburn or with Greta Gustafson, his teenage discovery from PUB. Ivar saw some of his own ambition in Greta, who was already raw with experience and had a reputation for running with an edgy crowd. It didn't take Greta long to charm not only Ivar, but all of his film industry contacts. At the Royal Dramatic Theater, where Ivar sponsored her acting lessons, Greta met Mauritz Stiller. Stiller was emerging from Sweden as one of Europe's leading directors, and he instantly saw Greta's potential. He cast her as Countess Elizabeth Dohna in his film epic *The Saga of Gösta Berling*. He also insisted that she abandon the surname Gustafson. Stiller took her to Constantinople, then Berlin, and, finally, arranged a trip to Hollywood, after Louis B. Mayer asked Stiller to direct a film there.[30]

Before Greta left for America, she attended a ball Ivar threw in Saltsjö-baden for Douglas Fairbanks and Mary Pickford. Ivar introduced her to the famous actors, though he kept Greta for himself as a dancing partner. Greta's eyes, like Ivar's, were capable of looking right through a person, and she looked right through Ivar. She shared his intense need for privacy, and she understood how a person's real personality could slip away as he or she formed a new on-stage persona for the public. Following Ivar's lead, she also would split her life in two.

Throughout their lives, Ivar and Greta would share this bond, as the two most famous people from Sweden during the 1920s. They loved each other, in a way, though neither found the idea of a permanent relationship with another person attractive. Like Ivar, Greta embraced the idea of love, but questioned the notion of marriage. As she put it, "Love? I have said over and over again that I do not know. There is always my overwhelming desire to be alone."[31] When Ivar and Greta saw each other, there was a deep connection, a kind of shared loneliness.

By the time of the Fairbanks-Pickford ball, Ivar's department store discovery was a new person, with a new name. She was Greta Garbo.

Even with Greta and other actresses drawing his attention from business, Ivar didn't give up on an American match deal. He wasn't spending much time in America, so he needed someone there to focus on direct talks with Diamond Match. Jordahl was busy and even more distracted, so Ivar delegated responsibility for future negotiations to one of his more junior New York employees, Eric Landgren. Ivar could not have chosen a worse person for the job.

Landgren was even wilder and less responsible than Anders Jordahl. He already had been involved in some shady efforts to persuade Congress to reduce import taxes on matches, efforts that ranged from merely aggressive lobbying to illicit payments of cash.[32] He also had run up extraordinarily high expenses, overdrawing his personal account by four times his monthly salary.[33]

Ivar arranged for Landgren to meet directly with W. A. Fairburn to hammer out the details of a transaction. Fairburn was underwhelmed by Landgren,[34] and clearly felt slighted to be dealing with one of Ivar's lackeys. Fairburn didn't trust this new man, and asked him to report directly to Diamond Match's auditors from Price Waterhouse & Co., one of the leading accounting firms at the time.[35]

Price Waterhouse's accountants were famously attentive to details, and they began submitting inquiries to Landgren about certain of American Kreuger & Toll's profits and expenses. For example, they immediately spotted, and questioned, Landgren's $4,428.68 charge for the use of an automobile.[36] When they discovered several irregular book entries, they began questioning Swedish Match's financial statements, too. Then the real trouble started.

When Landgren concocted false figures to explain some of the numbers in

the financial statements, the auditors quickly found the fabrication and negotiations fell apart. W. E. Seatree, a lawyer and an accountant with Price Waterhouse, dashed off an angry letter directly to Ivar, in the formal style of
someone who had proudly mastered the disciplines of both law and accounting during the early twentieth century:

> You will note that we did not certify the balance sheet. Mr Landgren's
> letter is obviously an attempt to make it appear to you that he had accom-
> plished something; but the fact that he had to resort to forgery to accom-
> plish his purpose is the best proof of his failure. The euphemism, that he
> was going to issue a so-called copy of our balance sheet leaving out parts
> which were of material importance, does not disguise the true nature of his
> action.[37]

When Price Waterhouse lost confidence in Ivar, so did Fairburn and
Diamond Match. Ivar tried to repair the damage by asking Jordahl to retain
an independent outside accountant to vouch for their new US business. Ernst
& Ernst, a reliable audit firm, completed a review of American Kreuger &
Toll's financial statements in June, but by then it was too late.[38] The damage
was done, and so were the negotiations.

Without a deal with Diamond Match, Ivar had no chance of an American
monopoly. On September 26, 1922, Ivar told Jordahl, "suggest putting off
negotiations Fairburn."[39]

By this time, Ivar's American business was a mess. His employees were out
of control. He was locked out of the American match markets. His film business was losing money. Jordahl had approached several banks about raising
new funds for American Kreuger & Toll, but he fared even worse with the
banks than he had with *Körkarlen*, the Swedish film. Kuhn Loeb & Co. said
no. The Warburgs were interested, but said the business was too young. Jack
Morgan, J. P. Morgan & Co.'s lead partner, wasn't about to risk sullying his
bank's reputation on a 39-year-old Swede. Jack might have been a pale imitation of his father, Pierpont, but, like many of the partners of Lee Higginson,
he didn't associate with self-made men. By the time Ivar stepped off *Berengaria* to meet with the media, he had run through nearly all of his options.

Ivar needed to put the starlets aside, come to America, and refocus on
matches. This was the reason he had sailed to America in 1922. This was the
reason he needed Donald Durant.

As Ivar traveled downtown to the Wall Street offices of Lee Higginson, he shifted gears. His pitch to Durant wouldn't be an American monopoly – that venture clearly had floundered. He certainly wouldn't mention film. Instead, Ivar would dangle a new idea before Durant: the prospect of Americans investing in *foreign* monopolies. Antitrust laws prohibited a match monopoly in the United States, but nothing prevented American investors from buying into monopolies abroad. Ivar's match monopoly in Sweden was a highly profitable model. It could be just the beginning.

Ivar recalled the extraordinary scheme orchestrated during the seventeenth century by Robert Harley, Earl of Oxford, who had formed the South Sea Company to assume England's national debt. The scheme had become known as the South Sea Bubble, for the sharp increase in the price of South Sea Company shares. In exchange for the South Sea Company assuming its debt, the British government had given the company a monopoly on trade to the South Seas. The deal helped keep England solvent, and led to a boom in the business and share price of the company.

It was an audacious deal, but a simple idea. And the idea could be replicated; it wasn't limited to England and the South Seas or to a time two hundred years earlier. In theory, if a government needed money and a company wanted a monopoly, both sides could benefit from a similar compact – anytime, anywhere, with any product.

Ivar's grand idea was to do just what Harley had done, except with matches instead of South Seas trade. Ivar would lend money to the governments of Europe in exchange for a monopoly concession for the production and sale of matches within their territories. It was a brilliant concept.

There was one immediate problem, though: Ivar didn't have enough money to lend millions of dollars to foreign governments. Ivar was wealthy, but not that wealthy. Much of his money already was invested in his companies, which were heavily in debt. This was why Ivar needed the backing of a major bank. If he could persuade Durant to raise the money, he was sure he could entice some foreign governments to give him a match monopoly.

This twist on the South Sea story was the pitch Ivar planned to make to Donald Durant. Like all of Ivar's speeches, this one would be a tapestry of bold ideas, with a single thread running throughout: Americans would lend money, through Ivar, to foreign governments, and in return everyone would make unimaginable profits from match monopolies.

Durant and Lee Higginson were ideal for Ivar's new plans. Durant's group had built a new sales force, and his partners were embracing new clients, especially from abroad. As Ivar put it,

> Lee Higginson & Co., with its extremely good sales organization – probably larger than that of any other American firm – is particularly well placed to handle issues for companies that have not previously been introduced on the American market, and therefore require energetic preparation of the market. As an example, this firm has single-handedly managed the financing of the American subsidiaries of the Shell Company, which seems to be the only instance of a European company raising American capital through a share issue. The Shell Company is – as is well known – the most important European business now extant.[40]

Ivar entered Lee Higginson's offices at 41 Broad Street, the center of the financial world, a few steps from the New York Stock Exchange. He stepped into a three-story banking hall framed by bronze-capped mosaic columns and a 225-foot-long seafaring mural.[41] The prestigious architecture firm of Cross & Cross had designed the space to grand effect. Durant, the master mariner, was obviously at home here.

But when the two men finally shook hands, it was immediately apparent who had the advantage. Ivar looked more like a Lee Higginson partner than did Durant. And Durant looked more like a Swede desperate for funding than did Ivar. Ivar mesmerized Durant with his knowledge of the match industry, his worldly sophistication, and his mastery and memory of financial detail. And, most importantly, he hooked Durant with his simple, brilliant idea: government loans in exchange for match monopolies. As Durant understood immediately, it was a plan that would change history.

3

THE SPEECH

Durant wasted no time arranging for Ivar give a formal luncheon presentation.[1] Lee Higg was a powerful firm but, like most investment banks of the era, it was small, a true partnership. When all of the partners were in New York, they could, and frequently did, gather in one room at 41 Broad. Their important business was done at lunch, with everyone sitting around a long conference table set with silver and crystal.

Ivar's lunch specch required a different kind of theater than his performance for the passengers on *Berengaria*. The bar was much higher now; the audience was more critical. Ivar knew of Lee Higginson's reputation for integrity and rectitude. He knew Frederic Allen and the Higginsons would resist associating their prestigious firm, and its deep Ivy League roots, with a self-made man from a remote town in Sweden. Ivar had attended a Stockholm engineering school whose name they could not even pronounce. He hadn't gotten anywhere near Harvard or Yale. Ivar knew he should not press too hard during this speech. He should not appear to be a salesman or suitor, but rather a wealthy businessman these prudent men should court.

Ivar needed the partners to see him as worldly and independent, so in addition to discussing his ambitious plans and perspectives, he planned to weave in stories about his past. He wanted to show them a picture of his character.

After the food was set, and brief introductions made, Lee Higg's partners sat and Ivar stood calmly in front of them. Ivar was about to use the two important oratorical lessons he had absorbed from giving hundreds of speeches to investors in Europe: speak from memory, and use lengthy pauses. First, he rubbed his hands together – a long-standing habit – to show he did not plan to use any notes. Second, he paused. And then he paused some more.

And then some more. Ivar had learned the power of silence. He liked to make eye contact with everyone in the audience, one by one, and he did so slowly, before he uttered a word.

Finally, when Ivar began to speak, he gave Lee Higg's partners a surprising piece of advice. He told them to forget about the American match market, including Diamond Match. Ivar viewed Diamond Match as a small-time company with limited upside. He didn't want to discuss the American match market at all. Ivar couldn't be sure he had contained the recent fiasco among Landgren, Fairburn, and Price Waterhouse. He wanted to distance himself from those efforts, just in case the partners from Lee Higg had heard anything about the failures of American Kreuger & Toll.

In place of an American match monopoly, Ivar laid out a far more ambitious plan: to play the role of "world's banker" by raising money in America and then lending it to Europe. In this role, he could satisfy the desires of three important groups that were now separated by geographic, political, and economic barriers: American investors, European governments, and the match industry.

As Ivar explained, the desires of the three parties were clear: American investors wanted high returns, European governments wanted US dollars, and the match industry wanted monopoly power. The resources also were clear: American investors had dollars, European governments had the power to grant monopolies within their territories, and the match industry had the potential for high returns. What was missing was a middleman, a statesman capable of bringing together these three disparate groups.

Ivar was that middleman, a capitalist with European sensibilities and a strong grip on the match industry. He could link the three groups by raising dollars from American investors, lending those dollars to European governments in exchange for match monopolies, and then using those monopolies to generate high returns.

The first part of Ivar's speech to the Lee Higg partners wasn't just about business. He wove in major ideas in political economy, international relations, and world history. He described how post-war Europe was crippled by inflation and unemployment. He discussed the monetary crises facing major European governments, as evidenced by their weakened currencies. By late 1922, the German mark sold for less than four cents, the Austrian crown was worth just half of that, and Russian currency was practically useless in trade. Millions of people were out of work in England, France, Italy, and Poland. Even Ivar's home country, Sweden, was struggling through post-war recovery.

Moreover, much of continental Europe had, as Lenin predicted, developed a hatred of capitalist "profiteers." European governments turned inward and emphasized the state over the individual. Productivity and trade declined. Ivar agreed with the conclusions of the leading economist of the time, John Maynard Keynes, who wrote, "We are thus faced in Europe with the spectacle of an extraordinary weakness on the part of the great capitalist class, which has emerged from the industrial triumphs of the nineteenth century, and seemed a very few years ago our all-powerful master."[2]

As the partners ate, Ivar crisscrossed all of these topics, frequently citing financial statistics and data from his own companies' quarterly reports. He did it entirely from memory. When he had finished, he stood quietly and met everyone's eyes one more time.

Then Ivar began the second, even more important, part of his speech. He told the men he wanted them to know something about his background. Ivar needed Durant's partners to see he was like them, a savvy businessman with a long track record. Ivar didn't deny he was a self-made man, but he wanted them to see his business success as a strong, continuous thread.

Ivar skipped the early part of his life: the lonely childhood, the awkward teenage years, the fruitless search for a job during his first trip to America after engineering school. The Lee Higg partners didn't need to know how Ivar had finagled his way into a menial position at Fuller Construction Company, the leading builder in Manhattan. He might have mentioned that he had worked on the Metropolitan Life tower, the Flatiron and Macy's buildings, and the Plaza and St Regis hotels, and that he had discovered and fixed critical skyscraper flaws.[3] But he would have skipped any description of his antics with Anders Jordahl, whom he met at Fuller.[4]

Ivar might have said something about traveling to South Africa with Jordahl to build the Carlton Hotel, then the world's largest commercial building. But he certainly would have left out the part about their gambling on diamond and gold shares in Johannesburg, or how Ivar briefly joined the Transvaal Militia and then went on a multi-year bender through Paris, India, East Africa, Toronto, and throughout the United States.[5]

During these early years, Ivar was constantly reinventing himself and reforming his personality. But he didn't want Durant and his partners to know about his efforts at self-improvement; he just wanted to show them the finished product.

For these men, the story of Ivar's life began in 1908, shortly after he learned that his first love, a young Norwegian girl, had suddenly died. Ivar should have given up on her already, after her father refused to grant permission to marry until Ivar became wealthy, and then she told Ivar even a large dowry might not be enough. Yet even after these rejections, he still had harbored hopes of marriage. When Ivar learned about her death, a part of him snapped. As one friend put it, "his love-life had to die away to make room for other things he had to accomplish."[6]

Ivar had been working on the pathbreaking Archbold Stadium at Syracuse University. He regarded his bosses there as inferiors, men who lacked the intellect and ambition of the stadium's namesake, John D. Archbold, the great capitalist, oil refiner, and philanthropist. Ivar wrote to his parents, "I cannot believe that I am intended to spend my life making money for second-rate people. I hate the American outlook, but I shall bring American methods back home. Wait and see – I shall do great things. I'm bursting with ideas. I am only wondering which to carry out first."[7]

Ivar told Durant and his partners how, as a 28-year-old working on the stadium project, he had met Julius Kahn, the inventor of "Kahn Iron," a specialized product used to make reinforced concrete. When Kahn mentioned that he had given a Swedish engineer named Paul Toll the contract to represent him in Europe, Ivar persuaded Kahn to recommend that Toll take Ivar on as a partner. Ivar then sailed to England and persuaded Paul Toll to do just that.

On May 18, 1908, Ivar and Paul Toll formed Kreuger & Toll in London. The business was small, with shoestring capital of just over 2,500 dollars, but they produced a superior product and had ideal timing.[8] Kreuger & Toll was part of a wave of migration to London after the market panic of October 1907. Pierpont Morgan had single-handedly rescued several Wall Street banks and indebted trusts from bankruptcy, but the ensuing legislation, which led Congress to create the Federal Reserve System, drove lending abroad. Pierpont sent his son Jack to London, to be groomed along with the world's leading financiers. The Morgans, and other bankers, shifted operations to London.

Ivar tapped into the new funds available there to finance construction projects throughout Europe. He developed superior technology and methods of engineering design, as well as novel contractual features. In particular, he was willing to change the standard terms of construction contracts to reallocate risks to him. His appetite for risk was unique among men in the construction industry.

For example, from his experience at Fuller Construction in New York, Ivar knew how frustrated builders became when there were lengthy delays. Construction firms had not been willing to take on the risk associated with delays; instead, they put that risk on their clients. But Ivar understood a fundamental proposition about the allocation of risk: both parties to a deal can gain when the party in the best position to bear a risk takes on that risk. Construction firms, not clients, were in the best position to reduce delays. Therefore, as Ivar realized, the best way to minimize construction delays was to shift the risk of loss that arose from such delays to him and Paul Toll. Then, Kreuger & Toll would have the incentive – and, crucially, the ability – to speed up a project. And here was the punchline: clients would pay more if they knew the job would be done on time.

Kreuger & Toll became the first firm in Europe to commit to finish projects by a fixed date.[9] After completing some small projects, building some beams and a viaduct, Ivar secured a deal to build a six-story "skyscraper." He promised that if construction wasn't finished by a particular date, he would give the client a partial refund of 1,200 dollars for each late day. (At that rate, Kreuger & Toll's entire capital covered just two days.) In turn, the client agreed to pay a daily bonus for early completion. Ivar then hired three shifts of laborers to work day and night. He personally took over the permitting process to streamline operations, and persuaded the police to ignore neighbors' nighttime complaints about searchlights and cement mixers. Kreuger & Toll finished early, and Ivar repeated this formula and earned completion bonuses for every project. Builders were happy to pay extra to know a high-quality project would be finished ahead of schedule.

Word quickly spread about the firm's reputation for quality, honesty, and timeliness. Paul Toll was smart and hard-working, but Ivar attracted the clients. Within a few years, Kreuger & Toll was regarded as the best building company in Sweden; a few years later, it was one of the top firms in Europe. Soon Kreuger & Toll was building major landmarks, including the stadium for the 1912 Stockholm Olympics and the renowned Stockholm City Hall, which many people considered the most beautiful building in Scandinavia. As the firm expanded, Ivar hired several employees, including Anders Jordahl and Krister Littorin, his closest friend from Tekniska Högskolan, the engineering school in Stockholm, who became the firm's typist and messenger boy.[10]

When Swedish lawmakers decided to permit banks to invest in industrial companies for the first time, Ivar struck a deal with Oscar Rydbeck, a rising star at Skandinaviska Kredit A.B., known as "The Swedish Credit Bank."[11] When Rydbeck said he would be willing to take Ivar's Kreuger & Toll shares as collateral for an investment in a new business, Ivar's thoughts turned to his family – and to matches. Ivar's father, Ernst August, had methodically saved enough money to buy stakes in two small match factories from their extended family's consortium, Mönsterås Matchworks. Ivar's brother Torsten now managed one of those factories in Kalmar, Ivar's home town.

The match business was highly competitive and not very profitable, but Ivar and the newly liberated Swedish banks agreed there was potential. Ivar saw that the match industry was in the same economic position oil, sugar, and steel had been in a few decades earlier. There were too many owners of too many factories. Competition was driving prices down so far that hardly any profit remained. Ivar knew his family, and the numerous other small factory owners, would never make much money this way.

However, if these factories could be consolidated, the owner of a Swedish match monopoly could raise prices and make a fortune. Some factories in Sweden recently had combined, to form the Jönköping-Vulcan trust, but the men running the trust were conservative and slow. Ivar was sure he could dominate them. He began using loans from the Swedish Credit Bank to buy match factories throughout Sweden.

During the next eight years, Ivar parlayed a few family match factories into a conglomerate. He modernized factories and expanded overseas sales. Production increased from 90,000 cases in 1914 to double that in 1916; his profits more than tripled.[12] He reduced costs by purchasing the companies that made his machines, as well as companies that supplied chlorate acid potash for the tips. The hardball tactics Ivar used to take over competitors must have reminded Lee Higg's partners of John D. Rockefeller, who used a similar approach to acquire competitors of his company Standard Oil.

To get the money for these expansions, Ivar turned to Oscar Rydbeck. The Swedish markets were going through their version of a speculative frenzy during 1914–15, and Ivar was able to raise 5 million kronor from Swedish banks. During the war, when exports to Britain closed, Ivar turned to Russia, where he not only exported matches, but purchased aspen wood (the best wood for matches) and paper mills. After the war, he bought up virtually all of his competitors in Sweden, using more cash borrowed with Rydbeck's help. He never gave up control. When he consolidated his match companies, he kept a majority of the voting shares.

Initially, Ivar's decision to enter the match business seemed foolish. Match factories were not profitable, particularly at the beginning of the world war. The Baltic and North Seas were filled with submarines, and Swedes had difficulty importing or exporting anything, including matches. Moreover, in August 1914, during the first weeks of the war, Britain had suspended conversion of sterling into gold, throwing the markets into disarray. Most businessmen thought it would be virtually impossible to raise capital for a new business during the war.

But Ivar took the long view. He believed matches were an important staple, like steel or sugar, and that match factories inevitably would be consolidated. He also foresaw that Britain's abandoning of the gold standard would open up international finance to newcomers, and that the war would not clog shipping lanes as much as people supposed. He thought that if he could manage the match business as well as he had managed construction, he would be able to acquire a monopoly on production. Then, he could raise prices and earn enormous profits. Just as Rockefeller controlled oil and Morgan controlled banking, Kreuger envisioned controlling matches, and thereby joining an élite group of global monopolists.

By 1915, Ivar controlled ten match factories in Sweden, including those held by his family. The operation was tiny at first: one small room in downtown Stockholm, where Ivar worked with Krister Littorin.[13] They lost money during the first year, but in 1916 he posted operating profits of precisely 2 million kronor.[14] Ivar paid his investors, including the Swedish Credit Bank, a dividend of 12 percent.

Ivar pressured owners of rival match factories to sell to him or lose any chance at making a profit. He took advantage of wartime conditions by negotiating "sweetheart" deals with the Swedish government, and by selling matches to the Germans, which no one else would do. He took over potash and phosphorus manufacturing and choked off his competitors' supplies.

By the beginning of 1917, Ivar's group was almost as large as the Jönköping-Vulcan trust; by the end of the year, he owned that trust. He finally settled on a name for his combined company: Svenska Tändsticksaktiebolaget, or Swedish Match Company. It became known simply as "Swedish Match."

During the world war, Ivar crushed Swedish Match's remaining competitors. He approached factory owners with a simple offer: sell to him or be ruined. Ivar destroyed anyone who refused to sell with ruthless tactics: he took over supply contracts, interfered with customers, and temporarily lowered prices below cost. Almost overnight, he transformed dozens of widely spread and struggling factories into a strong and profitable monopoly. Within a few years, he controlled nearly all of the match industry in Sweden. Swedish Match was one of the few European businesses that remained profitable throughout the war.

Finally, Ivar persuaded Paul Toll to convert Kreuger & Toll into a holding company, which would own a portion of Swedish Match. Paul Toll would remain on Kreuger & Toll's board, but Ivar structured the deal so that Toll would give up his voting stake in the holding company in exchange for control of Kreuger & Toll Building Co., a separate entity that Ivar soon abandoned. To keep Toll happy, and busy with other matters, Ivar arranged for him to become Sweden's Consul General to Lithuania.

After relating what sounded like the life story of a sound businessman, Ivar told the Lee Higginson men he was confident he could dominate the global match business. He concluded that,

> There are many reasons why the match industry is particularly well suited for cooperation between the various manufacturers. This is primarily due to the difficulty of establishing new factories and the great advantages in pricing that can be obtained through the elimination of competition. This in turn depends on the fact that the unit price is so low that the consumers will hardly notice even considerable price increases. This is why Swedish Match has made it its objective to bring together all the match manufacturers of the world. These efforts have already advanced so far that a complete success may be considered assured.[15]

Ivar finished the second part of his speech by describing how his match interests had grown steadily, even as the world confronted financial turmoil and world war. By 1922, Kreuger & Toll had increased its dividend to 25 percent. He paused after saying that – a dividend of 25 percent per year – to let it sink in. Swedish Match's dividend also was in double digits. Ivar's companies were among the most profitable in the world. And this was only the beginning.

The men studied Ivar carefully. It was apparent that he was a genius. But even more important, he appeared to be a gentleman. His suit was dark, and he had brought a cane and a black dispatch case.[16] His tie, though not old school by Boston standards, was a conservative pinstripe of impeccable taste. Ivar wasn't exactly like the Lee Higg partners – he was fit and thin, from a strict diet and an obsession with his weight, and like Durant he was missing a moustache – but otherwise he matched them beautifully. He spoke five languages fluently, including near-perfect English. His receding hair made him look older than he was, and his eyes shone with experience. The reaction of one partner was that "here was a dignified Swede who could match patrician bearing with any man, just the kind of solid businessman who was deserving of the aid and backing of one of the nation's most respected banking and brokerage houses."[17]

As the staff removed the plates, the men were riveted by Ivar's plans to build a new "Match Palace" in Stockholm, a mansion that would double as an office. It would be a masterpiece of art and architecture, with a hundred more rooms than the average apartment or house of a Lee Higg partner.

Notwithstanding Ivar's modest background, he now seemed to belong with the whitest of the white shoes. He behaved like an old-line banker, and the partners were surprised that he neither looked nor talked like a Swede (one allegedly remarked, "And he has brown hair!"[18]). By the time Ivar finished answering questions, the hook was set. When he mentioned his ambition to double the size of his businesses, and his promise to pay a very high dividend in the United States – not the 25 percent Kreuger & Toll paid in Sweden, but certainly something in double digits – Ivar was ready to reel in one of America's leading banks.

Frederic Allen, the senior statesman from New York, summed up the views of the partnership after the luncheon with Ivar. They found him to be "all that they had expected, a brilliant business head, full of compelling ideas, and a gentleman to boot."[19] The partners had been right to bet on Durant; he had discovered precisely the kind of man they needed. Ivar shook hands with Durant's partners. He knew they would be proposing a deal soon.

There were many compelling reasons for Lee Higginson to support Ivar. His character, smarts, and connections. His brilliant idea for bringing together American capital, European governments, and match monopolies. But perhaps most persuasive was the notion that Ivar would give the men a chance to one-up their key rival, J. P. Morgan & Co. For Durant's partners, that reason alone was nearly enough.

Morgan still dominated the financial world, but since Pierpont Morgan's death the firm had faced a wave of fresh competition. Jack Morgan was a pale imitation of his late father, and Lee Higg was constantly looking for any opportunity to take business from its rival, and to unseat young Jack. They knew Jack had refused to do business with Ivar, following Pierpont's practice of transacting only with men he already knew and trusted. Jack's blinkers might be Lee Higg's opportunity.

Moreover, Jack Morgan seemed to be losing his grip, not only on the firm's business, but often on reality. The most recent symbol of Jack's weaknesses, and his firm's, was a terrorist attack. As bankers learned about Jack's response to this attack, it appeared that he was more vulnerable than ever.

Two years earlier, in 1920, just a few seconds after the Trinity Church bell tolled noon on a pleasant Thursday in September, a massive shrapnel bomb shook the corner of Wall and Broad Streets in New York.[20] The blast set fire to awnings twelve stories above, sprayed hundreds of slugs into the façade of the Morgan building, and killed thirty employees instantly. The cloud of greenish smoke that rose from the explosion darkened the area for several minutes. When the dust cleared, George Whitney, one of the six Morgan partners, walked outside and found that a fragment of window sash weight had pinned a woman's head and hat against the bank's scarred north façade. He reported, "I'll always remember that. It hit her so hard that it just took her head off and it stuck right on the wall."[21]

At the Stock Exchange, sixty paces around the corner, brokers rushed to the center of the trading floor to avoid falling glass, and trading was suspended within one minute, as William H. Remick, president of the Exchange, mounted the rostrum and rang the gong.[22] Trading on the Curb Market also halted immediately; the downtown area became a mob scene. The boys with the telephones attached to their heads weren't just swinging down from windows – now they were jumping. Brokers scattered, and federal troops rushed from Governors Island to Wall Street.

When the bomb hit, Jack Morgan was away vacationing at his Scottish shooting lodge. Jack already had been paranoid, even before this attack on his bank's headquarters. Just before the war, a mysterious German man had attempted to assassinate him, and he had almost succeeded. Although Jack had recovered from the gunshot wounds, he still suffered from the emotional blow. He was obsessed with his personal safety and gripped by fear that he had become a terrorist target. He had hired a group of former Marines as bodyguards, and scampered into hiding whenever he heard reports of an escape from a prison or mental asylum.

Now, after the shrapnel bomb, Jack descended into full-blown panic. When Justice Department authorities investigated the blast and pursued dozens of suspects, but could not pin the crime on anyone,[23] Jack concluded that he must have been the target. If he hadn't been off hunting in Scotland, he would have been killed. Who was after him? Would they ever stop?

He posted thirty private detectives to watch his brownstone on Madison Avenue.[24] He also began to view competition from other banks as more than merely business rivalry. He spun elaborate conspiracy theories involving the Bolsheviks and German-Jewish financiers. Jack and his friends were on one side of Wall Street; on the other side were the enemy bankers – Kuhn Loeb, Lehman, and Goldman Sachs – many of whom were Jewish. Jack Morgan neither trusted nor liked Jews. When Harvard president A. Lawrence Lowell sought to fill a board vacancy, Jack, who was an overseer of Harvard and a devoted alumnus, warned that "the nominee should by no means be a Jew ... the Jew is always a Jew first and an American second."[25]

Unlike Jack, investors ultimately shrugged off the bomb. The new Federal Reserve Bank reduced interest rates and added money to the financial system after the attack. The new Treasury Secretary, Andrew Mellon, brought confidence with a proposal for lower taxes. Investors came to see that neither war nor terrorists could defeat American optimism.

The Lee Higg partners were especially interested in the business of foreign lending, and here they saw more cracks in Morgan's foundation. Earlier, during the war, J. P. Morgan & Co. had arranged over $1.5 billion in loans to the Allied forces.[26] Immediately after the war, the United States government wanted to become more involved in reparations, but said it could not do so without Morgan, which controlled lending to governments. Only Morgan seemed to have access to sufficient funds to rebuild Europe, and no foreign leader could imagine borrowing money without Morgan playing a leading role.

For example, the French government, like most of Europe, had been interested in obtaining loans to help rebuild after the war. French officials had considered trying to arrange loans without Morgan, but they quickly became reconciled to dealing exclusively with Morgan. Baron Emile du Marais, a financial advisor to President Raymond Poincaré, wrote that "one can in no way manage without their support. It is a fact about which we can do absolutely nothing. In these conditions, wisdom seems to dictate that we accept the *fait accompli*, and try to give Morgan's the impression that we have full confidence in them."[27] Consistent with its historical dominance, Morgan recently had loaned 100 million dollars to France at a rate of 8 percent.

Before the attack on Morgan's headquarters, it was inconceivable that anyone other than Morgan would arrange future financing for France, or even that Poincaré would meet with someone else to discuss a loan. But the shrapnel bomb shifted momentum. As foreign officials learned about Jack Morgan's increasing paranoia, as well as the successes of other American bankers, they considered looking elsewhere for loans. The threat of competition in foreign lending went deeper than Jack Morgan's concern about Jewish bankers. Yes, there were able Jewish bankers poised to take business from Morgan. But there were plenty of Yankee bankers as well. Lee Higginson, for instance, was the ultimate Yankee bank, with Boston and Harvard roots, and it, too, was eager to arrange loans to Europe. Ironically, although the extent of Jack Morgan's paranoia about his personal safety was largely unjustified, from a purely business perspective, he wasn't nearly paranoid enough. Suddenly, in the foreign loan business, Jack was being fired at from all sides.

For better and worse, during the early 1920s the public came to see Jack and his British country squire lifestyle as a symbol of Wall Street's dominance and extravagance. American investors might not yet know Ivar Kreuger, but they recognized Jack's black eyebrows and white moustache anywhere. A picture of Jack's plump face in the newspaper was usually attached to some opulent leisure activity. Even Jack acknowledged that he tended to loaf, and was not as engaged in the business as he should have been. He preferred gardening and yachting to banking. Being in Scotland on vacation during the attack was typical of Jack. Although he had worked long hours during the war, and was a reasonably skilled international negotiator, Jack lacked Pierpont's drive, as well as his uniquely sharp financial mind. Jack once likened his own brain to a "soft, overboiled cauliflower."[28]

If Lee Higginson embraced Ivar's plan, it could strike at the heart of Morgan's franchise. Ivar was suggesting to Lee Higg's partners that they could replace Jack Morgan as the leading financier in Europe by helping Ivar give cash-starved European governments better loan terms and lower interest rates, perhaps a full percentage point or more below Morgan's. At the same time, Ivar also offered foreign governments something Jack Morgan did not: a chance to earn significant profits from an important local industry. When a government gave Ivar a monopoly, it would receive both a loan and a share of monopoly profits from the sale of matches.

Ivar's plan seemed too good to be true. The timing was perfect, Morgan was vulnerable, and Lee Higginson was well positioned. It was the idea of a lifetime. Ivar's speech had done the job. Lee Higg's partners gave Durant permission to begin soliciting American investors.

Durant confronted skepticism at first. Ivar had no track record as an international lender, and he didn't have any deals lined up. Swedish Match had been an active exporter throughout Europe, and Ivar had developed strong relationships with government officials. But his operations outside Sweden had not yet risen to the level of monopoly, or anything close. Ivar had been more of a borrower than a lender.

Still, Durant could cite many selling points to prospective investors. Ivar had a thriving match business and a history of paying high dividends, as high as 25 percent. The monopoly-for-loan idea certainly was ingenious. Even if it did not generate profits right away, the plan seemed likely to succeed at some point. Like General Motors or RCA, Ivar's new venture was a bet on the future. Increasingly, American investors liked gambling on the future more than tracking the past.

Ivar joined Durant on road shows, and interest grew as Ivar repeated his speech throughout 1923. By the fall Durant believed he finally had found enough investors, and Ivar and Lee Higginson began preparing to close a deal. They followed the same procedure as anyone seeking money. First, they created a new firm, called International Match Corporation, and incorporated it in Delaware. During the late nineteenth century, states had begun competing for corporate charters, the formative documents that corporations are required to file when they are created. Delaware had recently surpassed New Jersey as the incorporation state of choice, and increasingly companies chose to file in Delaware, even if their operations were in another state. Delaware judges took a hands-off approach to business, and would be unlikely to second-guess Ivar's decisions. By incorporating International Match in Delaware, Lee Higginson would give Ivar and themselves maximum flexibility.

Next, Durant and Ivar chose the initial shareholders and directors of International Match. The two original shareholders would be Swedish Match and a syndicate of Swedish banks; they would contribute start-up capital of 30 million dollars and receive the company's shares, in equal amounts. As shareholders, Swedish Match and the bank syndicate would vote for the company's board of directors, as well as other major business decisions.

The shareholders would elect five directors to oversee International Match's business: Ivar; Krister Littorin, Ivar's engineering classmate from Stockholm; Donald Durant; Frederic Allen, Lee Higginson's senior statesman and head of the firm's New York office; and Percy A. Rockefeller, a nephew of John D. Rockefeller. Percy Rockefeller owned the World Match Company of Walkerville, Ontario, and recently had met Ivar while negotiating the sale of a Canadian match manufacturing plant to Swedish Match.[29] The two men had impressed each other, and Ivar saw that Rockefeller, who then served on more than sixty other boards, would be the ideal director of International Match: he was well connected, wealthy, generally familiar with the match industry, and far too busy to care about any details. Ivar had idolized the Rockefellers since he was a boy in Kalmar; now, a member of that family would serve on his board.

Once these pieces were in place, Ivar and Durant needed to decide which type of financial instrument International Match would issue to new investors. Ivar wanted a customized investment that would appeal to the relatively cautious mindset of many investors, but that also offered a substantial upside. However, Ivar didn't want to give away control of International Match. Ivar had experience designing innovative contract features in the real estate and construction industries. Now, he would tailor a financial instrument to the needs of investors while preserving his interests.

Ivar and Lee Higginson decided to have International Match issue new securities called convertible gold debentures. "Debenture" was just a fancy term for "bond" – debentures were a fixed claim on interest payments by the corporation plus a return of the principal amount on the maturity date, which in this case would be twenty years. Debentures had a limited upside, but were safer than shares. These "gold" debentures were safer still, because they were payable in either dollars or gold, at the holder's option. If International Match became bankrupt, holders of debentures would be repaid first, before shareholders received any money. These debentures gave investors the right to receive annual interest payments of 6.5 percent from International Match, an attractive rate at the time.

Finally, these debentures were convertible, which meant that they could be converted into shares. If International Match performed well and the value of the shares increased, investors could switch from the debentures to the more valuable shares. The convertible feature made these securities particularly attractive: they had both downside protection and upside potential, the best of both worlds. Ivar and Lee Higginson had designed their first financial mousetrap.

The prospectus for the International Match gold debentures described these new securities as a conservative investment, although it also highlighted the potential upside. The stated purpose of the new issue was broad: "to acquire additional investments and to provide working capital."[30] In other words, investors would give cash to Ivar, and trust him to use it to generate yet more cash. That was a straightforward proposition, even if it required an act of faith.

As investors learned about the gold debentures, Ivar was inundated with requests for meetings and social engagements. Word spread about the now legendary speech he had given at Lee Higg, and businessmen throughout the country wanted an audience with Ivar to connect with him and hear the themes in person. He spent a Sunday at T. L Higginson, Jr's estate in historic Wenham, a North Shore Massachusetts town where the Higginsons had owned property for nearly three centuries.[31] He was invited to the annual dinners of the Fifth Avenue Association at the Waldorf-Astoria,[32] and the Council on Foreign Relations at the Ritz-Carlton,[33] as well as an event in his honor hosted by Donald Durant at the Racquet & Tennis Club on Park Avenue. When Ivar accepted that invitation, Durant gushed, "I am so glad you are giving me the opportunity to have some of my friends meet you."[34]

Ivar received fan mail from the masses as well, a surprising number originating because he had charmed some American man's wife or daughter on a cruise. Chauncey P. Colwell congratulated Ivar and invited him to lunch should he ever be in Philadelphia; Ivar had met Mrs Colwell on the *Berengaria*.[35] Edward B. Robinette, whose daughter had met Ivar at sea, was so desperate to send Ivar a fruit basket that he guessed which ship Ivar would be taking home to Europe for the holidays. When the guess turned out wrong, Mr Robinette sent Ivar an apology note, on Christmas Eve, just in case there was still any chance for his daughter to see him.[36]

Ivar's popularity helped Lee Higginson sell 15 million dollars of International Match gold debentures, at a price of $94.50 for each $100 of principal amount. Investors paid $94.50 in return for the right to receive interest of $6.50 per year for twenty years (6.5 percent of the $100 principal amount). After twenty years, International Match would return the investor's principal amount of $100. Investors who sold before the twenty-year maturity date might receive more or less than the $94.50 they paid, depending on how International Match was doing. Overall, the deal raised a total of $14,175,000 (94.5 percent of $15 million).

The financial press buzzed with news about Ivar and his newfangled gold debentures. The *Wall Street Journal* reported on October 26, 1923 that the new International Match issue was "spoken of with great admiration among the bond houses. It is probably the finest piece of bond salesmanship we have seen in years."[37]

It was one of the largest securities issues of the year, and certainly the hottest initial public offering. As one analyst later described a different kind of IPO, "it was like touching a match to a bucket of gasoline."[38]

Once International Match had the money, Ivar turned to his trusted circle of Anders Jordahl, Krister Littorin, and his brother Torsten. Each of these three men would play a crucial role in his expansion to America.

Anders Jordahl would continue to head Ivar's American operations and, perhaps more importantly, would arrange Ivar's social life during his time in New York. Krister Littorin would be Ivar's right-hand man, based in Stockholm, and also would become president of Swedish Match. Torsten Kreuger, Ivar's younger brother, would play the role of ambassador. As children, Ivar and Torsten had constructed elaborate imaginary schemes, and Ivar had always promised Torsten that some day he would engineer a real-life plan for both of them. Finally, Ivar was in a position to do it.

Although in 1923 Torsten was still in his thirties, he easily could pose as a distinguished businessman twenty years older. He was balding, well dressed, and even better mannered. When Ivar invited him to take a motorboat to Finland to discuss their plans for International Match, Torsten showed up in a grey three-piece suit with a starched tab collar and a black tie.[39] That level of formality would be crucial in Torsten's new position as Ivar's emissary.

Ivar updated Torsten about his recent success with the Americans. Ivar stressed the importance of securing a deal with at least one foreign government quickly, to lend some credibility to his grand plan of trading loans for match monopolies. Lee Higginson had raised millions of dollars based on an idea. If Ivar didn't convince American investors he actually could obtain match monopolies for loans, as he had promised, the first International Match debenture issue would be his last. Unlike Charles Ponzi, the small-time operator in postal reply coupons, Ivar would need to show real results before he would be able to raise any more money.

Ivar charged Torsten to find a government loan. His first stop would be Poland, which Ivar thought held the greatest promise of a deal. Ivar had been working with government officials there for several years, and already had some of Poland's match business. He arranged for Torsten's introduction to the finance minister and his staff.

Ivar would be available to assist Torsten with negotiations. But first Ivar needed to answer a pressing question. With one speech, Ivar had reeled in Lee Higginson, one of the biggest fish in the sea of American investment. International Match now held millions of dollars of cash, which would be at his disposal if he actually could close a foreign government loan.

There was one problem, though. That cash was sitting in an American bank. The fish was in a barrel, but it was the wrong country's barrel. That predicament was the reason for Ivar's important question. It was simple, but outrageous. Even asking it would have alarmed his new investors.

The question was this: How could Ivar get the millions of dollars Lee Higginson had just raised for International Match out of the United States?

4

TROUBLE AT HOME

Ivar put the handful of people he trusted into two categories. First was his circle of Torsten, Krister Littorin, and Anders Jordahl. Ivar knew these three men better than anyone. The only other person who came close to this group was Ivar's personal secretary, Karin Bökman, an attractive red-haired woman who spent more time with Ivar than even his three closest friends. These people trusted Ivar for what one might call the right reasons: they had come to love and respect him, and to believe in his mission and ambition. They were a major part of his life, and he was a major part of theirs.

But there was another type of person Ivar felt he could trust even more. By 1922, Ivar secretly had hired a handful of men with no previous connection to him or his companies. These men trusted Ivar for all the wrong reasons: because he had saved them from prison or bribed them or paid them five times what they deserved. Ivar could ask these men to do things he would never ask of friends. Sometimes Ivar needed a person he could trust for reasons more dependable than human love or respect, someone he could rely on as a master relies on a well-trained attack dog. Then, if one of Ivar's schemes unraveled, he could lay the blame on an out-of-control animal.

Getting International Match's money out of America required help from someone in the second category. Ivar wanted to hire someone new, unknowing, and anonymous, so he did what he typically would do when he needed to find an absolutely reliable new man: he placed an advertisement in the New York newspapers.

Ivar didn't tell his friends about the want ad, and he didn't use his name or the name of one of his companies. He interviewed applicants on his own, and went with his instincts. Ivar usually could tell whether a man would work out simply by staring him in the eye.

This time, one of the men who answered the ad had the given name Ernst August, the same name as Ivar's father. That caught Ivar's attention right away. Was it coincidence or fate? How ironic would it be if, after forty years, someone named Ernst August would come to play an influential and positive role in Ivar's life. His father, who still toiled away at a dead-end middle management job in one of Ivar's match factories, certainly had not.

Ernst August Hoffman's application fit the job description perfectly: he was a Swiss-American with some experience as a secretary and a few months working in a New York bank.[1] He spoke several languages. He was educated, but not too educated; smart, but not too smart. Ivar arranged a meeting, and was pleased to see that Ernst August didn't flinch at his stare. Ivar instinctively felt he could trust the young man, and he hired him on the spot.

At first, Hoffman didn't do much as Ivar's employee except collect and cash paychecks. Ivar gave him a few tasks, to test his trustworthiness. Ivar said it wasn't necessary for Hoffman to do more. He should just wait patiently. Ivar had something big planned.

Finally, when Ivar felt the time was right, he sent his new hire to Zürich to study the Swiss financial and tax laws. He told Hoffman of a plan to reduce International Match's taxes, and said it should be kept absolutely secret. Under no circumstances was he to mention Ivar's name or any of Ivar's companies to anyone.

By late 1923, it was getting difficult to track Ivar's multinational network of interlocking subsidiaries, most of which were linked in some way to Kreuger & Toll and Swedish Match. Now, Ivar had added International Match, a company that was half owned by Swedish Match. Ivar's interests were becoming a many-legged spider, with financial pedipalps extending into an increasing number of businesses and countries.

It was straightforward for Ivar to add an appendage to this network, and he did so frequently. Forming a new company was as easy as filling out a piece of paper. Then, Ivar simply transferred capital from one of his existing companies to the new company – also just a matter of paper instructions. To staff a new company's board of directors or management, Ivar picked one or more of his anonymous men. He had plenty of choices. The structure and personnel didn't matter anyway. It always was clear that Ivar remained in charge.

When Ivar decided to set up a new Swiss company, to be called Continental Investment Corporation, he told just one person: Ernst August Hoffman. The two men met in London, where Ivar told Hoffman what he needed to know about the plans. As Hoffman's research had confirmed, Switzerland was still a banking and tax haven. If a businessman wanted to keep his dealings secret, forming a Swiss company was a good place to start.

The two men boarded a train for Zürich, and Ivar showered Hoffman with praise. He needed a man he could trust, who could keep secrets, and who was good with numbers. Hoffman was off to a superb beginning. When Ivar said he had decided to appoint him as the sole director of Continental, the young man was stunned, but honored. When Hoffman asked, "How much capital will the new concern have?" Ivar simply pointed to a small hand bag he had carried onto the train.[2]

When they arrived for their scheduled meeting in Zürich, Ivar removed the contents of the hand bag: 1 million Swiss francs in cash, 9 million in checks, and a single sheet of paper. Ivar showed Ernst August the paper, a guarantee from the Swedish Match Company in the amount of 50 million Swiss francs. Ivar signed it. That guarantee was the bulk of Continental's initial capital.

With the stroke of a pen, Ivar had put in place the next step of his plan: he had formed a Swiss company with 60 million Swiss francs of capital. More money would be coming. Swedish Match owned Continental's shares, and Ivar would control Continental through its single board member, chief executive, secretary, and accountant, Ernst August Hoffman.

When Ivar returned to Stockholm, he met with his brother Torsten, who described a recent trip to the Duchy of Liechtenstein. Torsten also had been looking for a secretive domicile for a subsidiary, a company that would hold some of Ivar's Berlin real estate. Torsten thought Liechtenstein was ideal: the laws were loose and he could negotiate a tax arrangement directly with the country's finance minister in its capital Vaduz. Ivar was elated by this news. Ivar said he had "always liked droll little countries with droll little laws."[3]

Although Swiss taxes were low, Ivar was forever open to a better deal. Armed with Torsten's insights about Vaduz, he secretly sent Ernst August to reincorporate Continental Investment Corporation in Liechtenstein. Now, Continental would be doubly hidden – no one could trace a trail from Zürich to Vaduz. The finance minister of Liechtenstein agreed to fix Continental's taxes at 60,000 Swiss francs for the first two years and 30,000 thereafter, regardless of how much money the company made. The arrangement was perfect. International Match's earnings would have been subject to tax in America. If Ivar could shift those earnings to Continental he could virtually eliminate any tax. In addition, Ivar met with all thirteen members of Liechtenstein's parliament, and persuaded them to sign a ten-year agreement to apply only minimal regulation and oversight to Continental, which would remain controlled by Swedish Match and Ivar, and managed by Ernst August Hoffman.

Continental wouldn't *do* anything; its primary role would be to help Ivar secretly transfer funds from America to himself without requiring any direct exchange of cash between International Match and Swedish Match. Once he sent money to Vaduz, it entered a black hole. American auditors might monitor checks and wires from International Match, but they could not see any evidence of Continental's transactions. Indeed, they wouldn't even know Continental existed. To the extent Ivar or any of his henchmen needed money for bribes or other clandestine activities, they could avoid the scrutiny of American auditors by going through Continental rather than International Match.

By the time Continental was incorporated, Ivar effectively controlled International Match. Swedish Match held half of International Match's shares, and Ivar's Swedish bank syndicate, led by one of his admirers, Oscar Rydbeck, controlled the other half. American investors owned debentures, not shares, which meant they did not have a vote. International Match's board of directors, and its investment bankers, agreed to everything Ivar asked. Lee Higginson already was more focused on International Match's next deal than on the details of what was happening within the company.

Ivar knew the offshore scheme was bold, and even with Ernst August and Continental in place he was nervous about getting caught. Just days before the gold debenture issue was finalized, Ivar wondered whether wiring money right away was too risky. He informed Oscar Rydbeck that "it may be inadvisable to remove money from America too quickly."[4]

When International Match closed its debenture issue in November 1923, and investors paid the company about 14.2 million dollars of cash, it essentially was up to Ivar alone to decide what to do with the money. Of that amount, about 2 million dollars was marked to pay interest and other fees International Match owed, including a substantial fee to Lee Higginson.[5] That left just over 12 million dollars – $12,244,792, to be precise.

As the head of International Match, Ivar debited that amount from the company's cash and replaced it with a credit to Continental Investment Corporation in the same amount. Suddenly, International Match's primary asset was an IOU from Continental instead of cash. Then, without the Americans seeming to care or even notice, Ivar wired $12,244,792 – all of the remaining proceeds from the International Match gold debenture issue, one of the largest American securities issues in years – to Continental's account in Vaduz.

Ivar was no Charles Ponzi. He wasn't going to abscond with the money. He just wanted the flexibility to use the funds as he pleased, and to buy time if things didn't go as planned. In a bad year, he could fudge the numbers and pay dividends out of Continental's assets. In a good year, he could understate earnings and save for a rainy day by hiding the extra income at Continental. Although Ivar needed US investors to fund his loan-for-monopoly plan, he didn't want to become a slave to them. Continental was the vehicle for Ivar to move his finances offshore, where Americans wouldn't see them. It would keep Ivar free.

Ivar had memorized every detail of his actual profits and losses, so he knew what the legitimate amounts were – he simply chose not to share that information with anyone else. He certainly knew his companies would need to generate greater profits to cover the huge dividends his shareholders were expecting. Those cash obligations were real, and it didn't matter whether the money came from New York or Vaduz. To meet those obligations, Ivar would need to raise more cash. To do that, he needed to persuade investors that his plans were a good bet. And to do that, Ivar needed to acquire some match monopolies in Europe.

Donald Durant and his partners had no idea how desperately Ivar needed the money Lee Higginson had just raised for International Match. Although Ivar's businesses seemed to be thriving, he had promised too much to his early investors. He had borrowed tens of millions of dollars from Sweden's leading banks, and both Kreuger & Toll and Swedish Match were paying double-digit dividends. The companies' profits alone did not always cover these obligations. Without new money every year or so, more cash was going out than coming in.

In order for Ivar's businesses to continue to succeed, they had to continue to grow. If they stopped growing, Ivar would not be able to repay his earlier debts or continue to pay high dividends. It wasn't rocket science: to pay a 25 percent dividend every year, you either had to earn 25 percent from your business or else raise more money. To grow by more than that rate, you had to earn even greater profits or raise even more money. The numbers were daunting.

Fortunately for Ivar, his reputation as a savvy businessman had permitted him to raise additional funds, every year. Investors believed he had a unique ability to choose investments, to buy low and sell high. Ivar seemed to make money on virtually everything he touched. And he seemed to touch almost everything, stretching from film to foreign currency speculation to real estate.

At least that was Ivar's reputation. The truth was more complicated. A large portion of the dividends recently paid by Swedish Match and Kreuger & Toll came from cash raised by International Match in America. In other words, the dividends paid to old investors came from proceeds raised from new ones. That pyramid approach, which had elements of Ponzi's scheme, couldn't last forever, and Ivar knew it.

Nevertheless, Ivar really was making money, a lot of it, from match operations throughout the world. Unlike Charles Ponzi's postal reply coupon scam, Ivar's profits were real. Swedish Match made and sold billions of boxes of matches every year. Kreuger & Toll built landmark buildings throughout Europe. Ivar had real investments in real businesses, ranging from matches to real estate to film. No one could fake that.

Ivar believed that if he kept raising cash to pay earlier debts his businesses would grow fast enough to survive, even if they continued to pay high dividends. This belief wasn't unreasonable. If Ivar really could control the production and sale of matches throughout the world, Swedish Match and International Match would be worth a fortune.

But first Ivar had to lock in some match monopoly deals before any obligations came due. He knew liquidity was crucial: even the very best ideas fail if a company runs out of money. Even if Ivar dedicated all of the proceeds from the American new gold debenture issue to business operations, his companies would burn through that cash in a year.

The immediate question was whether Ivar would be able to use the $12 million of new American money to keep his ventures running, or whether he would need it to repay his loans from the Swedish banks. Oscar Rydbeck, Ivar's banker from Skandinaviska Kredit, the Swedish Credit Bank, already had loaned Ivar more than either man could afford. Rydbeck had become one of the most distinguished bankers in Sweden, in large part by building his career on Ivar's successes.

Rydbeck was less conservative than most bankers, particularly in Sweden. He looked the part of a banker, though, with rounded jowls, a high forehead, and a neatly trimmed moustache. He dressed the part, too, with a traditional Gladstone collar, gold cufflinks, and a neatly folded front pocket handkerchief. But Rydbeck, like Ivar, was a big picture man and a dreamer. He had cozy relationships with banking regulators, who had permitted him to lend money to Ivar in novel and unconventional ways.

Ivar had raised most of the money that generated his early fortune from Swedish banks, with Rydbeck as his point man. Although Rydbeck had been lending money to Ivar and his Swedish companies for nearly two decades, he still wasn't sure whether to think of Ivar as a friend. Notwithstanding his central role in Ivar's success, Rydbeck hadn't made it into Ivar's closest circle.

Ivar and Rydbeck had pioneered an early version of "off balance sheet financing," loans that a company obtains without showing any debts on its balance sheet. The debts are real, but because they are "off" the balance sheet, the company appears healthier than if it had taken out a straightforward loan.

The techniques the men used to justify keeping the debts off the balance sheet varied, but they typically involved the use of companies that were loosely related to Kreuger & Toll and Swedish Match. Their argument was that the debts really belonged to those related companies, not to Ivar's companies, and therefore they did not need to be listed on the balance sheet. Swedish Match became one of the first companies to borrow millions of dollars through a complex web of interlocking and related corporations and partnerships without recording those borrowings as liabilities on its balance sheet.

During the second half of 1919, Ivar and Rydbeck had suggested to a group of bankers the idea of "a syndicate apart from the Swedish Match Company."[6] The key word was "apart." Swedish Match would obtain funding through private side deals with several banks. Ivar would use the money for a range of purposes: pay dividends and interest, expand match exports, buy new factories and raw materials, and invest in new industries. Then, Swedish Match would record any gains from these activities in its financial statements. However, it would not record any corresponding liabilities. In other words, the banks would "lend" Swedish Match money, but they would do it in a way that did not appear as a "loan" in Swedish Match's financial statements. Swedish Match got potential gain without the pain.

To engineer these deals, Ivar and Rydbeck employed financial derivative instruments known as options, which gave the holder the right to buy shares at a specified time and price. The linchpin of Swedish Match's option transactions was that they were separated from the company: they were "apart" from Swedish Match and therefore were legally distinct.

Specifically, Ivar and the Swedish banks signed a three-year syndicate agreement, and agreed to set "apart" about 60 million kronor for investments. During the first year, Swedish Match would have the right (here was the option) to take over all of the syndicate's assets for 125 percent of the original amount.[7] From that point on, the banks would have the right (again, an option) to force Ivar to buy the assets for the same amount.

Meanwhile, Ivar retained control, as he typically did, and he invested the money on behalf of the syndicate. He also was responsible for bookkeeping. As Ivar reasoned, because the syndicate was legally separate, Swedish Match's financial statements did not need to show any of the syndicate's losses or liabilities. Those numbers would not appear on Swedish Match's income statement or balance sheet.

During its first year, the syndicate Ivar and Rydbeck created lost more than 4 million kronor. But Swedish Match found a way to hide those early losses. In a report to the syndicate, at the end of September 1920, Ivar assured his bankers that the losses were offset by gains on other investments, and that it would be foolish to sell those investments because the gains would be taxed. Better to keep all the money in the syndicate for now. He confidently wrote that "it can be said with certainty that the intrinsic increase in value of the shares belonging to the company fully corresponds to the losses shown in the annual accounts, so that it must be considered completely justifiable to increase the book values for the companies."[8]

Ivar knew that "book value" accounting, a traditional approach, generally required that companies record their assets at cost. If a company bought land for 10,000 dollars, it would record the value of that land in its financial statements as 10,000 dollars. Following basic accounting principles, that recorded book value would remain constant, even if the value of the land went up or down. In other words, even if the market value of the land changed, Ivar would not "mark to market" that value.

In his 1920 report, Ivar was arguing that the syndicate should abandon the traditional approach to book value. His reasoning was persuasive: if you know land is now worth 15,000 dollars, why would you continue to record its value at 10,000 dollars? The same was true of other investments. If the actual value of an investment increased, why shouldn't the recorded value of that investment also increase? Thus, as Ivar argued, it was "completely justifiable to increase the book values." He was simply marking those values to market.

For example, the syndicate had purchased shares of one company for just over 4.4 million kronor. Ivar argued that those shares had increased in value to 6.8 million kronor. Why show the investment as worth just 4.4 million, when everyone knew it was worth 50 percent more? Ivar didn't wait for Rydbeck or the syndicate members to endorse his "mark to market" reasoning. Instead, he simply increased the recorded, or "marked," value of these shares to reflect the gains. A year later, he again increased the marked value of the same investment to 11.4 million kronor.[9] Once more, he argued, the value of the investment had gone up, so the financial statements should show that.

Ivar also used the banks' funds to gamble on foreign currencies. He seemed to have a deep understanding of the factors influencing exchange rates. Either that, or he was really lucky. Ivar's currency bets were a major source of profits for Swedish Match and Ivar's personal accounts. In one trade, he made a 250 percent profit – 10 million kronor – by buying US dollars in 1917 at a cheap rate of 2.34 kronor and then selling them three years later at a much more expensive rate of 5.70 kronor. Oscar Rydbeck and the syndicate members apparently believed Ivar had unique skills and knowledge, and a special ability to win these bets.

In 1920, the Swedish Bank Inspection Board discovered the creative approach Ivar and Rydbeck had taken with the banking syndicate. Svenska Handelsbanken, one of the syndicate members, commissioned Oscar Sillén, a public accountant and professor at the Stockholm Business School, to investigate Ivar's investments, and the Inspection Board members saw some of the details from that investigation.[10] The Swedish regulators also learned that Ivar had persuaded the banks to lend money based solely on Ivar's personal surety, or guarantee of repayment. In particular, the only security for many of the bank loans was Ivar's personal stake in Swedish Match.

Sillén published an initial report in December 1921, stating his aim "to raise the veil" from Ivar's companies. By the time of his second report, in April 1922, Sillén had discovered many items that belonged in the financial statements of Swedish Match but instead were listed in the statements of other companies. He found that important assets "did not show up in the balance sheets." Even after Sillén found what he thought were all of Swedish Match's assets and liabilities from the syndicate, he still could not put a value on Swedish Match overall, in large part because of the complexities of the company's exposure to various countries' foreign exchange rates.

In other words, just before Ivar raised money from American investors in late 1922, an astute public accountant in Sweden had found that Swedish Match's finances were so complicated that he could not unravel them. The Swedish banks in the syndicate had not truly understood their exposure to Ivar. Sillén concluded that the Swedish Match consortium of companies should be called "The Greatest Speculation Venture in Sweden."

Sillén also found that "too much responsibility rested on Kreuger alone."
He wrote:

> Kreuger, whose qualifications I have no reason to call in question, is the
> only one who really is in command of the whole business. If, for any reason,
> the company would lose his manpower, then – as far as I can judge – enor-
> mous values would be at stake. It is thus of vital interest for the whole
> group, that a man is placed at Kreuger's side. This man must be capable of
> representing Kreuger in the management of the company when Kreuger is
> away abroad.

The Swedish authorities were horrified. Their job was to protect the
banking system, and they criticized the banks for lending so much money to
Ivar without adequate security. The regulators' conclusion was simple: the
syndicate had exposed the banks to too much risk, and it should be dismantled. The banks needed to diversify their exposure to Ivar. One banking
inspector reported that "the match concern's leading man is in debt to various
banks for approximately 22 million crowns, where the security appears largely
to consist of match shares, in addition to which he has contingent liabilities
amounting to 42.6 million crowns."[11] In December 1922, the Swedish Banking
Inspectorate concluded: "Therefore, it is evidently high time that the banks
arrange for an extraordinary, completely impartial, examination of the whole
group."[12]

Only someone with Rydbeck's influence could have calmed the regulators.
Rydbeck used his close contacts to persuade the Inspection Board not to
intrude right away on any banking relationships. He argued that self-
regulation was a more flexible and safer approach. The regulators should trust
the banks to do the right thing. After all, Rydbeck argued, it was in the banks'
self-interest to survive. There was no need for costly new rules.

The final Inspection Board report reflected Rydbeck's influence. The regulators concluded that "It seems as though all paths should be exploited to free
the banks from these credits, for example by their conversion to share or bond
loans or their transfer to foreign financial institutions."[13] However, the report
was phrased as merely advice; the regulators ultimately did not require that
the syndicate disband or take any specific action to reduce its exposure to Ivar
and Swedish Match. They accepted self-regulation.

With Rydbeck's assistance, the syndicate continued until 1922, the year of
Ivar's meeting with Durant. Indeed, the banks desperately wanted it

to continue. Even if Ivar's accounting methods had been questionable, the syndicate was making the banks a fortune. And the banks were not only lending money to Ivar; they were his biggest shareholders. When Swedish Match reported annual profits of about one-fifth of its capital, and paid hefty dividends, much of that money went to the banks. Even as the post-war global recession weighed on other companies, Swedish Match's financial statements defied economic gravity. Ivar reported profits from investments, currency speculation, and, most of all, the sale of matches throughout the world.

In 1922, Swedish Match showed profits of more than 9 million kronor and paid a dividend of 12 percent. Kreuger & Toll, Ivar's parent company, paid a 25 percent dividend.[14] During the first three years of the syndicate, the banks had doubled their money. Not surprisingly, the bankers adored Ivar. They called him the "Match King," for good reason.

Still, the regulators had made the bankers nervous and raised questions they couldn't answer. How, when Sweden's post-war economy was in serious trouble, did Ivar's companies continue to make so much money? Were Ivar's strategies sustainable? Could he continue to raise money? The bankers knew Swedish Match's financial statements were fishy. But how fishy?

Oscar Rydbeck estimated Ivar's net worth at the time as at least 25 million kronor, which made Ivar one of the wealthiest men in Europe. Nevertheless, Rydbeck wasn't sure whether Ivar could afford to prop up his companies with personal guarantees and new cash. The Swedish financial markets were relatively small, and Ivar already had raised as much capital as anyone could raise there. Rydbeck knew Ivar had to find a new source of funds.

Rydbeck began suggesting they wind down the syndicate. Svenska Handelsbanken and Skandinaviska Kredit, two of the leading participant banks, asked Ivar to settle their loans, and return their money. It wasn't urgent, and the banks agreed to remain invested in Ivar's companies in the interim. But the Swedish bankers wanted to be prudent. They couldn't lend *all* of their money to Ivar, and there simply wasn't enough money left in Sweden to support his ambitious plans. They gently mentioned to Ivar that he might want to consider raising funds somewhere else.

Ivar was insulted. This was the time when he had increased his focus on American bankers, and had asked his broker Lagerkrantz to set up a meeting with Donald Durant. Ivar called the Swedes "blockheads." He told one Swedish banker, "You haggle about giving me money. But when I get off the boat in New York I find men on the pier begging me to take money off their hands."[15]

Durant and Lee Higginson hadn't known about Sillén's report or the concerns of the Swedish banking regulators. Nor had they realized that Ivar had tapped the capacity of the Swedish markets. They were focused more on Ivar's future match monopoly deals than on his previous sources of funds.

As to those new deals, there really wasn't anything to concern Lee Higg. Nothing had happened yet. When Ivar finally closed a loan to a foreign government, they would watch it closely. Until then, what could possibly happen to International Match's cash?

Like other American investment bankers, Durant and his partners relied on auditors to notify them of any problems. Durant assumed that a top accounting firm would spot anything significant, and notify him immediately.

During the early 1920s, the law didn't require that foreign firms use accountants before raising capital in the United States. Nevertheless, Lee Higginson, like other top-tier banks, wouldn't touch a company without an independent audit from a leading accounting firm. They were suspicious of any client who even questioned whether such an audit was necessary.

Ivar understood Lee Higginson's perspective, and he had been proactive in hiring an auditor. His primary concern was to avoid Price Waterhouse, the firm that already knew too much about him from his difficulties with Diamond Match. He was concerned that Price Waterhouse employees might tell Durant and his partners about Ivar's previous dealings with them. Ivar resolved not to repeat the disaster from 1921, when W. E. Seatree of Price Waterhouse had caught Ivar's aggressive sidekick, Eric Landgren, falsifying financial figures in negotiations with Diamond Match. Ivar had learned an important lesson from that fiasco. He needed to remain in direct personal contact with his accountants. He needed to find an American accountant he could trust and control.

Ivar therefore recommended Ernst & Ernst, the accounting firm he had asked Anders Jordahl, his Norwegian sidekick, to hire when they first ran into trouble with Diamond Match. Ivar wasn't happy about the added intrusion into his business, but Ernst & Ernst was the least bad alternative. Moreover, by insisting that International Match hire a top accounting firm, Ivar impressed the American bankers and investors with his forthrightness.

Donald Durant agreed with the choice. Like Lee Higginson, Ernst & Ernst had an unassailable reputation. The Ernst brothers audited Coca-Cola, Firestone, and Chrysler, and their firm was nearly as prestigious as Price Waterhouse. Like Durant and Ivar, the Ernsts were self-made men.[16] Ernst & Ernst had a humbler beginning than other top firms. The Ernsts were from

Cleveland, not Boston, and they hadn't attended Harvard or Yale. Alwin Ernst was Ivar's age, and had worked as a bookkeeper for four years after high school before founding the firm with his older brother Theodore in 1903.

But Ernst & Ernst was an innovative firm. The Ernsts were the first accountants to advertise, and they blazed the path of combining audit and consulting services. The Ernst brothers understood that financial information was valuable, not only to investors, but also to managers, who could use the data to improve their business decisions.

The Ernsts further saw the benefit of giving combined audit and tax advice. When the federal income tax was established in 1913, Ernst & Ernst immediately set up a tax department. If the Ernst brothers were concerned about potential conflicts of interest from simultaneously attesting to an audit and advising on taxes, strategy, and disclosure, they kept that to themselves. The Ernsts were visionaries, and had no time for prudish accounting old-timers. When the American Institute of Certified Public Accountants, a long-established accounting trade group, accused the Ernsts of violating its rules against soliciting and advertising, the brothers resigned their AICPA membership.[17]

The Ernsts hired only the sharpest graduates from top schools, men who were quick and careful with numbers. With their vision and a backbone of smart employees, they made nearly as much money as Lee Higginson's bankers. Alwin Ernst ultimately would leave an estate of 12.6 million dollars (although, ironically, Alwin's estate would lose more than 7 million dollars to taxes and costs due to poor financial planning).

When International Match hired Ernst & Ernst, the Ernsts assigned one of their most junior auditors to the new account. Although they knew Ivar's European businesses were substantial, his American business would be a relatively small start-up company, at least at first. The American audit would cover International Match only, not Kreuger & Toll or Swedish Match. Such a limited audit wouldn't require much expertise.

The given name of the junior auditor assigned to Ivar was Albert D. Berning, but the men of Ernst & Ernst didn't know that. Albert didn't like his first name and he hid it from people outside his immediate family. His colleagues knew him only as "A.D."

Ivar met A.D. Berning and the men looked into each other's eyes. Ivar couldn't have been more pleased.

5

THE GREEN EYE SHADE

By the time Ivar formed International Match, A.D. Berning had worked at Ernst & Ernst for two uneventful years. Berning had graduated from the Cooper Union for the Advancement of Science and Art in Manhattan. He recently had passed his Certified Public Accountant examination, and had joined the national and state CPA institutes. Berning held the entry-level title of Assistant Manager at Ernst & Ernst, a junior role with limited responsibilities.

Berning was a quiet man, married and conservative. Unlike Ivar, he was not experienced in the world. Berning had not traveled extensively, and he certainly had not sailed luxury ships in first class or cavorted with movie stars. While Ivar was out with Douglas Fairbanks, Greta Garbo, and Mary Pickford in New York or with politicians and bankers at the finest restaurants in Europe, A.D. Berning dined at home with his wife.

Berning was the sort of person Ivar knew he could control. Like the other junior boffins at Ernst & Ernst, Berning saw every new client as an opportunity to advance, to prove to the Ernst brothers that he was partnership material. The International Match account was an exciting opportunity, Berning's first major chance at a promotion from the firm's lowest ranks. Although Berning had the qualities of a fine auditor, he was not a businessman. He was persistent, with a sharp eye for detail, but he was also cautious and careful. You could see Berning's personality simply by looking at his small and precise handwriting. There was no chance of confusing a "2" with a "7," which was always neatly crossed, like a "t."

Berning's job on the new International Match account was an odd admixture of simple and impossible. On one hand, Ernst & Ernst was to give only a qualified statement of opinion based on inputs from Ivar's companies abroad. In this way, Berning's primary job was straightforward, not so different from watching over the mechanized sorting and packaging of matches. Ivar's Swedish accountants had done all the difficult work, determining the value of International Match's share of the assets of Ivar's other companies and calculating how much of those companies' profits should be attributed to International Match.

Most of the details of Ivar's assets, liabilities, and income were in the financial statements of those other companies, outside the United States. Berning's job was simply to check the math, to be sure the individual numbers from Sweden added up to the sums from Sweden. Any decision requiring judgment already had been made. Viewed this way, International Match's financial statements might be the tip of an iceberg, but Berning was responsible only for that tip.

On the other hand, performing a *real* audit of International Match was impossible. How could Berning know whether the Swedish numbers really were accurate? How could he protect American investors from inaccuracies in the financial statements? In this way, too, his job was like that of a sorter and packager of matches. How could anyone ensure that every match would be safe or free from defects? Without extraordinary effort, it simply could not be done. From his vantage point at Ernst & Ernst in New York, Berning could not even assess the size of the iceberg growing out from under International Match, much less its specific composition or the dangers it might pose.

Accordingly, Ivar and Berning understood that International Match would be a small account for Ernst & Ernst, an account that would not require much oversight. The financial statements would be brief and straightforward. Because the Swedish accountants already had performed an audit, Ernst & Ernst would play only a limited role. Essentially, the Americans would simply verify whether the Swedes had added and subtracted correctly, and would rely on the accuracy of those numbers in certifying International Match's financial statements. If Berning wanted to generate additional fees from Ivar, they wouldn't come from spending more time on the audit, but instead would have to come from tax or consulting advice.

From the beginning, Ivar personally took control of International Match's relationship with Ernst & Ernst. He spoke directly to Berning, not his bosses, and made it clear that Berning should speak directly to him. Throughout 1923, the year of International Match's gold debenture issue, Ivar and Berning communicated directly by letter and cable regarding a wide range of issues, including some of the most mundane particulars of International Match's accounting. At first, no detail was too small for either man. On June 8, 1923, Ivar wrote to Berning to confirm a few fine points about minor working expenses, including stamp duties and registration fees.[1] Berning must have been elated by all this attention. Assistant managers typically spoke to other assistant managers, not to famous international business leaders.

Ivar also made it clear to Donald Durant that any attempts to assess the particulars beneath International Match would be pointless. Ivar said International Match would act as a conduit for bringing American capital into his other businesses, particularly Swedish Match and Kreuger & Toll.[2] International Match would not have any substantive business distinct from those other companies. Nor would it need many employees. Like Continental Investment Corporation, Ivar's secret Liechtenstein subsidiary, International Match wouldn't actually *do* anything.

Ivar told Durant and Berning his plan was to have profits from new government match concessions "about equally divided between International Match and Swedish Match."[3] However, no one signed an agreement requiring an equal division. Indeed, the documents for the twenty-year 6.5 percent gold debentures did not even require that International Match receive any of the profits from Ivar's other businesses. The allocation of profits to International Match was left entirely up to Ivar.

Berning was baffled by this arrangement. He couldn't decipher the financial statements Ivar sent. Were the measures of International Match's profits accurate? Did the company's balance sheet entries include the assets and liabilities of Swedish Match's subsidiaries? There was no way to tell. He had to rely entirely on Ivar's numbers, which changed more frequently than a careful accountant would hope or expect. Berning sent Lee Higginson one set of financial statements in October 1923, just before the gold debenture issue was sold, based on information provided by Ivar. But soon after investors had purchased the debentures, Berning had to send a corrected version, which reflected revised numbers from Ivar.[4] Fortunately, the only surprises were positive ones: the numbers had gone up.

Although Berning was frustrated by Ivar's shifting lack of precision, he didn't let Ivar know it. Instead, he tried to build a closer working relationship, even a friendship. He shared details from his personal life, and inquired about Ivar's. Berning was particularly interested in Ivar's travels. He asked about Ivar's recent trip to Canada; he wished him a good time in Chicago.[5] He had never visited either place, though he and his wife planned to do so, some day.

Berning also kept close tabs on International Match's payments within the United States, so that he could help if there were any questionable transfers of money. When Berning confirmed that Eric Landgren, the renegade employee who had blown Ivar's negotiations with Diamond Match, was taking advantage of Ivar and using firm money for personal purposes, Ivar fired Landgren and asked Berning for a full report.[6]

Ivar appreciated Berning's diligence on the Landgren matter, but he wasn't looking for a new friend. Although Ivar would focus intensely on the details of accounting issues, he barely knew who Berning was and didn't seem to care. While Berning spent a good portion of each day thinking about Ivar and his companies, Ivar found it difficult even to keep track of Berning's first name, and mistakenly called him A.L. instead of A.D. for nearly a year.[7]

When Berning approached Ivar with an inquiry from the securities division of Wisconsin's Railroad Commission about International Match's gold debentures, Ivar brushed Berning aside. Wisconsin? Railroad Commission? Berning couldn't be serious.

But he was. During the 1920s, the states, rather than the federal government, played the most active role in securities regulation. Wisconsin was among the most aggressive state regulators.

Companies were required to comply with state "Blue Sky" laws, so named because of the concerns of a Kansas legislator that investors were buying securities backed by no more than the atmosphere. The railroad commissions of many states governed investments, a continuation of previous decades during which most securities sold to investors were backed by railroads. Ivar found this regulatory approach antiquated and annoying.

Because some residents of Wisconsin had purchased International Match's gold debentures, Wisconsin securities examiners wanted to be sure those purchasers were getting something more than blue sky. Given Ivar's experience with building permit officials and banking regulators in Sweden, an examiner from the Railroad Commission of Wisconsin must not have seemed much of a threat.

When Berning sent Ivar a list of questions from Commissioner O. Hibma of the securities division, Ivar ignored them. What could some bureaucrat from Wisconsin possibly do to Ivar? Besides, the questions were unreasonable. Hibma was asking for more information than Ivar had ever given anyone about his businesses.

But Commissioner Hibma didn't like being ignored, and Berning soon notified Ivar that Hibma was requesting even more information:

The latest request comes from Wisconsin, for detailed statement of expenses for 1921 and 1922 for all constituent Companies, together with their consolidated balance sheet at December 31, 1922. I am today writing them again, trying to appease them. They have already requested, and will undoubtedly do so again, a detailed statement of consolidated earnings, surplus and balance sheets of the constituent Companies for 1923. However, we can discuss this with you when you arrive here, and can then determine the best way to accommodate them.[8]

Ivar had no interest in discussing these details. Nor did he want to see Berning during his time in New York. Ernst & Ernst was supposed to play only a limited role in International Match's life. It was Berning's job to get rid of a minor nuisance such as a Wisconsin securities regulator.

Ivar tried dangling a carrot in front of his auditor. He invited the Bernings to sail with him from Canada to the Far East, all expenses paid. It had become obvious to Ivar that Berning was jealous of his international travels. Mrs Berning also coveted the trips her husband told her about, especially Ivar's time in five-star hotels, restaurants, and luxury cruise cabins. She was delighted by Ivar's invitation and the couple eagerly accepted. The next month, when Berning gently reminded Ivar that the Wisconsin regulators had not gone away, Ivar suggested that they simply send them updated versions of the financial statements with no additional detail. Berning agreed, even though it was obvious that Wisconsin wanted more.

Indeed, Commissioner Hibma responded immediately that "The statements do not give us the required information."[9] Ivar was surprised that Berning had been unable to appease the regulators. He could not understand why they needed so much detail. Ivar replied to Berning, "I note with regret that you are still being annoyed with demand for all sorts of information and figures and shall try to have some statements compiled for you within the near future."[10] It was already May, six months after the gold debenture deal, and Ivar still had given Berning nothing except the promise of an exotic vacation.

As Berning continued to ask Ivar for the details during June and July, Lee Higginson learned of the delays and began pressuring Ernst & Ernst to respond to Wisconsin. Durant wanted to know when International Match would be in compliance with state blue sky laws.[11] Given this pressure, Berning's requests to Ivar became more specific: "Wisconsin requests details costs of sales and expenses suggest statement showing half dozen major items under each classification with interest taxes separately."[12]

When Ivar finally sent some additional information a few weeks later, it was obvious that the statements had been hastily and not very carefully prepared. For example, Ivar sent balance sheets for International Match for 1921 and 1922, showing that the company had 1 million shares outstanding. But International Match had not even existed during those years. Surely a securities regulator from Wisconsin would catch that mistake. Berning certainly did, and noted, "In view of the fact that this company was incorporated in July, 1923, we thought it advisable to cover the point in the letter accompanying the exhibits."[13]

Berning also noted that the foreign exchange rate assumptions in International Match's financial statements had changed. Because Ivar's business was predominantly outside the United States, most of his cash flows were denominated in foreign currencies. The assumed basis for converting those currencies to US dollars affected the results for International Match.

For example, Ivar previously had used a rate of 26.80 Swedish kronor per US dollar. That meant International Match's claims on 268 million Swedish kronor of assets were worth 10 million US dollars. But now, suddenly, Ivar reported a rate of 26.55. At the new rate, the same amount of assets suddenly appeared to be worth 1 percent more – about 100,000 US dollars of extra value.

Why the change, Berning wanted to know, given that the statements covered the same date? Ivar gave no explanation. One percent might not seem like a huge difference, but it would have mattered to an accountant trying to respond precisely to an inquiry from a state securities regulator.

Yet instead of asking why Ivar suddenly had increased International Match's assets by 1 percent, Berning accommodated the change. He explained to Ivar that "The difference is quite small, and I hope that the statement made in this respect in the attached report meets with your approval. If not, it can be readily changed."[14] Hopefully, Commissioner Hibma would not notice the difference. In any event, Ernst & Ernst would continue to send investors only an abbreviated version of International Match's financial statements, so they would never see any details about foreign exchange rates. Berning sent the revised documents to Wisconsin, and the Bernings began planning for their trip.

Ivar appreciated Berning's reconciliation. The message from Ernst & Ernst was that if Ivar decided he didn't like some numbers, they easily could be changed. As the old joke went, when an accountant interviewing for a job is asked, "What is two plus two?" the best answer is not "Four," but "What do you want it to be?"

In his next telegram, Ivar advised, "Contemplate sailing Japan with Empress of Asia leaving Vancouver September twenty-fifth will this date be convenient for you and Mrs Berning."[15] The Bernings must have reread this cable a hundred times. Berning responded, 'Suggested date entirely satisfactory."[16]

But if Mr and Mrs Berning were elated by the prospect of largesse from Ernst & Ernst's new client, they were soon to be disappointed. After dangling the trip in front of Berning, Ivar snatched it back. He seemed to be punishing Berning for the trouble with Wisconsin. On August 21, 1924, after International Match finally was in compliance with Wisconsin's blue sky laws, Ivar cabled Berning that "On account very important and urgent business proposition which has come up unexpectedly it will be necessary for me to still further put off my trip to Japan."[17] The Bernings would have to wait.

At the end of 1924, International Match was a strange-looking operation. Ivar had produced two financial statements for the company: a "Statement of Assets and Liabilities" and a "Consolidated Profit and Loss Account." These two statements corresponded to what investors generally knew as the balance sheet and income statement. The balance sheet was a snapshot of the value of a company's assets and liabilities at a particular time, such as the end of a year or quarter. Typically, the values of assets were recorded at their original cost on the balance sheet. For example, if a company bought a building for 1 million dollars, it would record the value at 1 million dollars at the end of the period, even if the value of the building had gone up or down.

If the balance sheet was a snapshot, the income statement was a moving picture. It depicted how much money the company earned and spent during a particular year or quarter. The income statement typically would include a list of how much revenue a company generated, as well as expenses such as salaries, rent, interest payments, and taxes.

International Match's 1924 Statement of Assets and Liabilities – the balance sheet – was a snapshot that could easily fit in a wallet. There were no detailed entries. The vast majority of the company's assets – 26 million dollars out of 33 million dollars total – consisted of a single line item for "Land,

Buildings, Machinery & Equipment."[18] There was no mention of the cash Lee Higginson had raised from investors just a year earlier, or any clues about where that money had gone.

The 1924 Consolidated Profit and Loss Account – the income statement – was an even less illuminating motion picture. The statement was not even typed, but instead was written out in longhand. All of the information came from Ivar. The company's income was broken into just two items: "Sales" and "Income from Other Sources."[19] The bulk of the income was from foreign companies, but there was no explanation of what the "other sources" might have been or of which companies the "income" might have come from. Indeed, there was no explanation at all.

The company's expenses for 1924 were small – just over a million dollars – and almost all of that (975,000 dollars) was interest owed on the 15 million dollar gold debentures. The remaining expenses were paltry: a few thousand dollars for salaries, a thousand dollars to pay rent, and 100 dollars of office expenses.[20]

Few people seemed to care that the information was incomplete. Indeed, International Match's cursory financial statements were typical of corporate disclosure at the time. Even companies with securities listed on the New York Stock Exchange gave up scant detail. Fewer than one-third of Stock Exchange companies published quarterly reports, and those reports were brief. Another third of Stock Exchange companies didn't publish any reports at all. There was even less disclosure from companies, such as International Match, with shares traded on the Curb Exchange.[21] Anyone who wanted to invest in those companies did so in the dark, or not at all.

Even without detail, anyone who carefully examined the limited information in the income statements of International Match would have seen some strange early signs. International Match reported net profit for 1924 as 2.2 million dollars. Its net profit for 1923 had been just a little less: 2.1 million dollars.[22] 1922 was 2.0 million dollars, and 1921 was 1.9 million dollars.[23]

These numbers flashed two red lights. First, the steady increase in earnings suggested that International Match was engaging in earnings management, that is, manipulating earnings to smooth them over time. The match business was highly volatile, particularly during and after the world war. Prices were fluctuating, moving up in areas where Ivar had acquired a dominant share of the market, and moving down where competition still raged. Yet International Match reported steadily increasing income during these volatile periods. Of course, Ivar wasn't alone. Earnings management was widespread during the

1920s, and even if investors noticed the smoothing it didn't seem to bother them.

But International Match's financial statements contained a second, more fundamental, warning. If International Match did not exist before 1923, how could it have had income during 1922 and 1921? Perhaps Ivar had included income from some predecessor companies. Perhaps the numbers were from American Kreuger & Toll, the failed effort led by Anders Jordahl that had focused more on being close to Broadway theaters than on negotiations with the American match industry. Investors could not tell which of Ivar's other companies might have been responsible for International Match's alleged income. Instead, they were led to believe that International Match had consistently been making money since 1921, more than a year before Ivar had sailed to New York to meet Donald Durant. Anyone who checked the dates would have known those numbers were wrong.

The partners at Lee Higginson weren't bothered by these details any more than the people who invested in International Match. On October 29, 1924, the directors of International Match, including Donald Durant, Percy Rockefeller, and Frederic Allen, the Lee Higginson partner who served as Director of War Savings and head of Yale's rowing committee, held a special meeting. But instead of questioning Ivar, or reining him in, they voted to give him new extraordinary powers. They formally authorized Ivar to transfer any amount of money out of International Match and to permit him to limit transfers into International Match to no more than necessary to meet the company's quarterly dividend payments.[24] Ivar had argued that they should keep all surplus profits outside of International Match, and therefore out of America, to avoid paying tax on those profits. The directors accepted that rationale and gave him the authority. They seemed unconcerned about where the money might go or what Ivar might do with it.

In December 1924, Lee Higginson arranged for International Match to raise more money, this time by selling an innovative financial instrument: participating preferred shares. Like gold debentures, participating preferred shares were a hybrid investment, part conservative and part aggressive. The "preferred" part meant that the investor would have seniority over "common" shares, which were still held by Swedish Match and the Swedish bank syndicate. This preference meant that if International Match became bankrupt, the preferred shares would be paid before the common shares. Thus, preferred shares were less risky than common shares.

But these were "participating" preferred shares, which meant they also participated in dividend payments along with common stock. Unlike the gold debentures, participating preferred shares could receive more than a 6.5 percent interest payment. If the common shares received dividends of, say, 12 percent, then so would the preferred shares – that was what it meant to "participate." This new hybrid investment had substantial upside.

Most investors had never seen participating preferred shares. Nor were they aware of anyone using new participating preferred issues to refinance or recapitalize by paying off previously issued debentures. Such a new issue didn't change the nature of Ivar's business or make more money available. Instead, it simply reallocated the financial claims to future profits, giving investors more risk and upside, but a less secure claim on corporate assets.

In 1923, when Ivar and Lee Higginson had closed the gold debenture deal, many investors were still conservative, particularly when they were considering America's first experience with a securities issue from Ivar. They had insisted on debentures, whose principal payment International Match was obligated to repay at a fixed rate during a fixed period of time. A year later, even the conservative investors had joined the mania coursing through the markets. Given their optimism, Ivar was able to switch to a more flexible capital base by refinancing. Unlike debentures, the 15.7 million dollars of participating preferred shares did not require repayment on a particular date. Effectively, International Match had shifted from a strict debt obligation to a more flexible equity obligation.

Ultimately, Lee Higginson sold nearly half a million participating preferred shares for $35 each, to raise a total of 15.7 million dollars. This time, though, Ivar kept the money in the country. International Match used the proceeds to pay off most of the outstanding gold debentures, at a price of $105.[25] The original investors in gold debentures had expected to receive a price of $100 (not $105) in twenty years (not one year). Not only did they receive the promised interest payments, but they also made an extra 5 percent return on their investment. These investors were ecstatic, and they spread word about Ivar in the same way early investors in the postal reply coupon scheme had spread word about Charles Ponzi.

Now that Ivar had converted his debentures into more flexible obligations, he was free to plan his future monopoly-for-loan transactions without a ticking clock. He had added to his track record of impressive returns for investors by giving American holders of gold debentures 5 percent more money than they expected, faster than they expected it. And he had demonstrated to

Lee Higginson, and other bankers, that he was a sophisticated financier. The bankers were impressed by his new recapitalization technique.

Of course, Ivar still needed to raise new money, not just to pay off International Match's previously issued obligations, but to meet the very large dividends that his European companies soon would owe. Swedish Match was scheduled to pay its investors a hefty double-digit dividend. Kreuger & Toll had promised 25 percent. Nevertheless, with the increased flexibility of financing in America, Ivar was confident in his ability to generate enough cash to make those payments.

He also was confident about where that money would go. His brother, Torsten, had been in Poland for more than a year, and that government seemed close to a deal.

6

POLAND FIRST

For centuries European governments had granted monopolies on all kinds of production and trade to their loyal subjects. These weren't gifts; the governments required payment in return, in the form of cash, interest, or a share of profits. These "fiscal monopolies" were an alternative to state control: industry remained in private hands, but governments received a steady stream of revenue, a kind of selective tax. The early fiscal monopolies included cigarettes, flax, gunpowder, liquor, petrol, playing cards, salt, and tobacco. For many countries, the tax revenues from fiscal monopolies were significant, as much as one-third or more of the overall government budget.[1]

France created one of the first match monopolies, in 1872, not long after the invention of strike-on-the-box Swedish matches. The transaction was straightforward: the French government simply leased the right to make and sell matches within France to a private corporation. Other countries soon followed France's lead. Belgium, Bulgaria, Greece, Portugal, Romania, Serbia, and Spain all established fiscal match monopolies during the late nineteenth century.[2] In France, when government officials finally realized how much money the private sector was earning from the match monopoly, they nationalized the industry. But elsewhere, the monopolies stuck.

Germany and Italy, two of the dominant economies in Europe, were late to the monopoly game. Germany taxed match sales, but didn't even try to establish a monopoly until after the world war and the Weimar Republic hyperinflation, when the currency markets finally stabilized. The German match industry was stagnant, match factories were in disrepair, machinery was obsolescent, and raw materials, including aspen trees and chemicals, were scarce. In 1924, Ivar and Oscar Rydbeck, his lead banker, met with Dr Hjalmar

Schacht, the Governor of the Reichsbank, Germany's central bank, and Dr Schacht requested a concrete proposal. Ivar agreed to work with the central bank to prepare one, but he correctly anticipated that the process in Germany would not gain momentum until the economy recovered and consumer demand returned.[3]

Italy also started late, and with far too much bureaucracy. The government created a public match monopoly, but refused to cede any control to the private sector. The Italian finance minister set prices, and a government agency controlled production and export. The costs of government control were too high, and the government dismantled the match monopoly in 1923.[4] By the time Ivar sent Torsten to focus on Poland, he had made no progress with the Italian government.

Ivar had been somewhat more successful with Spain, although competition, taxes, and restrictions on foreign investment were hurting Swedish Match's export business there. When the Spanish government imposed strict preferences for local industry, Ivar marshaled some creative tactics to overcome those obstacles. Before 1922, the Spanish government had controlled the match monopoly, but still permitted Swedish Match to export matches to Spain. Then the government shifted course and signed a fifteen-year lease with a Spanish company, Compañia Arrendataria de Fosforos (CAF). It also began enforcing a decree that match interests could only be held by Spanish citizens or companies owned by Spanish citizens. From that time on, CAF would control all match production and sales within Spain. As a foreigner, Ivar was not permitted to own shares of CAF.

But Ivar refused to be locked out of the Spanish market. He began buying shares of CAF through Spanish intermediaries, and even created a front company in Spain, Sociedad Financiera de la Industria Española (SAFIE).[5] The share purchases were time-consuming and expensive, and even by 1924 he was a long way from taking control of the Spanish match market. SAFIE gave Ivar a presence, so that Swedish Match could make some money from exports to Spain, but a Spanish match monopoly seemed unlikely anytime soon. Like Germany and Italy, Spain would have to wait.

By 1924, Ivar was in negotiations with a dozen governments, with little or no success. Ivar had tried for a monopoly in Turkey, but lost that bid to a small Belgian firm. His talks with the Bolivian president were at an impasse, and the Hungarians had suspended negotiations. Ivar was traveling constantly, yet even after logging all those miles, he had gotten nowhere on the path to match monopolies.

Ivar needed to forge much closer ties with government officials. Merely acquiring match factories, as he had done in Sweden, was not enough. Outside his home country, competition seemed to sprout quickly and from anywhere. Every time Ivar bought one factory, another competing factory sprung up in another location. For example, Ivar had managed to purchase every match factory in Belgium by 1920. Yet just a few years later, thirteen new factories had appeared.[6]

Just as businessmen realized it was cheap and easy to set up match factories, governments had seen that it was even cheaper and easier to adopt measures protecting local industry. Legislators raised tariffs on match imports, to stimulate local production. Many countries followed Spain's lead and blocked foreigners from owning match factories. Now, both governments and private competition threatened the dominance of Swedish Match.

Swedish Match's economic advantage also was deteriorating. Aspen, the wood most suitable for match production, was scarce in Germany but plentiful throughout eastern Europe. The demand for matches continued to grow outside of Sweden. Perhaps most importantly, as the value of many currencies fell, particularly in eastern Europe, exports became cheaper while imports became more expensive. There was no way Ivar's companies could continue to pay high dividends if they didn't overcome these problems.

Given the challenges elsewhere, Poland presented Ivar's best opportunity. The population of almost 30 million was well educated and hard working. The economic minister had just established the zloty as a single common currency for the country. Poland had active ports and a history of prosperity and trade.

Before the world war, the match industry there had been small – just five match factories in the provinces that later united to form Poland. In 1921, these five factories produced just 2,000 cases of matches a month, barely enough to meet one-third of the area's demand. Swedish Match had secured a toehold in the region by then, and it covered much of the remaining demand by exporting matches to Poland.

Then, suddenly, without any stimulation from external investment, Poland's match factories began reproducing, just as private factories had sprouted up in Belgium. In 1922, this parthenogenesis led to seven new factories. A year later, there were seven more. By the time Torsten arrived, match production had grown to nearly 125,000 cases a year. There were four times as many factories as there had been before the war. Virtually overnight, Poland was exporting matches.

Ivar followed these developments closely. The new match factories were driving down prices and taking away Swedish Match's export business. Ivar hired a few men to send him regular reports about developments in Poland. The competitive landscape there was rocky, and the threat to Swedish Match was serious. One expert called the situation "alarming."[7]

There were too many independent Polish factories and too little government support. Ivar tried the approach he had mastered in Sweden, dramatically reducing the price of matches sold in Poland, to undercut competing local factories. He forced a few of the new factories out of business, and offered to buy others. But he and Torsten still needed to secure the assistance and trust of key government officials. Only then could they organize a sales cartel with local manufacturers, to maintain high prices and restrict production.

Poland's political volatility made it a more attractive candidate for a monopoly.[8] From the moment Torsten arrived, Polish officials faced so many crises that the right person would be able to slip them a match monopoly without much scrutiny. The government was in chaos. The final borders of the Second Polish Republic had been established two years earlier, and the new constitution just a year before that. The reborn interbellum Poland was fractured into competing sects. President Gabriel Narutowicz had been assassinated in late 1922, and the country had sworn in four different prime ministers that year (and another two the following year). At first, it wasn't even clear to Torsten which officials he should approach, or who was in charge.

Then, through the bedlam, Torsten met Dr Marjam Glowacki, a senior finance ministry official. The two men immediately bonded and became friends. Torsten appeared to be a distinguished businessman with extensive experience in international finance. Their talks moved quickly. Dr Glowacki saw that a significant loan from International Match could resolve many of the country's humanitarian and fiscal needs. Even a few million dollars would greatly assist Polish reparations from the world war.

Moreover, Torsten was offering a compelling deal. International Match would pay a regular royalty from its match sales in Poland to the Polish state treasury, and the proceeds of the royalty would secure the loan to the government. The loan payments would be calculated so that the amount of the royalty payable to the government would cover the annual debt service and leave the government a profit margin of 25 to 50 percent. In the worst case the monopoly-for-loan deal would pay for itself. In the best case it would generate substantial profits. As Ivar described the proposal, "It may even be said that the loan itself is nothing but an advance of future royalty payments."[9] It was an offer Dr Glowacki couldn't refuse. And fortunately for Torsten and Ivar, Dr Glowacki was the right man.

Once Dr Glowacki agreed to the deal, the specifics didn't take long. International Match agreed to lend 6 million dollars to the Polish government at an interest rate of 7 percent. The extant Polish match factories were nationalized, combined, and leased to International Match for twenty years; ownership of the factories would revert to Poland after that. During the twenty-year monopoly period, the income would be shared among Swedish Match, International Match, and Poland. The Polish government would use its share of the proceeds to fund relief work following devastating floods in Upper Silesia, as well as to bolster the country's finances more generally.[10]

Dr Glowacki signed the agreement and pushed the deal through the Polish government. Technically, International Match would not have its first functioning public monopoly for several months, until the law went into effect in October 1925. But that didn't stop Ivar from broadcasting the deal to America right away.

Ivar began hinting to Lee Higginson and Ernst & Ernst that in addition to Torsten's "public" deal with Poland, Ivar also was negotiating a "private" contract with Dr Glowacki, in which International Match would obtain additional rights to sell matches at even higher prices in Poland. No one was to mention this private agreement, which was preliminary and should be kept a secret – even from Torsten.

When Ivar received a copy of the signed documents, he did something rather unusual. Apparently, he thought it might be useful to be able to replicate Dr Glowacki's signature in the future, so he took a signed copy of the contract to a stamp shop and ordered a rubber stamp that would produce a facsimile. Ivar had been skilled at forging signatures as a child, but now he decided he wasn't good enough. From then on, he would obtain rubber stamps of official signatures for nearly all of his match deals.[11] Dr Glowacki's stamp was his first.

The public deal with Poland generated great excitement in the United States. Both Lee Higginson and International Match's investors were pleased with Ivar's quick progress, and Durant sensed a growing appetite as he pitched a new deal for International Match. Durant wrote to Ivar that "for the third time in about three years you have gone to the public and asked them to double overnight the amount of their investment in your Company, and each time this has met with success. We recall no other company with such a record."[12] Lee Higginson had introduced International Match to American investors in 1923 with a conservative gold debenture, and then converted that investment into a slightly riskier participating preferred stock deal in 1924. Now, investors were clamoring for more.

There were still a few outstanding gold debentures from International Match's first deal – not all of them were redeemed in 1924 – and they were in high demand because they were convertible into shares. A.D. Berning excitedly wired Ivar that Lee Higginson had found a potential buyer for a large block of International Match debentures. There was one catch: the buyer wanted to know the amount of dividends Swedish Match had received from its subsidiaries during the previous six years.[13] That was the kind of detailed question Ivar previously had refused to answer.

Ivar dodged it again, responding that "the working conditions during the years immediately after the war were so extraordinary and exchange conditions so confusing that our accountants consider it absolutely impossible to give out any figures regarding profits earlier than year 1921 which we have already given you."[14] Yet even after this brush off, the customer bought anyway. International Match debentures were quoted at $129, a high level for a security that would repay just $100 in eighteen years. The price was so high because of the conversion right. According to Berning "practically all debenture holders" had converted into common shares.[15]

Ivar's next challenge was to decide how best to raise more money from optimistic American investors. He still objected to selling common shares of International Match, because common shares held a vote and he was wary of giving up any control. He felt the same way about selling direct investments in common shares of Swedish Match, International Match's parent. Ivar claimed that Swedish law prohibited foreign interests from owning a stake in a company that owned real estate in Sweden, which Swedish Match did.[16] In reality, Swedish law only prevented foreign investors from acquiring a controlling stake, not a minority stake. But the law was a good excuse to continue to sell securities without votes to Americans, and it was some protection against the threat of Americans acquiring control of International Match.

Ivar had faced a difficult question: How could he raise capital from investors who wanted a share of his company's upside without giving them too much power over how the company was to be governed? Ivar didn't want foreigners intruding on his Swedish companies, but he wanted their money. How could he get more cash from investors without giving them control?

Historically, companies had tried various responses to this quandary, with little success. During the late nineteenth century, many companies had been resigned to the fact that they would have to give votes to all of their investors. Even the preferred shares of major industrial trusts (Steel Corporation, the American Woolen Company, and the American Shipbuilding Company, for example) had voting rights.[17] Nearly every corporation gave votes to all of its shareholders, including both common and preferred shares.

Years earlier, Coca-Cola had devised one awkward solution. It was a publicly listed and widely owned corporation, but 251,000 of its 500,000 shares were held by the Coca-Cola International Company, which was owned by a knot of insiders who held control.[18] A few companies had followed Coca-Cola's two-company approach: Associated Gas and Electric Securities Corporation held a controlling stake in Associated Gas and Electric Company; Armour and Company of Delaware was controlled by Armour and Company of Illinois.[19] But that structure was clumsy and raised legal uncertainties about the relationships between parent and subsidiary.

Ivar devised a more elegant solution to this problem. It was an ingenious piece of financial engineering that would survive the test of time.

Ivar decided to introduce a new type of security, which he called a "B Share." Ivar began with Swedish Match. He divided its common shares into two classes. Each class would have the same claim to dividends and profits, but the B Share would carry only 1/1000 of a vote, compared to one vote for each A Share. It was a simple, but profound, insight. B Shares could be sold to investors without affecting control.[20] Ivar could double the size of his capital, while diluting his control by just a fraction of a percent.

Would investors be willing to buy shares that didn't carry a vote? Ivar was sure the answer was yes. In 1924, Ivar and Lee Higginson arranged for the sale of 900,000 Swedish Match B Shares, mostly on the British market. The B Share issue raised 90 million kronor, doubling the share capital of Swedish Match.[21] Some Americans bought into the deal, through British intermediaries. Ivar's bankers praised his financial brilliance.

After Ivar's initial issue, B Shares blossomed as numerous other companies followed Swedish Match's lead. Investors in large public companies already had realized that their relatively small voting stakes didn't matter much. That was true even if they bought A Shares. Few investors held enough shares to justify attending corporate annual meetings, or bothering to vote. Even a 1 percent vote, a huge stake for one person, wouldn't matter. It made economic sense not to care about votes. Not voting was rational apathy.

Soon companies as diverse as the Dodge Brothers, Inc., Industrial Rayon Corporation, Universal Chain Theaters Corporation, and Southern Gas and Power Corporation had B Shares.[22] Then, the natural extension of B Shares with 1/1000 of a vote was B Shares with no vote at all. Such non-voting shares also became common during the mid-1920s. The practice spread so widely that Harvard Professor William Z. Ripley dubbed 1924 the "Year of the Vanishing Stockholder."[23]

The elimination of shareholder voting rights led to a minor backlash, but not enough to change state or federal law. Not even the New York Stock Exchange required that listed companies give every shareholder an equal vote. A protest poem, entitled "On Waiting in Vain for the New Masses to Denounce Nonvoting Stocks," was published in the *New York World*. It is not a very good poem, but there are so few poems on corporate law issues that it is worth reprinting here in its entirety:

Then you who drive the fractious nail,
And you who lay the heavy rail,
And all who bear the dinner pail
     And daily punch the clock –
Shall it be said your hearts are stone?
They are your brethren and they groan!
Oh, drop a tear for those who own
     Nonvoting corporate stock.[24]

After the B Share deal, Ivar asked Lee Higginson to begin soliciting investors in another participating preferred issue of International Match. The previous preferred issue, which carried no votes but participated in dividends along with common stock, had sold for 35 dollars per share in late 1924. Donald Durant saw that those shares already had increased substantially in value, and thought they might raise as much as 40 dollars per share with a new issue.

An initial question was whether the new preferred shares would be listed on the Curb Market or the New York Stock Exchange. International Match's previous issues had been listed on the less prestigious Curb Market, which had lower standards and didn't require the same degree of care with respect to financial statements and auditing. Lee Higginson had a good reputation to preserve at the New York Stock Exchange, and the firm wanted to have greater confidence in International Match before it would apply for a listing there.[25]

The directors of International Match, including Durant and Frederic Allen of Lee Higginson, had some questions about the company's financial statements. They were scheduled to meet to declare a dividend in early 1925, but decided to postpone the meeting when it became clear that Ivar and his accountants would not be able to prepare a balance sheet and income statement in time.[26] Lee Higginson pressed Ernst & Ernst with questions. Why the delay? How confident was A.D. Berning about the numbers?

By this time, Ivar and Berning had developed a much cozier relationship. Ivar had given up on getting Berning's first name right, but at least he addressed letters with an honorific now, as in "My dear Mr Berning."[27] Berning had gotten over the scrubbed trip to Japan, and instead was focused on an upcoming trip to Europe with his wife, at Ivar's expense. He wrote that "Mrs Berning and I are looking forward with a great deal of anticipation to our visit to Sweden."[28]

A.D. Berning's responses to detailed inquiries from Durant ranged from murky to non-responsive. What, Durant wanted to know, did International Match's income statement entry of $4,318,827.84 for "income from other sources" represent? Berning cryptically answered that the "other sources" entry "represents all the income of the corporation other than from sales. It includes dividends and interest received on investments, interest received on advances, accounts receivable, etc., profit on exchange and other miscellaneous items."[29] Whatever that meant, it could not have inspired much confidence.

Durant also asked about "investments" listed on the 1924 balance sheet, which also were calculated to the penny. Given the vagueness of the terms, how could these numbers be calculated with such precision? Did "investments" actually include all of International Match's investments?

Berning advised that the "investments" entry "consists almost entirely of investments in companies engaged in the match manufacturing and related industries, but in which the holdings of the International Match Corporation are not of an amount or character to warrant their assets and liabilities being consolidated."[30] Apparently, Ivar was using the same rationale he had used several years earlier to keep the liabilities of his earlier Swedish bank syndicate "off balance sheet."

If a company did not own a majority of a subsidiary's shares, it didn't make sense to "consolidate" that subsidiary by reporting all of its assets and liabilities. Berning treated International Match's minority stakes in other companies as investments in special purpose entities, which could be excluded from International Match's financial statements. Why would International Match consolidate the debts of a minority investment? If it bought some shares of RCA, would it need to include RCA's debts as well? No, Berning said. Such debts were deemed to be off the balance sheet.

Durant was conflicted about the new preferred issue they were planning. Ivar's financial statements were sloppy and incomplete. Yet investors nevertheless clamored to buy securities of International Match. The story about Poland was widely publicized. Although details in International Match's financial statements were vague, even dubious, the Poland deal was real. The Polish government would be granting International Match a match monopoly in exchange for a 6 million dollar loan – that was an easily verified fact. Moreover, this monopoly seemed likely to be the first of many. Even if the financial statements had holes, sharp investors wanted to get in early. They didn't care what was off or on the balance sheet.

As Durant explored the Poland deal, though, he realized that its terms were uncertain as well. It wasn't even clear how Ivar would get the money to Poland, or even whether it already was there. Had Ivar personally loaned Poland 6 million dollars? Would the money come from Swedish Match? Or perhaps another of Ivar's rapidly multiplying subsidiaries? Durant didn't yet know about Continental Investment Corporation, the secret company Ivar and Ernst August Hoffman had set up in Liechtenstein to shelter International Match's income. Durant wondered whether some of Ivar's various unnamed subsidiaries – the ones whose balance sheets were hidden from view – might play an important role in Poland. No one knew the answers to these questions, and Ivar said he wouldn't divulge details until a second, secret deal with Poland was closed.

Ivar made it clear, though, that the money from the new participating preferred share issue would be used in some way to cover the loan to Poland. Ivar also said he was making good progress on the second Polish agreement, which would require more capital than he or his other companies could afford. It was apparent to Durant that, without new money from American investors, International Match wouldn't be able to cover any payments that would be owed from that secret deal.

Although the terms of the second arrangement with Poland emerged only slowly, it appeared that the contract would give Ivar and his companies a monopoly to sell and distribute matches in Poland at a much higher price than the current market price, in exchange for a cash payment of $25 million.[31]

(Torsten's agreement had covered only match production, not sale and distribution.) Ivar and Dr Marjam Glowacki, the finance ministry official, negotiated the terms during the summer of 1925, while at the same time Durant solicited new investors in International Match.

According to Ivar, he and Dr Glowacki reached a final agreement on July 2, 1925, just days before the new participating preferred shares were to be sold. Ivar's assistant, Karin Bökman, said she witnessed the signatures to the secret deal; she certified the translation of the original contract, as did a Polish notary. Dr Glowacki signed on behalf of the "Treasury of the Polish State," and Ivar signed on behalf of International Match Corporation.[32] Ivar apparently didn't need to use the stamp he had prepared with a facsimile of Dr Glowacki's signature.

Like the B Shares, this contract was a marvel of financial innovation. First, the agreement provided for the creation of a new Dutch company called N.V. Maatschappij Garanta, or Garanta for short. Garanta would be incorporated in Amsterdam, and its shares would be owned by Polish citizens nominated by Dr Glowacki. Garanta would take over the entire match industry in Poland, from production to sale.

Garanta also would assume "certain exchange losses which have been sustained by International Match Corporation in connection with financial transactions in Poland. This item is to be carried as an asset on the books of Garanta."[33] Apparently, Ivar had continued gambling on foreign exchange rates during 1925. This time, though, he had used International Match's money, and this time he had lost. The secret agreement shifted those losses from International Match to Garanta. Durant and Berning were unaware of these losses, or their transfer.

The contract provided that International Match would lend 25 million dollars to Garanta in exchange for staggeringly high annual interest payments. Ivar promised to pay Poland 24 percent, a rate that was almost as high as Kreuger & Toll's dividends. The first 17 million dollars would be due on October 1, 1925; another 8 million dollars would be due the following July.

There was one major problem with this provision. International Match did not have 17 million dollars. Indeed, International Match did not have any money.

Remember that Ivar previously had moved all of the cash International Match had raised from the gold debentures to Continental, the Liechtenstein subsidiary. Then, he had used the cash from the participating preferred shares to repay the gold debentures. That meant all the money was gone. In order to comply with the secret Poland contract, International Match would need to raise another 17 million dollars right away. In other words, Ivar had signed a promise to give Poland 17 million dollars he didn't have.

The second Poland agreement also contained some extraordinary protections for International Match, terms that would have impressed Lee Higginson's bankers, if they had seen them. For example, Ivar obtained an agreement that if "for one reason or another" Garanta did not earn enough profit to pay the 24 percent interest payments due to Poland, those payments would be covered by "the income of the Polish Alcohol Monopoly or ... the Polish Tobacco Monopoly."[34] In other words, Ivar obtained a promise of payment supported not only by the match monopoly, but by unaffiliated monopolies on alcohol and tobacco. Ivar also included a binary foreign exchange option, a kind of derivative contract, to protect International Match from any declines in the value of the dollar: "International Match Corporation shall have the right to obtain payment of interest in Dutch guilders or US dollars according to its choice and for all such payments one dollar shall be counted as 2½ guilders."[35]

Given that Garanta's shareholders would be nominated by Dr Glowacki, how would Ivar retain control of Garanta? Here, as well, Ivar created another innovative financial provision:

> During the first four years until October 1, 1929, International Match Corporation shall have the right to appoint the managing director of Garanta who is alone entitled to sign for the company. On or after October 1, 1929, International Match Corporation has the right to acquire 60 percent of the shares at par.[36]

This option term secured both initial control over Garanta and the right to own a majority of Garanta's shares in the future. Either way, Ivar, not Dr Glowacki, would have control.

When Donald Durant asked to see this Garanta contract, Ivar said no. The deal was too sensitive for him to reveal anything but the most general terms. Ivar said he was using an intermediary corporation domiciled in Holland, not Poland, because of "unsettled Polish political conditions."[37] Like Switzerland and Liechtenstein, Holland did not impose currency restrictions, so it would be easy for Ivar to transfer money in and out of the country. Moreover, there was no annual auditing under Dutch law and no taxes on undistributed profits. Durant always had appreciated the tax angle, so Ivar emphasized that.

Ivar also explained to International Match's directors that their company would not pay any cash to the Holland company. Instead, International Match would pay 17 million dollars to Swedish Match, to wipe out a prior debt, and Swedish Match would then pay 17 million dollars to the Holland company. International Match would still hold the right to receive interest payments from the Polish government at a rate of 24 percent, but it would do so indirectly, through Swedish Match. Ivar argued that International Match nevertheless should list the Polish loan as an asset on its balance sheet. Liabilities might belong off balance sheet, but assets looked better on.

This arrangement might have seemed strange to the directors, and the interest rate of 24 percent looked usurious. Yet everything worked, just as Ivar said it would. International Match began receiving quarterly interest payments on the debt, about 1 million dollars each quarter, just as the agreement with Poland provided.[38] As more cash flowed in, the directors' questions went away.

In late July 1925, International Match sold 450,000 new preferred shares for 45 dollars per share – a full 10 dollars more than the issue just eight months earlier. Including dividends, investors in the previous issue already had profited by almost 30 percent. With that track record, it was easy for Lee Higginson to raise an additional 19.6 million dollars for International Match.

After paying expenses and other obligations, about 17 million dollars remained. That was exactly the amount of Ivar's obligation to Poland. At Ivar's direction, the cash banked like a billiard ball from International Match to Swedish Match to Garanta to Poland – from New York to Stockholm to Amsterdam to Warsaw. It was a complex transaction, but the pieces seemed to fit.

Or did they? Did the money make it through those last steps? Did Ivar initially send Poland only the 6 million dollars that Torsten had agreed to lend, the initial amount that the Polish government had approved? Or did he also send the additional amounts that supposedly were part of his secret agreement with Dr Glowacki, but were not yet approved by the government? No one in America knew, and Ivar intended to keep it that way.

In fact, the main reason Ivar had insisted that the money move to Swedish Match in Stockholm first was that he didn't want to have to answer too many questions about the Polish deal. He didn't want his bankers and auditors to know about Garanta, his Dutch subsidiary. Like Continental, Ivar's Vaduz subsidiary, Garanta was to remain secret.

Although Ivar's relationship with A.D. Berning was improving, at this point he couldn't trust Berning to audit, or even to know about, Garanta. He could use a paper trail to show Berning the details, if he ever discovered Garanta. But Ivar needed to hire an entirely different kind of person to perform an audit – or at least an "audit" – of Garanta.

When Ivar first saw Karl Lange, he had to agree that, indeed, the man looked exactly like Santa Claus. Lange was elderly, with a thick white beard and an imposing torso. Unlike Santa, he recently had been fired from a Stockholm bank after arranging a secret loan to himself.[39] Ivar was a director of this bank, and when he learned about Lange's firing and the secret loan, he immediately offered Lange a job. Like Ernst August Hoffman, the underqualified head of Continental, this man seemed to fall into the category of people Ivar could trust.

As with Hoffman, Ivar gave Lange a few small jobs at first, as tests. Lange happily did whatever Ivar asked: travel to Berlin, help promote a stock, assist one of Ivar's Swedish brokers.[40] Ivar opened a two-room office in Amsterdam and installed Lange as the new chief financial officer and auditor of Garanta. For months, Lange's primary job was simply to stay in Amsterdam and collect checks. Lange was not yet ready to "audit" Ivar's new Dutch company.

Finally, during fall 1925, after Garanta had funneled the loan money to Poland, Ivar asked Lange to travel to Sweden and meet him at his apartment in Stockholm. Ivar's apartment was a private lair, and had been off-limits to virtually everyone save a few women. Ivar kept most of his colleagues, particularly his bankers and accountants, at a safe distance. Lange was about to get a rare glimpse of Ivar's private life.

Ivar lived at No. 13 Villagatan, in one of Stockholm's most distinguished neighborhoods, a short walk from Tekniska Högskolan, the engineering school he had attended during the late 1890s. Kreuger & Toll had been the construction firm for the apartment building, and Ivar had followed the plans carefully. When the firm's workers had finished the structure six years earlier, Ivar took over the penthouse maisonette flat on the west half. Villagatan was, in every sense, Ivar's creation. He designed the plantings and shipped in statuary. He even arranged for Ingeborg Eberth, a dark-haired and attractive longtime female companion,[41] to buy the mirror apartment on the east half. It was easy to drop in for a quick visit, and even easier to hear her piano across the hall.

The rare visitor entered Ivar's public rooms on the building's fourth floor. The front door opened to a dining room with a wide wooden staircase leading to the private rooms on the upper floor. Ivar spent most of his time up there, either in his library or in a winter garden on the roof, which he reached by climbing a narrow corkscrew staircase. The rooms upstairs were formal and spotless. Both his bedroom and bathroom were laden with Italian marble. There was an additional, smaller dining room upstairs, where Ivar usually ate, alone.[42]

Although Ivar had staff, he didn't like being waited on. He still carried his own luggage, answered the telephone, greeted visitors, and opened his copious letters and cables. Ivar preferred to spend most of his time in Stockholm by himself, in silence. He had not lost the extraordinary memory skills he had as a child, and he spent much of his time devouring information about his companies, politics, and the global economy, all of which became permanently lodged in his mind.

Now in his forties, Ivar had become a creature of habit and discipline. He was anxious not to become fat, so he ate little throughout the day. Ivar preferred vegetarian dishes, especially fruit. He rarely drank alcohol, and never at lunch, though he was capable of consuming large amounts of vodka, usually without the slightest sign of being drunk. Ivar didn't smoke in the apartment either. He was a highly disciplined man, his one weakness being a fondness for sweet things, especially jams, marmalades, and all kinds of desserts, which he rarely kept at home.[43]

Ivar also had developed a habit of giving good luck taps to his favorite items in the flat. When he passed a small carved Renaissance table in the hall, he would say, "This is the loveliest table in the world," and tap it with his finger. He was superstitious in other ways, too – or at least he liked people to think he was. Ivar was credited with spreading the story that using one match to light two cigarettes was fine, but a third was bad luck. Whatever the source, that idea caught on and boosted match sales. But if Ivar really was superstitious, he was selective about it. For instance, his address at Villagatan was apartment No. 13, and he once remarked that "For me, even thirteen is a lucky number."[44]

If the morning of Lange's visit was typical, Ivar would have woken at six a.m. and immediately weighed himself on the scale in his bathroom. For breakfast, he might have had a few cherries, his favorite fruit since childhood, and maybe a piece of toast. When he walked downstairs, he would have stopped on the last step, as he always did, to pat the heel of the small wooden bear on the lowest banister of the handrail. That little bear's foot was worn smooth and shiny from Ivar's patting.

Ivar, not a servant, would have answered the door for Lange, and welcomed him into a formal reception room adjoining the dining room on the lower floor. The men likely would have sat in straight back chairs facing away from a grand piano. That was where Ivar received his rare visitors. Ivar might have mentioned some of the contemporary Swedish artwork that covered the walls: etchings by Anders Zorn, a realist, and paintings of wildlife by Bruno Lilje-fors. Zorn and Liljefors were two of Sweden's most famous artists, but Ivar typically was modest when he described the collection. In any event, Lange probably would not have appreciated the work, unless he intended to steal it.

The men quickly got to the business of Garanta's audit. Ivar showed Lange a balance sheet for Garanta listing millions of dollars of assets and liabilities and abruptly asked him to sign, attesting that the figures were correct. That was it – then he could go.

What was Lange to do? He told Ivar he'd like to look over the balance sheet first, as such huge sums were involved. According to one account, Ivar stared at him stone-faced in response, and, when Lange mumbled that it would be nice to know where all the money was going, Ivar said it was being spent secretly in Poland and shouldn't be mentioned. Ivar told Lange, "If you don't believe me, go to Poland and see for yourself."[45] Lange nodded, and signed. Ivar had always treated him well. Why would this time be any different?

Then Ivar told Lange he was closing the Amsterdam office of Garanta, ostensibly to save costs, although part of the reason was to make it more difficult for others to trace Garanta and its records. Ivar asked Lange to keep the corporate books at his home or, better yet, carry them around with him. Even the most suspicious investigator wouldn't suspect that Garanta's financial statements were in the bag of a man who resembled Santa Claus.

Lange had never handled any cash, and he never would. When the 17 million dollars flowed to Garanta from Swedish Match, and Lange wasn't sure how to adjust the accounts, Ivar told him, "Just debit it to me."[46] That was precisely what Lange did. Ultimately, Garanta's books showed that it had received a total of 25.4 million dollars from International Match and Swedish Match, and that it had paid all of that money to Ivar. Some of the money eventually went to Poland. But no one would ever be able to trace it all.

When Ivar finished his instructions to Lange, he showed the burly man out. They would have remained on the downstairs floor throughout the visit; male guests never saw Ivar's upstairs rooms.

After Lange left, Ivar would have resumed his evening habits, reading his mail upstairs while nibbling at dinner. If Ingeborg Eberth was in town, he might have stopped in to hear her play a piano sonata or some jazz, or just for the comfort he drew from her smiling, enigmatic eyes.[47] Frau Eberth set a lovely calm in him, the kind of simple peace he rarely received from other women.

After tea or coffee in his apartment, Ivar would take his evening stroll. Walking was his primary form of exercise and he loved it, just as he had as a young man. Sometimes, when Krister Littorin was in town, they would walk together. But more frequently, Ivar would go alone. Every night he spent at Villagatan, Ivar would step out past the Carl Milles sculpture in the courtyard, turn his collar up so he wouldn't be recognized, and wander the streets and parks of Stockholm for hours.

In 1925, A.D. Berning and his wife finally got the summer vacation Ivar had been promising. Ivar arranged for the trip to coincide exactly with the closing of the new International Match financing and the Poland deal with Garanta. Berning discussed the trip with the Ernsts, and got permission to be away while the details of the participating preferred deal were finalized. Berning wrote, "Mr Ernst felt that it was rather important that there should be a clear understanding of all of the essential factors so that the International Match Corporation's financial record here be proper in every respect, particularly in view of the plans for its future which you have often mentioned to me. Mrs Berning is indeed pleased at the prospect of the trip."[48]

Ivar arranged for the Bernings to sail for Southampton on June 9. He booked them on *Aquitania*, the longest-serving member of the Cunard fleet, an elder sister to *Berengaria*, the liner he had sailed to America in 1922. The Bernings had never seen anything like *Aquitania*. The ship's walls were adorned with English seaport prints and portraits of royalty. The public rooms were stylized versions of galleries from a major museum: the main restaurant in Louis XIV style; the grill room in Jacobean style; and the first-class drawing room in the Adam style, copied from Lansdowne House in London. There was even a smoking room modeled on Greenwich Hospital with oak panels and beams.[49] Mrs Berning must have been so pleased with her A.D.

Always a details man, Berning had been careful to arrange travel instructions from Southampton. Instead of consulting maps or a book on European travel, he asked his new friend Ivar directly: "As I am somewhat unfamiliar with the best route to take in order to reach Stockholm, I would appreciate it very much if you will let me have your suggestions."[50] If Ivar was surprised that an assistant manager of an accounting firm would ask him for directions, he didn't let on. He gave Berning several options, and advised that the "best and most convenient route from London or Paris to Stockholm is Berlin–Sassnitz–Trälleborg," a trip he estimated would take some forty-eight hours.[51]

When the Bernings arrived in London, A.D. received a cable from Ivar suggesting that they should meet. It sounded like there were some exciting developments in Poland. Ivar asked the Bernings to go to the Savoy Hotel, where he had arranged a suite for them. Ivar said he would travel from Stockholm soon. Meanwhile, perhaps the Bernings would enjoy some time in London at his expense?

Several days later, Ivar cabled that his trip to London had been canceled and asked the Bernings to go to Paris instead. Ivar wrote, "I am expecting news from Poland every day and if you can conveniently do so I would ask you kindly to stay in Paris until further so as to be prepared to return Stockholm if we decide to go ahead with business now."[52] Meanwhile, perhaps the Bernings would enjoy some time in Paris at his expense?

Finally, on July 23, six weeks after the Bernings had sailed from New York, Ivar and Krister Littorin, his engineering school classmate, cabled Berning at the Hotel Continental in Paris. The Bernings should come to Stockholm, now that the latest International Match issue of preferred shares had closed. Ivar said the "issue was made last Tuesday at $45. It has been very well received by the market. We thank you for your valuable cooperation and wish Mrs Berning and yourself a pleasant trip."[53]

The money Ivar had spent on the Bernings' vacation was well worth it. As the details of the new preferred issue were being finalized, Ivar's auditor – the one man who might have asked penetrating questions about the accounting details of the deal – had been just where Ivar wanted him: strolling the streets of London and Paris with his wife.

Ivar said he wanted A.D. Berning to meet Krister Littorin in Stockholm. He also wanted to take care of Mrs Berning. Ivar advised that "Miss Littorin asks if Mrs Berning should like to stay with her in the south of Sweden a couple of days in which case she would meet you in Malmoe."[54] Mrs Berning was delighted to receive such royal treatment.

In Stockholm, Ivar even invited the Bernings to see his apartment, where they had the same experience as Karl Lange: the Carl Milles statue of Diana at the entrance, the straight back chairs, the grand piano, the Zorn and Liljefors paintings. They saw everything Lange had seen, but they certainly did not see Lange. Nor did A.D. Berning see any of the Garanta financial statements

Lange had signed and now carried with him. In fact, Ivar and Berning hardly discussed business during the visit, and Berning left Stockholm with no keener sense of Ivar's companies. He still didn't even know of the existence of Ivar's key subsidiaries, Continental and Garanta.

The only new items on Ivar's agenda had been some additional cash payments to Ernst & Ernst, and to Berning. Ivar agreed to pay an extra 6,000 dollars a year of consulting fees to Ernst & Ernst, in addition to other fees he already was paying. He also agreed to pay an extra 3,000 dollars of "special expenses" related to the Bernings' trip to Europe.[55] Those payments alone were more than A.D. Berning's annual income. With this new money, Ivar had made A.D.'s year.

The Bernings left Sweden and spent a week in Switzerland, the original home of Garanta, before Ivar had moved it to Vaduz. Finally, they sailed home on *Berengaria*. The ship was quiet without Ivar on board, and the radio shack was less used than it had been during Ivar's 1922 trip. But the first-class cabins were just as luxurious and by the time the Bernings arrived in New York, in August, they were glowing. Berning met with Durant for an update on the participating preferred issue, and then wrote to Ivar:

> Messrs. Lee Higginson & Co. are naturally much pleased with the manner in which the public received the new offering of securities and the splendid market which the shares have maintained. Everyone seems to be quite enthusiastic. Mrs Berning and I enjoyed a very delightful return voyage and have many pleasant recollections of our stay in Sweden.[56]

Back at work, Berning was dismayed to see that his previous correspondence with the Wisconsin regulators had not made them go away. Instead, Commissioner Hibma continued to press for details, to see if International Match was performing as the company's reports claimed it would. That meant Berning would have to get more information from Ivar. He reluctantly wrote to Ivar, who even more reluctantly responded, with a pithy summary of International Match's first half of 1925. Berning thought he could dress up this new information in a way that might satisfy Wisconsin. He thanked Ivar and wrote, "[W]e hope that you will have no further annoyance from this source."[57]

Berning was wrong yet again. Wisconsin immediately rejected the summary and asked for a more detailed statement of International Match's earnings for the first six months of 1925. It was early December and Ivar was in New York, so Berning reported the bad news and requested to see Ivar in person.[58] Ivar promised to meet, but said he couldn't do it right away. They set a date, and meanwhile Ivar sent five lines of more detailed information for Berning to work with.

The categories were broad, but each item was carried out to the penny:

Interest on Advances, Bank Accounts, etc.	$2,763,463.57
Profit on Exchange	$1,129,568.16
Interest on Investments and Sundry	$323,449.19
Dividends	$102,346.92
Total	$4,318,827.84

Before sending the revised information to Wisconsin, Berning checked to see how Ivar's new numbers compared to what Lee Higginson had sent to investors a few months earlier. Berning also sent a request to Lee Higginson, seeking to confirm the details of International Match's income for the first six months of 1925.[59] In its investor circular, Lee Higginson had represented, also apparently based on information from Ivar, that earnings for the first six months of 1925 were "in excess of $4,400,000." However, when Berning checked the numbers from the new lines of information Ivar sent, they summed to a total of just $4,318,827.84. Anyone could see that this number was less than $4,400,000. That shortfall was a serious problem. It suggested the previous numbers had been inflated.

The discrepancy would raise eyebrows in Wisconsin, where the regulators certainly would notice that the new reported income for the first six months was less than the income set forth in the investor circular. If Commissioner Hibma saw this shortfall, he would open an investigation into whether International Match had misrepresented its earnings. Was there any chance he wouldn't notice? Ivar had not expected a Wisconsin securities regulator to have a sharp financial mind. Yet Hibma was the only person Berning and Ivar had been unable to shake.

Berning concluded that he couldn't run the risk of using Ivar's new numbers. He simply had to find a way to send the Wisconsin regulators something that added up at least $4,400,000, the amount Lee Higginson already had told investors was International Match's income.

In an extraordinary auditor-to-client letter, Berning wrote to Ivar on December 11, that "In view of the fact that the circular stated that the earnings for the first six months 'were in excess of $4,400,000', I thought it best to increase this amount slightly." *Increase this amount slightly?* Yes, at Berning's request, Ėrnst & Ernst reported net income for International Match of $4,475,000, a nice round number that was higher than the income Ivar and Lee Higginson previously had reported to investors. In a letter to Lee Higginson, Berning did not highlight the fact that he had adjusted the earnings. Instead, he merely noted, somewhat opaquely, that "the figures shown on the attached are subject to any necessary adjustment upon the final closing of the books of the various companies at the end of the fiscal year."[60]

Meanwhile, Berning and Ivar still had not met in New York. Berning summed up his most recent work in a letter to Ivar: "It is therefore to be sincerely hoped that the enclosed will be the final chapter with respect to the State of Wisconsin."[61] Indeed, with the "adjusted" numbers, it was.

Ivar received Berning's good news before he sailed to Europe on a New Year's cruise. Berning was performing just as Ivar had hoped. Ivar resolved to send the man and his wife on an all-expenses-paid trip to Europe every year. However, while Berning relished his face time with Ivar, Ivar didn't feel the same affection. Now that Berning had resolved the inquiry from Wisconsin, Ivar saw no need to see him, and he canceled their meeting in New York. Like a dog missing his master, Berning wrote, "I am very sorry that I did not have an opportunity of personally wishing you a very happy and prosperous New Year before you sailed."[62]

7

LE BOOM

The mid-1920s were a time of great mirth and movement in America, book-ended by the death of President Warren Harding and the Great Crash. From 1923 to 1929, Ivar tripled his funds raised from American investors; he persuaded the New York Stock Exchange to list his securities; he pulled even with Morgan as a leading lender to Europe by securing match monopolies in several countries, including France; he built his 125-room Match Palace in Stockholm; and in general he got really, really rich. The six years leading up to 1929 were a blur, a period when Ivar's story was the story of a newly prosperous America. In six short years, Ivar wove his way into the fabric of American culture.

After the exhausting years of war and tension under Woodrow Wilson, President Harding was a relief. His first official act was to throw open the locked gates in front of the White House and let sightseers roam the grounds. If they pressed their noses to the windows, they might catch him in a favorite unofficial act: playing poker, practicing his golf swing, smoking a cigar, or even violating the laws of Prohibition. Harding was Midwestern handsome and small-town good natured – "just folks," he liked to say. Cigar-smoking lobbyists from oil and banking swarmed him and his cabinet, a fraternity of laissez-faire businessmen led by Andrew Mellon and Herbert Hoover.

Harding's administration left a trail of scandal, but also an improving economy that boosted the mood of American investors. The reaction to his funeral, in 1923, was more about the future than the past. New issues of securities of industrial companies would increase from 690 during the year after Harding's death to nearly 2,000 in 1929.[1] Brokers' loans to investors and share ownership would quadruple by 1929.[2] The number of Americans who paid tax on income of a million dollars a year also would quadruple.[3]

The new optimism about the future led to a boom in consumer spending. Radio sales doubled in 1923, then tripled in 1924. On average, nearly every family had a car, and drivers were branching out from black Model Ts to an assortment of new makes in colors ranging from "Florentine cream" to "Versailles violet." Average people bought items they hadn't imagined spending money on just a few years earlier: from Listerine mouthwash and crossword puzzle books to vacuum cleaners and meat slicers to new golf clubs and even property in Florida.[4]

Prosperity changed the culture. Suddenly there were traffic lights, filling stations, and new concrete highways with chicken dinner restaurants and tourist rest stops. Giant broadcast radio stations with nationwide hookups brought Graham McNamee's play-by-play or the Happiness Boys or reports on the Scopes Monkey Trial into more than one out of three homes. More Americans followed politics now, including the presidential nominating convention, which was covered live from Madison Square Garden.[5]

The legendary newspaper editor William Allen White, who had found President Harding "almost unbelievably ill-informed,"[6] found it more difficult to criticize his replacement, Vice President Calvin Coolidge, who was easily reelected in 1924. Coolidge was so hands-off there simply wasn't much to say. Even friends called him "silent Cal." The best White could manage as criticism was an observation that the aloof Coolidge always seemed to be "looking down his nose to locate that evil smell which seemed forever to affront him."[7] Even Dorothy Parker, the witty founder of the Algonquin Round Table, couldn't skewer the president. As the story went, at a dinner party she asked him, "Mr Coolidge, I've made a bet against a fellow who said it was impossible to get more than two words out of you." His famous reply was, "You lose."[8] (Parker got the last word, as she typically did. When told in 1933 that Coolidge had died, she quipped, "How can you tell?"[9])

Like Andrew Mellon and Herbert Hoover, who remained as Secretaries of Treasury and Commerce, respectively, President Coolidge believed that individuals and markets, left alone, naturally would produce the best decisions and the greatest wealth. Together, these three men reduced income taxes, deregulated industry, and encouraged borrowing and spending. Coolidge's famous statement, often misquoted, was that "the chief business of the American people is business." From 1923 to 1929, he was right.

Along with America's new wealth came a hunger for sophistication. College applications spiked, as did international travel. The most popular nonfiction books included *Outline of Science*, *The Story of Philosophy*, *Why*

We Behave Like Human Beings, and Emily Post's *Book of Etiquette* (the top seller). The now-literary-minded masses read an astonishing rush of new novels during this period: F. Scott Fitzgerald's *The Great Gatsby*, Ernest Hemingway's *A Farewell to Arms*, Herman Hesse's *Siddhartha*, Franz Kafka's *The Trial*, and Virginia Woolf's *Mrs Dalloway*. Newly minted intellectuals tried to parse James Joyce's *Ulysses* or T. S. Eliot's *The Waste Land*. New fans of the arts listened to George Gershwin's *Rhapsody in Blue*, and saw plays by Eugene O'Neill, who won three Pulitzer Prizes during the 1920s.

One sure way for both men and women to appear sophisticated was to smoke cigarettes. Advertisers depicted pretty girls, cigarettes in hand, imploring men to blow smoke their way. Tobacco manufacturers announced that "now women may enjoy a companionable smoke with their husbands and brothers."[10] Women had earned the vote and entered the work force; now millions of women of all ages exercised their right to take up smoking. Blue tobacco smoke wafted through theater lobbies, where Greta Garbo's most important silent movies – *Flesh and the Devil*, *The Temptress*, *The Torrent*, and *Love* – appeared in 1926 and 1927, just as talking movies débuted. Sports fans smoked as they watched Babe Ruth, also a smoker, hit sixty home runs in 1927 for the New York Yankees; his teammates, known as "Murderers' Row," easily smoked their way through the World Series that year. Prohibition also fueled smoking, just as it increased illegal alcohol consumption. The more people drank, the more they craved a smoke. And, most important to the story of Ivar Kreuger, the more they smoked, the more they needed, and thought about, matches.

During the decade prior to 1929, US cigarette production doubled. Ivar didn't have a monopoly on match sales in the United States, although Swedish Match accounted for a significant share of US match imports. Still, each time an American lit up was an advertising opportunity for investments in International Match. As Americans smoked more, so did the rest of the world, particularly Europeans. What could be a better bet for newly sophisticated American investors than the securities of a company with a monopoly on match sales abroad?

Harvard Professor William Z. Ripley began warning as early as 1924 that, although the stock market kept going up, trouble was brewing. He first focused on the sharp rise in real estate prices and the surge in mortgage lending. While the price of land increased, the profits from land fell, particularly for farms (then the predominant use of land). Even during the prosperity of the mid-1920s, many farms were defaulting on their debts, and these defaults were creating a minor crisis at some regional banks. In seven states, nearly half of the banks doing business as of 1920 failed *before* 1929. Ripley believed these regional difficulties in the mortgage markets would soon spill over to the stock markets.

Ripley also pointed out that, although investors were flocking to buy shares, even shares without votes, they were doing so based on little or no information. According to Ripley, the sketchy disclosures by International Match continued to be typical of those by leading companies. National Biscuit Company's income statement from 1925 was just three-by-four inches, and didn't need even that much space – it included just a single entry labeled "Earnings, Year 1925."[11] The Royal Baking Powder Company didn't issue any financial statements at all.[12] Many corporate reports contained disclaimers that the official income account "does not by any means give a clear picture of the annual earning power" or that "the balance sheet by no means discloses the true value of the company's fixed assets."[13]

In 1926, only 242 of 957 companies listed on the New York Stock Exchange published quarterly reports.[14] Nearly a third of listed companies did not issue reports at all, primarily because they had been members of the Exchange for many years and had nondisclosure agreements that were grandfathered from when they first joined. Newly listed companies filed quarterly reports, but they lacked detail. Listing requirements varied by company and were open to negotiation.

Even the minimal New York Stock Exchange requirements were too much for many companies, which instead listed securities at the Curb Market. Shares of major companies, such as Singer Manufacturing, traded at the Curb, and those companies did not publish quarterly reports either. International Match traded at the Curb because it had not yet met the Exchange's minimal requirements.

According to Professor Ripley, the stock price boom couldn't possibly be based on reality because investors lacked basic information about companies. Before 1929, virtually everyone thought he was wrong. National Biscuit, Royal Baking Powder, and Singer Manufacturing were real companies that made real products. So were RCA and General Motors. Share prices were rising because companies, like most Americans, were prospering. Moreover, these companies were backed by leading investment banks and accounting firms. Why did investors need to see detailed financial statements when prestigious firms such as Lee Higginson and Ernst & Ernst were vouching for the companies? The average investor wouldn't understand the details anyway.

Meanwhile, Lee Higginson and Ernst & Ernst were too busy serving current clients, and soliciting new ones, to consider the doomsday scenarios of some Harvard professor, or to worry about giving investors more information than they wanted. Indeed, in one surprising instance, Lee Higg even neglected to disclose the commissions Ivar had paid to the firm. At the beginning of March 1926, A.D. Berning cabled Ivar to let him know the mistake. Lee Higg had received the commissions, but Berning hadn't deducted the amount from International Match's reported earnings. Ivar suggested that Ernst & Ernst simply shift some money away from earnings over a several-year period to cover up the missing commissions. "In this way the deferred charges will disappear in a relatively short time."[15] That seemed like a reasonable solution to everyone. Investors would never know the difference.

The bankers and accountants had a similarly casual approach to International Match's annual meetings. Most companies arranged for shareholders to meet once a year, typically in the early spring, to vote on major business decisions, such as the election of directors. In advance of this meeting, companies typically sent shareholders and directors annual statements summarizing results from the previous year, however terse those statements might be, so that everyone could make informed decisions.

Yet, as late as April 1926, it remained unclear when International Match's annual meeting would take place. There were still no financial statements for the year, and Donald Durant cabled A.D. Berning to ask if some kind of a report – anything – would be forthcoming soon.[16] On April 21, Ivar said he had prepared a summary letter to shareholders.[17] The annual report was finally printed in May.

International Match's annual meeting that year was perfunctory. Ivar still controlled the common shares. American investors didn't have votes, and in any event Ivar and the other board members were easily reelected. The directors covered just two items of interest at the meeting. First, they discussed the fact that International Match's financial statements were intended to be only general summaries; all of the details would remain off the balance sheet. Berning reminded the directors of the rationale for keeping any other liabilities out of the annual report. He reported that "it is only customary to consolidate the assets and liabilities of companies in such a balance sheet when a substantial majority of the outstanding shares are owned by the parent company. Where less than such a majority is owned, the shares are included as investments."[18] Everyone agreed that this off balance sheet approach was fine.

Second, Durant and Frederic Allen asked Ivar to change one line of the report, a reference to an asset worth $5,293,113.38 that Ivar had labeled "Advances to Governments and Government Monopolies." They didn't object to the amount or question how such a broad item might have been calculated with to-the-penny accuracy. Nor did the directors question the rationale for including the value of such "advances" as assets without listing more specific information. Everyone presumed that the money related to Poland and the match monopoly there.

Instead, what the directors objected to was Ivar's use of the term "government monopolies."[19] "Monopoly" was a dangerous and sensitive word in the United States, and the Lee Higginson partners were nervous about tipping off some overzealous antitrust prosecutor. It didn't matter that the word was accurate, or that the entry actually reflected a real monopoly. At their request, "monopoly" was removed before the report was publicized on the Curb Market.

A.D. Berning thought he was now on a much friendlier basis with Ivar, although he still didn't see the man very often. In his letters to Ivar, Berning retained a level of formality, addressing Ivar as "My dear Mr Kreuger,"[20] but Ivar's responses and behavior suggested that he was permitting Berning to inch closer to his inner circle. Ivar asked Krister Littorin to remain in New York after International Match's annual meeting, to spend a few fine summer days with Berning. Berning showed Littorin a copy of the *Bawl Street Journal*, the farcical newspaper Donald Durant still oversaw. The men had a good laugh over the columns lampooning financial people they knew. Littorin insisted that Berning send Ivar a copy, which he did, noting that "it has some amusing references to some of your friends here."[21] Ivar responded that he found the *Bawl Street Journal* "very amusing and have read with a great deal of interest."[22]

Berning and Littorin also discussed future business, including the possibility of other monopolies in Europe in addition to Poland. Berning's future looked bright. Ivar already had agreed that Berning could charge International Match separately for consulting services Berning would perform in addition to his audit, and Berning was preparing to send Ivar a separate bill for "$6,000 covering general consultation work in connection with the International Match Corporation."[23]

Berning introduced Littorin to the Ernst brothers, and they gave him permission to accompany Littorin on an upcoming trip to Germany.[24] The Bernings were looking forward to more travel, but unfortunately Mrs Berning became ill.²⁵ That, plus the rush of work at Ernst & Ernst, prevented the Bernings from returning to Europe in 1926. The Ernsts needed every assistant manager at 27 Cedar Street, the firm's office in New York.

At the end of the summer, Berning, who had only seen Ivar once that year, wrote that the "continued easy money market has prompted many financings, mergers and reorganizations."²⁶ All of those deals required accountants, so Berning and his firm were prospering along with everyone else. Berning had less time to devote to International Match, which was just fine with Ivar.

The next year, International Match sold another block of 450,000 participating preferred shares, this time for 50 dollars per share, the highest price to date. Ivar wrote that the money was "to be used for transactions in Greece, Portugal, Algiers, Norway and Manila."²⁷ Once again, there were few details and the cash quickly left America. The vast majority of the funds raised, more than $16 million, went directly to Continental Investment Corporation, Ivar's Liechtenstein subsidiary. This time, a portion of the money – 3 million dollars – migrated to Swedish Match in Stockholm. The rest went to pay dividends and fees.

While Berning was updating International Match's reports to reflect this new preferred share issue, he discovered a reference to Garanta, the Dutch company that Karl Lange, the Santa Claus lookalike, had been "auditing." Berning was surprised to see that Garanta owed International Match 17 million dollars. That was a lot of money. He asked Ivar for some assurances about Garanta. What was it? Did this company make any profits or have any assets? Would it actually be able to repay? Why hadn't Ivar told him about Garanta?

Ivar reassured Berning that Garanta's income during 1925 was 46 million Dutch guilders, and that it owed the equivalent of just 45 million Dutch guilders to International Match.²⁸ Garanta made enough money in one year to repay the entire debt. That was plenty of cushion. Besides, Garanta was just a conduit for sending cash to Ivar's businesses outside the United States. The debt owed by Garanta was an unimportant detail, a nit. There was no reason for concern.

What was Berning supposed to do? Should he be suspicious of Ivar, who had brushed aside Berning's inquiry about Garanta and a 17 million dollar debt as if they were minor issues he had simply overlooked in previous discussions? The Garanta obligation was International Match's primary asset, and Berning hadn't even known it existed. That certainly was alarming. But was it so serious that Berning should accuse his most important client of hiding crucial information? Even a hint of accusation would destroy Berning's improving relationship with Ivar, and that would ruin Berning's chances of making partner. Ivar had treated him well, and there was at least a chance that Ivar really had simply overlooked Garanta. Wasn't there?

Ivar paid his bills on time, and his fees to Ernst & Ernst were rising, particularly now that Berning was giving him tax and consulting advice. Berning was even recommending American companies that Ivar might consider pursuing.[29] He recently had sent Ivar the annual report for the International Telephone and Telegraph Corporation, noting that it "may be interesting to you."[30] Ivar was considering a major transaction with IT&T. Did Berning want to risk losing the fees from such a deal?

The match monopoly in Poland was real, and Ivar's reputation was unassailable. One only had to open a newspaper or ask any businessman to understand that. Ivar was negotiating match monopolies in Ecuador, Estonia, Greece, Hungary, Latvia, Peru, Portugal, Yugoslavia, and those negotiations also were undeniably real. Ivar met regularly with government leaders, most recently with Raymond Poincaré, the distinguished French statesman who had been prime minister during the early 1920s, and retook the job in 1926. Given these facts – and they were facts – Berning was reluctant to accuse such a reputable man of anything. He told himself Garanta wasn't important. It couldn't be.

Berning had toured Ivar's apartment, but not his factories. Durant hadn't even seen the apartment. Indeed, no one from Lee Higginson or Ernst & Ernst had ever inspected Ivar's business, either to check on the efficiency of his operations, or even to see whether the factories Ivar said he owned actually existed. Instead, they had relied entirely on Ivar's word, and on a surprisingly thin stack of paper.

At the beginning of 1927, Durant asked to send someone to visit Ivar's match factories in Sweden. Previously, Ivar had refused to permit inspections, citing concerns about confidentiality. Some of Ivar's obsession with trade secrets seemed justified, but at times his stories seemed far fetched, not unlike the conspiracy theories of Jack Morgan. Had Japanese spies really traveled to Jönköping to steal the secrets of Ivar's Lagerman automatic match-making machine? Had an American engineer really "accidentally" dropped his hat into a tank of chemicals at one of Ivar's plants to get a sample he could analyze and copy?[31] Ivar's competitors might have been ruthless, but he seemed a bit paranoid.

Ivar finally agreed to an inspection, but insisted that Durant send a businessman, not an auditor. Ivar was willing to have someone who understood the match industry look at his factories, but he didn't want that person to ask annoying questions about the intricacies and complexities of Swedish accounting. Ivar, Ernst & Ernst, and Lee Higginson already had agreed that the American audit would be limited in scope. Berning was to rely on Ivar's audit in Sweden, and he wasn't to look into, or even question, what Swedish auditors said about Ivar's subsidiaries and operations in Sweden.

Ivar didn't want to pay for the same audit twice, and he especially didn't want to answer irritating questions about accounting niceties, as the Wisconsin securities regulators had forced him to do a few years earlier. He cabled Berning, "Regarding the International Match Corporation, it has always been understood by Lcc Higginson that you based your report on the figures given you by Mr Wendler, who is a Swedish Chartered Accountant, and this method of working has been accepted by Lee Higginson."[32] Ernst & Ernst had agreed to this approach, but no one from the firm had met or spoken with Anton Wendler, even though they had been relying on his written audit statements since 1922.

Given Ivar's preference for a businessman over an auditor, Berning and Durant chose to send F. Gordon Blackstone, a consultant Durant knew who had experience in the match industry. Ivar responded that he was busy negotiating with French officials, but would be willing to discuss Blackstone's visit with Durant's British associates during an upcoming trip to London. Ivar also wanted a chance to look Blackstone in the eye. He wrote in a letter to Berning that "While it is quite probable that Mr Blackstone will be ultimately accepted, it is understood that I shall have opportunity to know him and pass judgment on him before it is decided if I find him suitable for the position and if I am prepared to give him any confidential information regarding our business."[33]

The look of this letter was especially curious. Ivar typically dictated his letters and cables, or at least he had since putting on the one-man telegraphing show for the passengers on *Berengaria*. But he typed this letter to Berning himself. Ivar apparently didn't even want his trusted assistant, Karin Bökman, to know the Americans were asking sensitive questions and seeking to inspect his businesses. The difference in the appearance of this letter, compared to letters he dictated, was striking. Unlike Miss Bökman's meticulous typing, some of Ivar's words were out of line, the "m"s were raised slightly, and there were "I"s in place of "1"s. The letter was dated "February 15th 1927."[34] Berning must have thought the letter looked a bit creepy, as if a madman had hunted and pecked each key.

Ultimately, the inspection was a non-event. Ivar met Blackstone, and approved him. Blackstone reported that the match factories did in fact exist, and were marvelously efficient. He noted that Ivar was widely known and respected in Sweden, and that no one there would question his word. There is no record of what Blackstone and Ivar did in Sweden, although something must have led the men to trust each other. In any event, Blackstone's glowing report satisfied Donald Durant, at least temporarily.

Ivar decided he needed to be more forthcoming to Berning about his Swedish accountants, or at least to appear to be so. He didn't want to risk losing Berning's loyalty, so he invited Berning to come to Sweden to meet Anton Wendler and get a better sense of the Swedish audit process. Berning booked a cabin on *Berengaria*, but Ivar asked him to take a different ship, *Homeric*, and to meet him first at his flat in Pariser Platz, Berlin.[35]

Meeting in Berlin was mostly for show, and to give Berning a trip to another country in Europe (albeit without his wife). Ivar showed Berning his apartment and the swanky neighborhood, including the Brandenburger Tor, the nearby embassies, and the famous Hotel Adlon. Ivar wanted Berning to see how the German locals were thrilled and proud to have him living nearby. A Berlin paper reported that Ivar's phone at Pariser Platz would start ringing within moments if the caretaker so much as opened the windows or turned on the lights.[36]

In Berlin, Ivar told Berning a secret. He understood Berning's suspicions, and he confided that, indeed, the financial statements for International Match were in error. There were mistakes. But not for the reasons Berning might have imagined. Instead, the financial statements were wrong because they massively *understated* Ivar's profits. Ivar told Berning he was involved in politically sensitive deals with numerous governments, many of which would generate substantial profits, and these dealings simply could not be disclosed to anyone. Ivar said Berning should draw comfort from the safety net of secret deals that were not even mentioned in his corporate accounts. The International Match financial statements weren't supposed to accurately reflect the value of Ivar's enterprises. They were merely a floor, a minimum amount that only hinted at the much higher, true value.

For example, Ivar showed Berning a copy of what he called the "Spanish contract," which appeared to be signed by Miguel Primo de Rivera, the Spanish ruler who had taken over from King Alfonso in a recent coup. Ivar suggested that he had met with King Alfonso in 1923, and he said Primo de

Rivera secretly had agreed to honor the terms of a loan-for-monopoly deal between Ivar and the king. Unfortunately, Primo de Rivera had abandoned his pre-coup promise to rule for only ninety days, and instead suspended Spain's constitution, established martial law, and imposed a system of strict censorship. But Ivar assured Berning that, even given this turmoil, Spain secretly continued to pay interest on the loan. There was no way for Berning, or anyone, to confirm or deny Ivar's assertions about such a secret deal. Berning understandably would have been reluctant to travel to Spain to try to verify Primo de Rivera's signature.

Ivar also showed Berning a certificate of deposit showing that the Nederlandish Bank held 400 million francs of French government bonds for the account of Continental Investment Company, Ivar's Lichtenstein subsidiary. When Berning said he hadn't heard of the Nederlandish Bank, Ivar explained that it existed "in order to keep certain transactions secret from Swedish and foreign bankers."[37] Ivar had hired Sven Huldt, an unemployed match jobber, to keep track of this bank's deposits. Included among the receipts Huldt periodically sent Ivar were not only entries for the French government bonds, but also items showing that Continental's account with the Nederlandish Bank included proceeds from secret match monopolies and a Spanish contract worth 144 million Swiss francs.[38]

Ivar's explanations about these secret assets made some sense. Why else would he have been so casual about financial issues, including important matters such as quarterly dividends? He *had* to avoid accurate disclosure, to preserve the secrecy of his match monopoly negotiations. The inaccuracy of his financial statements was a boon, not a worry. It reflected the fact that Ivar had secured many secret deals, and therefore additional secret cash flows.

Moreover, Ivar behaved like someone who understated, not overstated, his income. One time, Ivar sent the money for International Match's dividends to America early, indicating to Berning that "we have so much money over here, you might as well have this now." Another time, Ivar sent an extra million dollars, and later responded, "Oh, we simply made a mistake. We have so much money here, we just can't keep track of it." These were either the acts of a crazed risk taker or a man in such solid financial condition that he really couldn't be bothered with minor seven-figure details. The latter explanation seemed more plausible: Ivar, and International Match, must have had substantial undisclosed assets.

Ivar's newly open approach reinforced Berning's view that Ivar's companies were strong. Once Ivar thought Berning seemed more comfortable, he introduced Anton Wendler, his Swedish accountant, who also was in Germany at Ivar's request. The men discussed Ivar's use of various subsidiaries such as Garanta and Continental. Wendler was an impressive figure. Like the Ernsts, he and his brother had started their own accounting firm, called Svenska Revisions Aktiebolaget. The firm was small, and the Wendler brothers had just two other partners, but they seemed more than capable of handling a complex audit. Wendler assured Berning that he had voluminous details about Ivar's various subsidiaries at his offices at 4 Västra Trädgårdsgatan in Stockholm.

Ivar said they should all to go Stockholm, and he insisted that Berning stay at the Grand Hôtel there, the most luxurious hotel in Scandinavia.[39] Ivar knew everyone at the Grand Hôtel, particularly its president, Torsten Segerstråle, who had just refurbished the public areas and created several new guest rooms. Ivar was an investor in the hotel, and he dined regularly in the great dining room, usually by himself.

Ivar showed Berning into the lobby, and they walked across the English porcelain-tiled floor, through pilasters of black and yellow-veined marble, and up the double staircase to the first floor. Ivar tapped the mahogany rail atop the cast-iron banister, just as he did at home. He then showed Berning the two-story dining room at the southern end of the building, where the Nobel Prize banquet was held before it moved to Stockholm City Hall, one of Ivar's buildings. Ivar then left Berning to dine alone, under the massive gas candelabra that hung from the 25-foot ceiling.

After spending the next day at Wendler's office, Berning was overwhelmed by the mountain of new information and sent a handwritten note to Ivar asking if they could meet to discuss how Berning might filter what he really needed to see. Ivar said he was too busy; Wendler and his stacks of paper would have to do. But there were so many documents that it was impossible for Berning to do more than simply scan through the lists of what was at Wendler's office. Berning took notes, but Wendler insisted on keeping the originals. There were no carbon copies. Berning would have been happy to stay in Stockholm, and spend a month at the Grand Hôtel. He would need that long to inspect the documents. However, the Ernsts needed him back in New York.

After Berning returned home, Wendler sent him some additional information about Ivar's foreign subsidiaries, as he had promised. As Berning scrutinized these new disclosures, he found that some of Wendler's calculations were incorrect. For example, Berning discovered that one subsidiary had paid about 400,000 dollars of dividends to Continental, but Continental had not recorded those dividends. He quietly corrected this mistake.[40] On balance, though, the deluge of paper in Stockholm persuaded Berning that Ivar's accounting there was reasonable. Perhaps it was even conservative, understating Ivar's income, as he had suggested.

At some point, Ivar would need to disclose more information, but Berning was confident Ivar would be willing to do that when it became necessary. Berning discussed his visit to Wendler's office with Donald Durant and the Ernsts, and together they decided they had enough confidence to support International Match's application for a listing on the prestigious New York Stock Exchange. Berning began preparing documents for the Exchange.[41]

There were two hurdles to overcome before International Match could list on the Exchange. First, Ernst & Ernst needed to prepare and certify quarterly financial statements for International Match. Berning would take care of that. Second, the company needed to establish a source of profits based on something more than one 6 million dollar loan to Poland. That was Ivar's job. He would have to show that he could secure a marquee deal, one that warranted a listing on the world's leading exchange.

Ivar thought he could overcome this hurdle. At the time, he was working on the largest monopoly loan in history, in one of his favorite cities in the world. For the first time in his life, he was close to competing with J. P. Morgan & Co.

Pierpont Morgan had always been the leading lender to France, and his son Jack had assumed he would inherit any French business. That assumption had been true through 1926. Both Jack Morgan and Ivar had made overtures to the French government during 1924 and 1925, but Jack had won the beauty contest each time. Ivar had made progress in some smaller countries, but the titans of Europe – France, Germany, and Italy – remained wedded to Morgan.

Yet in July 1926, when France fell into financial crisis and Raymond Poincaré was reinstated as prime minister, Poincaré immediately sought help, not from Jack Morgan, but from Ivar. The reasons were both financial and personal. France already owed J. P. Morgan & Co. 100 million dollars at an interest rate of 8 percent, and Morgan had refused to lend any more. Jack Morgan in particular worried that the French franc might follow the German mark's plunge into oblivion.

Unlike Morgan, Ivar was willing to offer a loan. And he was willing to accept a lower interest rate than 8 percent.

During the previous decade, Ivar quietly had built a strong relationship with

France in general and Poincaré in particular. He advised Poincaré about the global economic scene and various industries the French government owned and administered. He assisted the dysfunctional French Monopoly Administration. Through Swedish Match, he sold matches, match-making machines, and raw materials to the French government. Most important, Ivar and Poincaré discussed France's fiscal needs. France's predicament was straightforward, but not easy to resolve: it needed to reduce its annual obligations so that it could afford various government programs without going deeper into debt. Ivar saw an opening here, and his chance to compete with Morgan.

With the rise of the investor class in America, the financial power base was shifting from banks to investors, and this shift was very much to Ivar's advantage. Previously, banks had played the primary economic and financial roles, and a handful of bankers, led by Morgan, had exercised control of the financial system. But now that investors were becoming more important, the bankers were losing their grip. Jack Morgan might have the minds of other American bankers, but Ivar had the hearts of American investors, and those investors now had the power. Ivar didn't need to lend his own money to France. Instead, he could act as an intermediary, raising money from the Americans and lending *their* money.

Once Poincaré was firmly in control of the French government, Ivar approached Durant and Berning with an idea for a fifth securities issue in the United States. Lee Higginson had sold International Match's gold debentures in 1923 and three different participating preferred issues for the company from 1924 through 1926. Overall, American investors had bought 70 million dollars of International Match's securities, which made Ivar's company one of the most widely held stocks in the US. Investors were delighted by Ivar's inroads into the match markets of Poland and other smaller countries, and the rising prices of International Match's preferred shares reflected their optimism about Ivar's future match deals.

Now, Ivar proposed something truly bold: one massive 50 million dollar issue backed by an arrangement with the French government. It would be one of the highest-profile deals in the history of the American markets. Ivar told Durant and Berning he finally was ready to close his first blockbuster loan to one of Europe's powerhouses.

It was an audacious proposal, but by 1927 Americans were ready for audacity. Everyone, including investors, was developing a taste for novelty and adventure. This was the year Charles A. Lindbergh flew from New York to Paris. It also was the year a record 270 new shows opened on Broadway, many of which would have been regarded as scandalous a few years earlier.[42] Even experts in the dismal science of economics were giddy in 1927: world-famous economist John Maynard Keynes pronounced that, "We will not have any more crashes in our time."

During that summer, the Federal Reserve lowered interest rates to 3.5 percent and flooded the market with cash by purchasing government securities.[43] Brokers made unprecedented amounts of call loans, which permitted investors to buy stock "on margin," borrowing a portion of the purchase price. Investors responded by purchasing record numbers of shares at record prices. The Dow Jones average of leading US companies' shares rose on twenty-four of twenty-seven straight trading days. At the New York Stock Exchange, as many as 3 million shares traded each day. On a single day, 651 of 1,100 separate issues were traded, a new record.[44] Previously, on a typical day for most companies, not even one share would change hands.

Poincaré was as bullish as the Americans, and he was intrigued by Ivar's loan-for-monopoly idea. However, most French government officials turned up their noses at the notion of a Swedish businessman telling them how to conduct business. At first, the manager of the French match monopoly rebuffed Ivar.[45] Marius Moutet, the socialist party spokesman, argued that Ivar was an unwelcome foreign intruder who would squelch their liberty: "If you wish to let the French government associate itself with a world power of this nature, do you really believe that this would be an arrangement between equal partners? That is why I say that the real issue is not what you are discussing, but whom you are dealing with."[46]

Initially, even Poincaré could not overcome this criticism. The Chamber of Deputies, the lower house of France's parliament, rejected Ivar's initial monopoly proposal by a vote of 281 to 243. It seemed that the French government's monopoly was too deeply cemented for Ivar to budge. As one journalist wrote, "*le Napoleon des allumettes* has met his Waterloo."[47]

Still, Ivar was determined. He knew that, without a French loan deal, his bold new securities issue would fail. American investors were primed to give him money. Berning, his auditor, was in his hip pocket. Durant, his banker, was as friendly as ever. All of Ivar's ducks were in a row. Except in France.

Ivar quickly took a new tack. He abandoned the monopoly idea, and instead persuaded Poincaré to propose a twenty-year contract that gave Ivar more limited rights. The new proposal would reorganize the country's match business, as Ivar originally had suggested, but no one would use the word "monopoly." Nor would Ivar take over any responsibilities from the officials who ran the French match business. Ivar's new proposal seemed far less intrusive: the French government merely would agree to pay Ivar higher prices for matches, match-making machines, and raw materials, and to buy more of each.

The French deal wasn't called a monopoly but it was one in everything but name: the agreement with the government gave him exclusivity and the right to charge high prices. The French government agreed to enforce the restrictions, too. If someone brought even a dozen foreign matches into France, they would pay a heavy fine.[48] Even the French left wing could accept this deal politically.

Meanwhile, Ivar argued to the Americans that the new proposal was a minor concession, given that Swedish Match already had been selling these items to the French government for years. International Match would make the same amount of money; it was merely a semantic change to persuade the French. Overall, the compromise was a brilliant political move.

Ivar also dangled a loan with unprecedented terms. He would lend France 75 million dollars at a rate of just 5 percent, a full 3 percent less than Morgan had been charging. France would have the right to redeem the loan early, but would not be obligated to repay the full amount for forty years.

Why would Ivar offer the French such incredibly attractive loan terms? He certainly wanted the fame, and he longed to unseat Morgan as the leading lender to Europe. He also believed that a revitalized France would be good for the global economy overall. But Ivar wasn't being entirely magnanimous – he planned to make some money, too.

Although the French public would see this loan as being for 75 million dollars, Ivar insisted that he issue the loan at a price of 93.5 percent of par. Par referred to the amount of the loan on the face of the loan documents. For each 100 dollars of par amount France agreed to repay Ivar in forty years, it would receive just 93.50 dollars today, substantially less than par. In other words, France actually would receive about 70 million dollars upfront, but would have to repay 75 million dollars. That higher repayment meant that the effective interest rate France would pay on the loan would be higher than 5 percent and would depend on when it repaid. If France actually repaid the loan over forty years, the difference in cost would be minimal. But if Poincaré decided to repay the loan early, Ivar would make a *much* higher return. In effect, Ivar would get an extra 5 million dollars if France prepaid its loan right away.

It was unclear whether the members of the French Chamber of Deputies understood all of these details. What everyone clearly saw was that France needed money and that Ivar's new proposal permitted the government to keep its precious match monopoly. With the last canards in place, Ivar closed the loan in November 1927. He promised to send 70 million dollars to France.

Jack Morgan followed these negotiations closely. Ivar was becoming a real threat, and his new proposal would harm Morgan's business. It wasn't just that Ivar's loan would erode Morgan's franchise in the area, though that was important. In addition, the Morgan partners were counting on the 8 percent annual interest payments from France. If Ivar's loan replaced the lion's share of Morgan's loan, Morgan would lose that income.

Indeed, Jack was right to be concerned, and Ivar's deal caused him some pain. In anticipation of receiving Ivar's money, Poincaré prepaid Morgan's loan, thereby releasing the government from its obligations to pay the higher 8 percent interest rate. Because Morgan's loan had not been issued at a substantial discount, like Ivar's loan, Morgan did not benefit in the way Ivar would from prepayment. By refinancing with Ivar, France raised an extra 5 million dollars – the difference between the amount of Ivar's loan and the portion of Morgan's loan it prepaid – and it reduced the government's annual interest burden by nearly 2 million dollars a year. That was money Jack Morgan had been expecting, but would not receive.

The deal brought hope to Paris. If Poincaré could maneuver loan negotiations so skillfully, perhaps he could save the economy as well. Not only did the French government now have money to spend, but the French people finally had some much-needed confidence. Soon French investors would be as optimistic as the Americans.

As usual for Ivar's match-for-monopoly deals, one question remained: How would he come up with the money? This question was especially important, given the size of the obligation. Ivar owed France 70 million dollars. Swedish Match and Ivar's various subsidiaries could cover almost a third of the loan.[49] But the remaining 50 million dollars would have to come from International Match. Indeed, "have to come from International Match" was a written commitment he had made as part of the deal with Poincaré. The directors of International Match had given Ivar wide-ranging powers to negotiate on their behalf, and Ivar had done so. He had contractually obliged International Match to cover 50 million dollars of the French government loan.[50] Ivar had made a similar promise before to Poland, but this new one was three times as large.

Obviously, Ivar now faced intense pressure to close a deal in America.

Without fresh capital from American investors, International Match wouldn't have enough money to pay France. If Ivar couldn't deliver the cash to Poincaré, his reputation would be ruined.

The new 50 million dollar issue of International Match securities would be Ivar's most innovative yet. He wanted International Match's payments on the new securities to match the interest payments promised from France as closely as possible, so that he could simply pass through to American investors any money he received from France while the loan was outstanding. The easiest way to match the 5 percent interest payments owed by France was to promise investors a 5 percent return. But he also wanted to build in some profit potential, both for investors and for himself. He invented a new financial gadget to achieve these goals.

Ivar designed a new kind of "convertible debenture derivative," with three key components. First, the "debenture" component would pay a flat interest rate of five percent, in the same way that International Match's first issue from 1923, the "gold debenture," had paid a flat rate in dollars or gold. (Given Ivar's stature, a promise to pay in US dollars was fine; investors no longer needed his promise to be backed by gold.) An investor who bought 100 dollars of the new debenture would receive 5 dollars of interest each year. That money would match the payments from France.

Second, the "convertible" component would give investors the right to convert their debentures into shares of International Match. For example, an investor with a 100 dollar investment might have the right to purchase one share of International Match common stock. As long as the price of that share was less than 100 dollars, the investor would just keep the convertible debenture, and pocket 5 dollars of interest payments every year. But if International Match's common stock became more valuable than 100 dollars, the value of the convertible debentures would rise, too. Theoretically, the investor's upside was unlimited. The higher the price of International Match stock, the more valuable the convertible debentures. These first two features meant that investors would both receive a 5 percent return and also would have the upside associated with International Match shares.

Ivar also added a third "derivative" feature, which gave investors yet more upside. The 5 percent interest payments would increase along with any increase in dividends paid by Kreuger & Toll, International Match's Swedish parent company. Specifically, investors would receive an additional payment of 1 percent for each percentage point of dividends above 5 percent declared by Kreuger & Toll. If Kreuger & Toll paid a dividend in Sweden of less than 5 percent, the holder still would be guaranteed the 5 percent interest payment from the first "debenture" feature, but if Kreuger & Toll paid a higher dividend, the holder would benefit one-for-one along with Swedish shareholders from this third feature. For the previous nine years, Kreuger & Toll had paid double-digit dividends, most recently as high as 25 percent, so there was substantial additional upside that was derived from Kreuger & Toll's dividends. If Kreuger & Toll paid 25 percent, investors in these new instruments would receive 5 percent interest plus an extra 20 percent.

Ivar had to decide how long these "derivative" payments should last. The French obligation to pay Ivar 5 percent interest was for forty years, although the government could prepay. Ivar decided on a twenty-year maturity with a feature known as a "sinking fund." The sinking fund meant that Ivar would return a portion of the investment periodically – he would allow it to "sink" over time – for twenty years. Ivar couldn't be sure when, or if, the French government would prepay its forty-year obligation, but, hopefully, the maturity of the debentures would roughly match the maturity of the French loan.

The convertible debenture terms were first publicized in November 1927.[51] The deal was widely advertised as backed by a Who's Who of Wall Street, including the era's most prestigious bankers (Lee Higginson, National City, Brown Brothers, and Dillon, Read) and lawyers (Ropes, Gray, Boyden & Perkins and Carter, Ledyard & Milburn). Everyone was involved. That is, everyone except Jack Morgan.

Would Ivar's new product be too complex for investors? Ivar thought people were ready for some financial innovation and would see and understand the potential upside. He was right. The convertible debenture derivatives looked too good to be true, and that was exactly what investors wanted. They were thrilled by the derivative component and the idea of payments linked to Kreuger & Toll's dividends. Similar instruments issued in Europe were trading at 650 percent of their face value. Americans gobbled up these new instruments, whether they understood the details or not.

Indeed, investors were so excited about the new convertible debenture derivatives that they agreed to pay more for the debentures than France would receive from its loan. In other words, Ivar would raise more money from the Americans than he owed France. Because investors were willing to pay so much for the expected upside from the derivatives component, Ivar was left with a substantial difference, which he could keep. It required only a little bit of math to see that Ivar would make a fortune from the new issue.

Whereas France would receive just 93.5 cents for each dollar of loan, American investors agreed to pay 98.5 cents for each dollar of debentures – or one extra nickel more per dollar. Those nickels added up, and the difference between what International Match received from investors and what it paid to France was 2.5 million dollars. It was simple subtraction:

International Match receives:	$49.25 million (98.5 percent of $50 million)
International Match pays:	$46.75 million (93.5 percent of $50 million)
International Match keeps:	$2.5 million

This profit of 2.5 million dollars represented one of the largest fees for any financial transaction in history. Ivar simply played the role of intermediary, putting together American investors who had money with a French government that needed money. The market regarded International Match's credit risk as substantially better than that of the French government, so International Match could raise 98.5 cents from the market, give 93.5 cents to France, and keep a nickel for itself. So long as the payments matched over time, and the derivative payments did not increase too much, International Match would retain the full amount of the upfront profit. Indeed, if France repaid the loan early, International Match might make even more money.

As with Ivar's other sales of securities in the United States, most of the money raised – all but 2.5 million dollars – left the country immediately. But this time, everyone knew that the money was leaving, and they knew where it was going and why. The 46.75 million dollars didn't go into some secret subsidiary in Liechtenstein or Holland. It didn't go to Ivar or even to Swedish Match. This time, it went directly to France.

With the French deal, Ivar saw that it would be possible for him to replace Jack Morgan as the leading financier to the world. Ivar had, as one writer put it, "bearded Morgan in his den."[52] The French people found Ivar to be a truly great and powerful man. The international media compared him to the Medicis and Fuggers, history's other great private funders of governments.

Ivar accepted praise from France with humility. He loved being worshipped, but didn't want to appear arrogant. When Prime Minister Poincaré awarded him the Grand Cross of the Legion of Honor, Ivar wore only a single medal to the ceremony. Traditionally, recipients of the award had come in full decorations, and the attendees were struck by Ivar's modesty.

Ivar explained that the medal he wore was "given to commemorate the Olympic games at Stockholm."[53] He didn't cite the fact that he personally had financed the Stockholm games; nor did he mention his numerous other awards and medals. The Paris media grabbed the story, just as Ivar thought they might. One editorial cited Ivar's one medal as a metaphor for his singular status as a financial hero. It noted that "The French miracle has elevated Ivar Kreuger to the position of superman of finance. From today, he is Olympian."[54]

8

THE MATCH PALACE

The French deal and the new 50 million dollar debenture issue catapulted Ivar to a new level of fame and respect. It raised the promise of a New York Stock Exchange listing for International Match, and cemented Ivar's reputation as a leading man in finance. He remained modest in public, but privately he became increasingly confident in his ability to dominate the financial markets. By late 1927, Ivar held match monopolies in nearly a dozen countries. International Match's preferred share issues had more than tripled in value since they were floated, from a price of 35 dollars to more than 100 dollars on the Curb Exchange. Ivar still controlled International Match; its common stock was still held by Swedish Match and some Swedish banks. Swedish Match now had 26,000 employees and more than ninety match plants throughout the world, including new factories in Algeria, the Philippines, and throughout South America. Ivar was working on yet more monopoly deals, with Guatemala, Lithuania, Romania, and Turkey, and even another one with Poland. Swedish Match had taken over the two largest match factories in Canada, and International Match had done a deal with Bryant & May, which controlled the British production and sale of matches.

Ivar also had used his highly priced preferred shares as currency to expand beyond the match industry by purchasing other businesses and paying the sellers with securities of his companies instead of cash. Ivar bought banks, mining companies, railways, timber and paper products firms, film distributors, real estate, and even a controlling stake in the Swedish telephone industry, then dominated by L. M. Ericsson & Co. He controlled half of the international market in iron ore and cellulose. He bought mines all over the world, including the Boliden mine in northeast Sweden, which had substantial gold deposits. He bought acres of land in central Berlin, and exclusive buildings in Amsterdam, Oslo, Paris, Stockholm, and Warsaw. Ivar paid taxes on income of over 2 million kronor per year, more than anyone in Stockholm. And, obviously, not all of his income was taxed.[1] All of these assets were real, and there was no question that Ivar or one of his companies owned them. He was, legitimately, one of the wealthiest and most powerful businessmen in the world.

Ivar traveled constantly, and was rarely in one city for long. In addition to his corporate real estate holdings, he kept large apartments in several cities in Europe, even though he did not visit some of those cities, including Warsaw, for years at a time. In London, he preferred a particular suite at the Savoy Hotel, which he kept booked for months, even when he had no plans to visit England. In Sweden, he owned three summer homes, which he reached in one of his fleet of cars and boats, including a power boat that was rumored to be the fastest in Sweden.

The apartments, as well as the fast cars and boats, were fleeting, temporary pleasures. Ivar wanted to make a permanent mark, to build something that would survive for centuries, like the castle in his hometown of Kalmar. Moreover, as Ivar's stock soared, he saw the risk of becoming unmoored. He wanted to retain his Swedish identity and keep Stockholm as his home base.

With the profits from the French deal, he now had the money to finish construction on a building that would become his legacy: a building to house his enterprise physically as well as in spirit. He decided to call it the Match Palace, a fitting title for the place that would symbolize Ivar's greatness.

Ivar's architect, Ivar Justus Tengbom, was one of the leading exponents of Swedish neoclassical architecture of the early twentieth century. Tengbom was a professor at the Royal Swedish College of Art, and already had designed many of the most beautiful buildings in Stockholm: the Stockholm City Hall, the Stockholm School of Economics, and the Stockholm Concert Hall. Tengbom also had worked with Kreuger & Toll on several projects – the Stockholm City Hall was one – and he was familiar with Ivar's respect for both aesthetics and efficiency. The Match Palace would be a masterpiece, of course. But like all of Ivar's buildings, it would go up fast. A year after the French deal closed, the Match Palace was complete.[2]

The long four-story structure was tucked behind heavy wrought iron gates at 15 Västra Trädgårdsgatan, which translates as "Western Garden Street," in central Stockholm, just west of the Kungsträdgården park.[3] From the street, a visitor could see a balcony running along the three windows in the center of the second floor. The blue-gray marble walls were lit at night, and pillars of granite surrounded the courtyard, which was paved with matching stone. The architecture was symmetrical, and there were subtle references to fire throughout. In a portion of the pavement, one could spot an inlaid mosaic of Prometheus, giver of fire.

In the center of the courtyard was a fountain designed by Carl Milles, with a statue of the goddess Diana, a huntress who also nurtured and protected the weak. The main sculpture echoed the smaller Milles statue outside Ivar's apartment in Stockholm. Diana was surrounded by the strange forest creatures she was waking to life, including a grateful bronzed wild boar. The statue, and the boar's feet, were off limits and would remain well preserved. No one, including Ivar, developed a habit of patting them.

The building next door had housed the original offices of Ivar and Paul Toll. When the Match Palace was completed, Ivar decided that employees of Kreuger & Toll and its subsidiaries should continue to work in the old building. The new building was for Swedish Match, exclusively. Just as Ivar had effectively walled Paul Toll off from Swedish Match, Ivar refused to permit the barrier between the old and new buildings to be pierced. If Kreuger & Toll employees wanted to speak to people at Swedish Match, or vice versa, they had to walk outdoors and cross the courtyard to the street entrance.[4]

Ivar didn't need all of this new space, but it was grand to have it. His corporate office had fewer than 150 employees, including liftboys and chauffeurs. His other 26,000 employees worked elsewhere.

By 1928, Ivar's closest colleagues – Torsten, Krister Littorin, and Anders Jordahl – were spread around the world. Now, he brought them back to Stockholm to celebrate the new building, and to encourage them to use it as a base. From then on, Littorin would spend most of his time there. Although Torsten would still travel throughout Europe, and Jordahl would focus on America, the Match Palace would accommodate them when they were in town.

The three men toured the building with Ivar soon after it was completed. The board room was the first and last stop on any tour. Tengbom had placed the board room in the curved front part of the building that enclosed the upper arc of the center courtyard's semicircle. The wall was broken into several flat panels to accommodate the curve.

For the wall panels, Ivar had commissioned a breathtaking work called "Dawn" from Isaac Grünewald, a famous expressionist painter from Stockholm.[5] The boardroom panels echoed the walls and ceiling of another Grünewald design for the Stockholm Concert Hall, Sweden's version of the

Sistine Chapel and the site of the annual Nobel Prize ceremonies. The panels depicted Prometheus on a winged horse, rushing down through a rainbow to bring fire to the men trapped in darkness below. The unmistakable impression was that the deity represented Ivar, bringing matches, and profits from matches, to the people. The unpainted sections of the walls were mahogany inlaid with walnut, and on each short side between the painted panels were fireplaces of marble from Gropptorp in central Sweden, each covered with heavy cast-iron plates. There were panels over each of the fireplaces in the room, made from forty-six different kinds of wood. One depicted Thor's struggle with the giants; another showed the "Five Continents" worshipping fire.

The boardroom table, made from citron wood, was just as elaborate as the wall panels. The seating places were marked with ivory inlays, each symbolizing one of the countries where Swedish Match sold matches. The leather desk pads were decorated in gold. It appeared to be an appropriately grandiose spot for Ivar's negotiations with heads of state, although the bulk of those meetings occurred outside Stockholm. More commonly, Ivar and his friends would have lunch there when everyone was in town.

The Match Palace was more than a visible reminder of Ivar's financial prowess. Ivar designed it to keep himself safe and secluded. On the fourth floor, at the end of a long corridor, Ivar had built a small private working space that became known as his "Silence Room." It contained a writing desk and a sofa but was otherwise unfurnished. The room connected to a dressing area, and – most importantly – the door locked from the inside. Ivar would shut himself in the Silence Room for days at a time. It was a special spot where his hidden demons could safely surface. Only Ivar and the janitor had keys.[6]

The executive suite at the Match Palace was a dark wood version of a military bunker. It was immediately opposite the tall windows of the boardroom, through a waiting hall facing the semicircular courtyard. There were twin offices for Ivar and Krister Littorin, and a room for Karin Bökman, his assistant, next to Ivar. The architecture told visitors it would be a high hurdle to get to Ivar. Outside Ivar's door was a green and red light, which indicated whether he could be disturbed. When a guest arrived it would shine red at first, and would switch to green only after Miss Bökman had called one of the phones in Ivar's office.

Ivar's office was designed for show more than work. Over the entrance was a wood mosaic of Sweden's oldest match factory, and a crest with two torches and three stars. Inside, the walls were covered with rosewood and mahogany paneling. Near the door, the paneling hid a safe in the wall, so that Ivar could playfully show guests where any secret documents might have gone. The safe was typically open and unlocked. In case of an emergency, Karin Bökman knew the lock's combination.

On one side of the room was a comfortable sofa with two armchairs and a small round table. To the side was a small library and a cupboard. Behind the sofa was a large Gobelin tapestry on the wall. The setup was every bit as formal and sophisticated as Ivar's apartment. It conveyed precisely the message he wanted, of a wealthy man with a clean, clear mind and impeccable taste. It looked like the two armchairs had never been used.

Ivar's desk stood near the first window on the left side of the room. This desk, too, was mostly for display. Ivar did much of his real work elsewhere in the Match Palace, but he liked to greet guests from behind a desk. Next to the desk was a table with three telephones. The phone on the right connected directly to Karin Bökman. The one on the left was one of the world's first speakerphones, known as a "chief's telephone," built by L. M. Ericsson.

The middle phone was a dummy, like the third funnel on *Berengaria*, a non-working phone that Ivar could cause to ring by stepping on a button under the desk. That button was a way to speed the exit of talkative visitors who were staying too long.[7] Ivar also used the middle phone to impress his supporters. When Percy Rockefeller, a director of International Match, visited the Match Palace, Ivar pretended to receive calls from various European government officials, including Mussolini and Stalin. That evening, Ivar threw a lavish party and introduced Rockefeller to numerous "ambassadors" from various countries, who actually were movie extras he had hired for the night. Rockefeller returned from Stockholm with a glowing report, telling his fellow directors, "That man is the salt of the earth. He is on most intimate terms with the heads of European governments. Gentlemen, we are fortunate indeed to be associated with Ivar Kreuger."[8]

When Ivar had real work to do, he would pick an unused room at the Match Palace and set up several tables, each for a country he was working on. He would move among graphs and statistics his assistants placed on each table, memorizing the numbers and cramming financial details for future use. Ivar was perfectly comfortable working among vast amounts of paper clutter.[9] He just didn't want any of that mess in his office.

The Match Palace reflected not only Ivar's tastes, but his mental state. Nearly three decades earlier, during his first trip to America, Ivar had reformed his "public" personality to suit his business ambitions. His "true" personality, if there was such a thing, became lost. It was no longer possible to connect the dots from the charming, persuasive Match King back to the introverted and poker-faced child from Kalmar. Over time, Ivar had locked away the bad memories of his childhood: of boys from school who mocked him for gathering flowers; of the teenage Norwegian girl who refused his hand in marriage; of the mother who avoided him and the father who underwhelmed him. One of the world's most powerful men had no use for such a past.

Overall, the protective surroundings of the Match Palace suggested that the real Ivar Kreuger was no longer easily accessible. It was now as hard to get an in-person meeting with Ivar as it was to identify who he really was. Even Ivar's closest friends, the people who had watched the transformation of his personality, found it difficult to understand who Ivar had become. When unwelcome thoughts came, Ivar escaped to the Silence Room to confront them alone. To all of the men in his life, Ivar was a closed book. The closest he came to opening up was when he dictated cables to Karin Bökman, danced with Greta Garbo, or listened to his neighbor Ingeborg Eberth play piano.

The Match Palace gave Ivar a new set of physical defenses. They went up much more quickly than his mental defenses, which had taken a lifetime. In his new fortress, Ivar finally could feel secure in body and mind. Or so he hoped.

Ivar didn't invite A.D. Berning to visit the Match Palace, at least not right away. In fact, even though Berning was arguably the most important person in Ivar's professional life, Ivar almost entirely ignored him during late 1927 and early 1928. After Ivar returned from an extended trip, and gave the first tours of the Match Palace, he finally wrote to Berning

> I have to acknowledge your three letters of November 10th, your letter of November 23rd, your four letters of December 3rd, as well as your letter of January 25th, and thank you for same. I have just returned to Sweden after nearly half a year's absence and this is the reason for my not having answered your different letters previously.[10]

Even Ivar's belated response to his auditor was abrupt. He focused on a few tax issues and a crucial task Ivar still wanted Berning to complete: get International Match listed on the New York Stock Exchange.

As Ivar settled into his new space, Berning finished the listing application. Since Ivar first visited the Exchange almost thirty years earlier, he had dreamed of having his own company's securities traded on the floor there. With the

French deal, Ivar's business was now big enough. Durant and Lee Higginson had agreed to support him. The remaining question was whether A.D. Berning could persuade the Exchange to agree that International Match's financial statements met the requirements for a listing.

After seeing the stacks of paper in Anton Wendler's office, Berning knew he could never get all of the details about Ivar's subsidiaries. Only Ivar, and perhaps Wendler, saw the entire picture. Ivar seemed to have memorized the assets, liabilities, income, and expenses of every one of his subsidiaries, quarter by quarter. He could recite those numbers from memory. Berning ultimately decided he had no choice but to rely on, and trust, Ivar.

Berning's faith in the Swedish audit was reinforced by the fact that Ivar indirectly owned half of the shares of International Match. Berning was preparing an application to list International Match's participating preferred shares, not its common shares. The preferred shares had priority over Ivar's common shares; they would receive payments before Ivar's common shares did. In other words, if International Match lost money, Ivar would feel the pain first before holders of the securities that would be listed on the Exchange. That made it easier for Berning, and Ernst & Ernst, to vouch for Ivar and International Match's financial statements. After all, he owned the company. If his financial statements were false, and the preferred didn't receive any money, neither would he. Why would Ivar cheat himself?

Berning didn't request much additional information from Anton Wendler, who was working on Ivar's audit in Stockholm.[11] Berning just needed enough to persuade the Exchange that the summary disclosures in International Match's reports were accurate. When Berning had gathered what he thought was a sufficient amount of detail, and the Ernsts were comfortable with the latest numbers, they filed the application.

The Stock Listing Committee of the Exchange immediately asked Berning for more detail about International Match's sources of income. Although they took a lax approach to many American companies, they must have been suspicious of Ivar and his foreign businesses. In particular, the Committee requested that Berning split out the company's income into different categories, so that investors could see how much profit was from the sale of matches compared to other sources. This was the same kind of question everyone had been asking for years, including Donald Durant, the Wisconsin regulators, and several large investors. Ivar had never given anyone an answer.

Some auditors might have pressed their clients for additional information. But Berning knew Ivar wouldn't give up the detailed disclosure requested by the Exchange. At this point, Ivar probably wouldn't even respond to one of Berning's cables, at least not for a while. So Berning decided to tell the New York Stock Exchange no. If the Exchange wanted to list Ivar Kreuger's securities, it could only do so on Ivar's terms. There were plenty of companies listed on the Exchange that did not give out much detail, and many of those companies were controlled by managers without substantial ownership, who had less to lose from lying about results. In contrast, International Match was essentially Ivar's company. Here was Berning's reply:

> It is my position that practically all of the International Match Corporation's income is derived from the manufacture and sale of matches and related enterprises such as chemicals, timber, technical services, etc. together with interest and other income on its investments required to maintain its position in those respects. It is therefore unnecessary to make any subdivision of the corporation's income and possibly inadvisable owing to the probable fluctuations which might occur in any substantial items which might be shown.[12]

Berning's position was aggressive, but by this point he would do just about anything for Ivar. He still wasn't a partner at Ernst & Ernst, but it was apparent that if he could get International Match a listing on the Exchange, he would be in an excellent position to be invited to join. Berning was now completely exposed to Ivar's word, and to Ivar's memory of the details of the numerous transactions among his various subsidiaries. Berning couldn't verify whether the underlying numbers were accurate; he simply had to accept them as a matter of faith. He eagerly awaited a response from the Exchange. It wouldn't take long.

June 1928 was a good month for America, and a better one for Ivar. Herbert Hoover, the Republican candidate for president, declared,

> The poorhouse is vanishing from among us. We have not yet reached the goal, but given a chance to go forward with the policies of the last eight years, we shall soon be in sight of the day when poverty will be banished from this nation."[13]

Even during a blip when the market declined sharply, it quickly recovered, and both International Match and Swedish Match, which also was still traded on the Curb Exchange, kept soaring. Berning reported to Ivar that "The securities of both corporations held up remarkably well during the recent severe slump, which practically all securities suffered in our markets here."[14]

This performance was remarkable, given that International Match had practically no money on hand and could barely meet its obligations. On June 30, 1928, Berning cabled Ivar that International Match "will require cash in time for July fifteenth dividend payment."[15] Ivar had to wire money quickly to New York so that his company, then the darling of investors everywhere, wouldn't default. Investors were optimistically betting on International Match's future; default seemed inconceivable. They didn't care how much cash the company had, and wouldn't bother to check as long as the dividend payments kept coming.

June also was a good month for A.D. Berning. The New York Stock Exchange backed down after Berning refused to give more detail about International Match's income. His decision to hold firm paid off, and he gleefully reported to Ivar that the Exchange had given up its objections:

I took the matter up personally with the Stock List Committee of the New York Stock Exchange and have convinced them as to the impracticability of such a course. The annual report of the International Match Corporation for the year 1927 will therefore be issued substantially in the form which we prepared together in Stockholm.[16]

Ivar learned the good news in Paris, where he was spending a few days with his assistant, Karin Bökman. The next time Ivar was in New York, he would visit the Exchange, and look down at a man standing at a specialist post trading the securities of one of Ivar's companies. It was, in every sense, a childhood dream come true. Some of the ticker tape confetti falling to the floor of the Exchange every day would be printed with the trading prices of participating preferred shares of International Match.

Ivar quickly arranged for a celebration at Restaurant Paillard, one of his favorites. Dozens of guests attended, even given the last-minute nature of the event. He and Karin Bökman clearly had a rollicking time. The receipt from Paillard included an expense for 105 bottles of wine.[17] Ivar must have savored every drop.

As usual, Berning was the last person to hear from Ivar, who sent a cable to Ernst & Ernst the day after the party: "It is with great satisfaction I learn that you have succeeded in getting the Stock Exchange to approve the Balance

Sheet, substantially as discussed by us in Stockholm and I greatly appreciate your work in this respect."[18] The Ernst brothers also were greatly satisfied, and they began discussing a promotion for young Berning.

Ivar was happy for Berning to continue to work on his accounts, but he still didn't want to meet in person. Now that Ivar had the Silence Room, he had become even more reclusive, and was even less inclined to see his accountants and bankers. Now that International Match was listed on the Exchange, Ivar asked Berning to prepare an application for Swedish Match to be listed as well. He dodged Berning in Europe and New York. Ivar didn't want to look him in the eye, or take a chance that Berning would see him flinch in response to a probing question.

Ivar also asked Berning for help with the Metropolitan Life Insurance Company, one of the largest and most sophisticated investors in the world. According to Donald Durant, Met Life was considering a large purchase of International Match securities. A major purchase by Met Life would have almost as much cachet as a listing on the New York Stock Exchange.

Before Met Life would buy, though, it wanted more information about International Match, in particular a breakdown of its income from various international subsidiaries. Insurance companies generally classified their investments by industry and country, and Met Life said that if it couldn't get enough information to do that, it couldn't invest.

Ivar asked Berning to prepare some details to satisfy Met Life. Berning understood that this information must be kept confidential, because International Match "operates to a large extent under special government concessions, there would be a possibility of criticisms of a purely political nature."[19] As he had before, Ivar cited concerns that competitors might obtain precious secrets, and that foreign officials would balk if any details became public.

Ivar reviewed Berning's memo and agreed to permit Durant to show it privately to Met Life.[20] It broke out the sources of International Match's income as follows:

26 percent France
23 percent Spain
17 percent Italy
11 percent Poland
6 percent Germany
17 percent Other

The list was remarkable. Five countries accounted for 83 percent of International Match's income, yet Ivar had secured match deals in only two of them (and France was not even a real monopoly). Ivar had mentioned to Berning and Durant that he was talking to officials in Spain, Italy, and Germany, but he hadn't made loans to any of those countries. In other words, the income described in Berning's memo couldn't have been from interest paid by these governments to International Match.

Swedish Match, which was the ultimate source of International Match's profits, didn't have monopoly deals in these countries either. It had reported record profits of more than 13 million dollars for 1928, up from less than 11 million dollars the previous year. It now operated in more than thirty-five countries, and the Swedish Match directors were proposing a special additional dividend of 10 percent, given the stellar year. But as impressive as Swedish Match's deals during 1928 had been, they were not with Spain, Italy, or Germany, either. What, then, was the source of the income from those countries? Were Swedish Match's sales there that great? Perhaps they were, but it was impossible to tell.

The "17 percent other" listing was odd, too. The "other" countries Ivar had dealt with during 1928 – Estonia, Yugoslavia, and Hungary – were too small to account for a large chunk of International Match's income or assets. Ivar secured a monopoly in Latvia, in exchange for a 6 million dollar loan, but, even with a few side payments to coax along the Latvian parliament, that deal was not ratified until December 20, 1928.[21] A 30 million dollar deal for Romania, which desperately needed funds to stabilize its plunging currency, was not approved until January 30, 1929.[22] Those deals were too late to be included in the memo to Met Life. Where, then, could that extra "17 percent other" have come from?

If these questions were not troubling enough, it also was apparent that any money, even for small government loans, could not possibly have come from International Match, for one simple reason: International Match didn't have any money. Nor did Swedish Match. Any funds must have come from Kreuger & Toll, the largest shareholder of Swedish Match, which was still making money from various businesses, including construction projects.[23] But if Kreuger & Toll had been the source of funds, why were the profits reflected in International Match's list of countries?

The relationship between Kreuger & Toll and International Match was ambiguous, but the dominance of Kreuger & Toll was clear. Like Ivar's other companies, Kreuger & Toll had continued raising money throughout the

1920s. According to one source, by early 1929 investments in Kreuger & Toll were the most widely distributed securities in the world.[24] Its common shares were selling at 730 percent of par, the stated value when the shares were issued; its convertible debentures were at 863 percent. Kreuger & Toll's investors had made a fortune, as had Ivar, the company's major investor. When New York "operators" drove up the prices of Kreuger & Toll on the Curb Market, where it was still traded, Ivar took advantage of the speculative frenzy by buying low and selling high.

If Ivar was concerned that this mania might end soon, like the South Sea Bubble or the Dutch tulip mania, he didn't show it. Instead, he increased his companies' payout to investors. He announced plans to increase Kreuger & Toll's dividend to 30 percent, and Swedish Match's dividend to 16 percent, although neither increase was yet approved. Those dividends would be sustainable only if Ivar started making significant profits in Spain, Italy, and Germany. Apparently, investors believed he was positioned to do just that.

In any event, Met Life didn't question Ivar's list of countries. Met Life simply needed the list; it didn't care whether it was correct. It didn't object to Ivar commingling assets, or ask what generated the income. International Match wasn't about Latvia or Romania – it was a much bigger bet than that. If the company really had a shot at Spain, Italy, and Germany, its preferred shares were a bargain. International Match was a growth company, like RCA or General Motors. Met Life was satisfied to know it would be able to account for its investment in separate categories, even if those categories didn't match reality. At the end of 1928, it bought into International Match.

Met Life's inquiry reawakened Donald Durant's concern that he really didn't understand Ivar's companies. In particular, he didn't know anything about Kreuger & Toll, which seemed to him a black hole. Meanwhile, Ivar wrote to Durant that he planned to expand Kreuger & Toll's international role "from a comparatively passive holding company into a company actively engaged in financial transactions."[25] That expansion worried Durant.

After Met Life bought participating preferred shares of International Match, Durant told Ivar he wanted to probe some of the details of Kreuger & Toll's financial statements, with the help of A.D. Berning. Ivar responded in mid-February 1929 that he would "have no objection to your consulting Berning."[26]

Durant didn't doubt that Ivar had secured match deals in numerous countries: Ecuador, Estonia, France, Greece, Hungary, Latvia, Peru, Poland,

Portugal, Romania, and Yugoslavia.[27] Nor did Durant doubt that Swedish Match was continuing to expand, taking International Match along with it. Most recently, Swedish Match had moved into Brazil, where it now controlled several Brazilian factories and was seeking to buy Companhia Brasileira de Phosphoros, which controlled most of the remaining factories there.[28]

There was no question that these assets and income were real. But the companies' liabilities were real, too. Durant wondered how much Ivar's companies actually were worth. The more he learned from Berning about Ivar's offshore subsidiaries and off balance sheet accounting, the less he understood how to approach that question. 1928 had been an astonishing year for International Match. But Durant couldn't understand why. It seemed impossible to get to the bottom of Ivar's financial statements. And he couldn't even guess what might happen in 1929.

Durant was particularly concerned that Ivar had reported profits for 1928 that were too high, or at least higher than they needed to be. If investors weren't paying attention to International Match's numbers, even as cursory as they were, why should Ivar report such high profits? Investors would be just as happy if reported profits were lower. And even the most sophisticated analysts wouldn't necessarily appreciate being surprised by unexpectedly high profits; surprises made them look like they didn't know what they were doing.

After talking to Berning, Durant had a radical idea. Why not report *lower* profits for 1928 and save the extra for 1929? On February 22, 1929, Berning reported to Ivar that "confidentially Durant believes nineteen twenty eight figures somewhat higher than necessary."[29] Would Ivar be willing to carry some of those profits over to the next year?

The three men began considering whether International Match should conserve some of its income from 1928, to create a kind of "prudency" cushion in case the following year did not turn out as well. Ironically, the financial statements Durant suggested they deflate were the same ones they were sending to the New York Stock Exchange as part of the application for the Swedish Match listing, which they were formally seeking now that the Exchange had agreed to list International Match. Berning was scrambling to prepare that application and needed Ivar to approve the financial statements. He sent Ivar a nine-page telegram filled with new numbers.[30] At Durant's suggestion, Berning had moved nearly a million dollars into a reserve account. Berning wanted to know if this approach was acceptable to Ivar, or if they should account for the additional funds in some other way, perhaps in a surplus fund.

Ivar was in Paris and couldn't have cared less about these details. He cabled back:

We approve of form and contents of Balance Sheet and Profit and Loss account mentioned in your telegram second March. It is immaterial to us if you take the ninehundredfiftysix thousand sevenhundredsixty dollars from Surplus or from Reserve Fund.[31]

Ivar wasn't alone. No one cared about these details. The New York Stock Exchange approved Swedish Match's listing, and investors rushed to buy that company's securities in addition to those of International Match. Durant abandoned his skepticism for long enough to underwrite yet another of Ivar's issues, a 26.5 million dollar deal for Kreuger & Toll, which would be listed on the Curb Market. Every major bank except Morgan joined the syndicate for that deal, and no one asked for any additional information.[32] Prudent or not, the way Ivar's companies reported income simply didn't matter.

Since his negotiations with the Exchange, A.D. Berning had become more anxious about relying on Ivar. Berning was a details man and preferred that every number make sense. But now, nothing added up. Berning would send an urgent request to Ivar for more information, and months would pass in silence. Ivar refused to see Berning, and rarely responded to cables. Yet Berning depended almost entirely on these infrequent communications from Ivar to prepare International Match's financial statements. It was apparent to Berning that Ivar was playing faster and looser with numbers than he ever had. It wasn't clear if Ivar was merely becoming more casual or if he actually was hiding bad news. It certainly was possible that Ivar was simply too busy to be bothered with details that no one cared about anyway.

Berning needed – and his wife desperately wanted – a vacation, which Ivar was happy to provide. But when the couple sailed from New York, it was impossible for Berning to unwind, even in first class on a luxury liner. When they arrived in Europe, Berning could not locate Ivar. Ultimately, the stress and uncertainty became too much for him to bear. During the Bernings' summer trip to Stockholm in 1929, he finally cracked.

Berning's nervous breakdown finally brought Ivar out of hiding. Ivar was no stranger to mental illness. Both his mother and her father had problems. More recently, Ivar himself had been battling his own bouts of mania and depression while locked in his Silence Room. So he probably could relate to the breakdown.

In any event, Ivar stepped in to arrange for appropriate doctors, and to give Berning some recovery time. Berning was grateful for Ivar's kindness, and, finally, for some personal attention. He wrote,

> Upon attempting to settle with the doctors, etc. for my recent "indisposition," I learned that you had taken care of it all. This was very kind of you, and I appreciate it very much. You have been entirely too good to me, and I do not know how to thank you sufficiently.[33]

Ivar expected a return favor from Berning, and he got it. Berning persuaded Durant to back down from his accounting inquiries. Berning's thank you to Ivar included the following pledge of protection:

> You mentioned the other day that Mr Durant had brought up the question as to auditors of Kreuger & Toll. If he should speak to me about it I shall say that we are quite generally informed about this Company's operations and its relationship with International Match and Swedish Match, and have discussed all relevant matters with you; also, that as Kreuger & Toll is a Swedish company its purely auditing work should probably be carried on by Swedish auditors as in the past, and that should any special occasion arise we can undoubtedly make arrangements to cover the situation. I will take the position that this is a continuation of arrangements which have been in effect for some time.[34]

In response, Ivar sent Berning an absurdly expensive personal gift; some debentures that amounted to more than a year's pay. Now, it was Berning's turn to type out a letter on his own, without anyone else's knowledge, on a Swedish typewriter. Like Ivar's earlier letter, this one was filled with overtyping and crossed out words. Apparently, Berning was no better typist than Ivar. Berning noted at the bottom: "Please excuse the typing; I am not a good typist on an American machine, and certainly no better on a Swedish instrument!"[35]

Even with the mistakes, the message of Berning's letter came through:

> I must have been weaker than I suspected on Monday when you handed me the debentures with the accompanying statement. When I looked over the

amount I was under the impression that the 230 debentures were the equivalent of our American certificates. Upon returning to the hotel I found the
matter quite different, and feel now that I did not properly appreciate at the
time what you were doing. Mr Kreuger, you have been entirely too generous, thoughtful and kind to me, and all of it is far more than I deserve. I
feel I shall never be able to reciprocate. Please be assured however of my
grateful appreciation, not only for the material things, but for the great help
that you have given me personally in so many ways.[36]

When Berning finally returned home from Sweden, he found yet more good
news. First, there was yet another gift from Ivar, this one a self-portrait.
Berning found the painting of Ivar's face stunning, and gushed that he was
"honored that I may be included among those who may have the privilege of
owning one."[37]

Next, the Ernst brothers told Berning they had an important matter to
discuss with him. After seven years, Ivar had become one of the firm's biggest
clients, and Berning deserved credit. He had persuaded Ivar to pay the firm
more for its audits, as well as additional fees for consulting and tax advice.
The Ernsts were proud of everything he had done, and they had decided to
offer him a partnership. From now on, his correspondence would read, in
block letters, "RESIDENT PARTNER."

The Bernings didn't revel at Restaurant Paillard, or order 105 bottles of
wine, but May Berning certainly was proud of her A.D. Now they could afford
a new apartment, at 40 Fifth Avenue, in Greenwich Village. They could afford
a new social set as well. The Bernings joined several of New York's most prestigious societies, including the Union League Club and Sleepy Hollow Country
Club.[38]

Yet neither the partnership nor these memberships relaxed A.D. Berning's
nerves. His promotion added more pressure than it relieved, and he didn't
have time to play golf. Unfortunately for Berning, the stress was only just
beginning.

After a modest celebration at his Greeenwich Village apartment, Berning
asked Anton Wendler, the Swedish accountant, to send him final statements
for 1928 for Swedish Match and Continental, Ivar's Liechtenstein subsidiary.
Durant had not accepted Berning's assurances, and asked him to assemble as
much information as he could. But if Durant was expecting significantly more
detail than he had seen in the past, he was seriously disappointed.

Berning and Durant thought they understood some of what Anton Wendler and his brother were doing with Continental, but when they saw the 1928 numbers, they were stunned. They hadn't realized how massive Continental had become. According to Wendler's documents, as of the end of 1928, Continental had roughly 125 million dollars of assets. That made this obscure secretive Liechtenstein company one of the world's largest businesses. Yet the entries on Continental's balance sheet were no more detailed than any other information they had received from Ivar. Here is what Wendler sent:[39]

Continental Investment Corporation Balance Sheet
Advances to Governments of $31 million
Land, Buildings, Machinery, and Equipment of $32 million
Advances for Investments in Match Concessions of $28 million
Stocks and Bonds of $15 million
Accounts Receivable and Others of $9 million

That was it. These disclosures contained more questions than answers, and they made Durant more nervous than Berning had been. In recent months, Ivar had been showering Durant with kindness. To supplement Durant's income as a director of International Match, Ivar had appointed him to the board of Kreuger & Toll as well.[40] Ivar and Durant had spent several extravagant evenings together in New York in May, around the time of International Match's annual meeting. Durant liked to be entertained, but he wondered why Ivar suddenly was being so generous with his time and money.

Ivar tried to mollify Durant by inviting Berning to inspect Ivar's businesses throughout Europe. Although Mrs Berning did not accompany him, and he spent much of the time working, this trip was his best one to Europe yet. Berning produced a four-page single-spaced memorandum setting forth the results of a personal inspection of Ivar's factories and facilities during a tour that covered Berlin, Copenhagen, London, Nürnberg, Paris, Prague, Vienna, Zürich, and, of course, Stockholm.[41]

A.D. Berning apparently resumed his faith in Ivar during this trip. He reported that he was "considerably impressed by the speed with which rough logs were converted into veneer, cut into splints, polished, treated and turned into finished matches. The inventory turn-over is extremely rapid as you undoubtedly have observed when comparing the balance sheet inventory total with the annual sales." Berning saw "capable executives" with an "exceptional grasp of affairs" and everyone was "keen, aggressive and capable."[42]

He concluded that

It seems to me that Mr Kreuger's policy is to carefully select the man for each post and then to give him complete responsibility for the duties therein involved. I was considerably impressed with the complete harmony with which the organizations function and the extreme confidence that each one has in the other. There seems to be throughout the entire organization a splendid spirit of loyalty and an unselfish devotion to duty. No doubt a considerable part of the accomplishments and amazing growth of this enterprise is due to these qualities.[43]

Berning tried to respond to some of Durant's questions about the size and boundaries of Ivar's companies. For example, Durant had asked, where did one of Ivar's companies begin and others end? Which liabilities belonged to International Match, as opposed to Swedish Match or Kreuger & Toll? How could they be sure Ivar wasn't allocating income among the companies in an arbitrary way? Berning wrote,

The operations of the three larger companies are closely related, as you well know, and the inter-company transactions are quite large. All of those transactions which have come under my notice have always been handled with the highest degree of fairness. During none of the many examinations which we have made of the affairs of International Match Corporation have we ever had occasion to question the fairness of any transaction which this company has had with any of its affiliates. I thought you would be interested in this observation.[44]

Berning also sent a copy of the memorandum to Ivar, so he would know the efforts he was making with Durant. Berning labeled each page "PERSONAL" and attached a handwritten note: "D.D. just got around to this matter, and here is a copy for your information. I hope you approve of it. Sincerely, A.D."[45] Ivar certainly approved. Berning had run hot and cold during recent months, and Ivar was delighted to know his auditor was in a warming phase.

Durant, on the other hand, began to wonder whom he could trust. He previously had been concerned about Ivar. Now, he was just as worried about Berning. Berning's repeated use of the word "fairness" was alarming. It wasn't a term many 1920s accountants were comfortable using.

In fact, Durant had more reason for concern than he knew. On August 16, 1929, Ivar sat down with Karin Bökman to dictate a letter to Berning. Perhaps the handwritten "D.D." note had made Ivar more confident of Berning. In any event, Ivar had arranged an inter-company account transfer that was not even close to fairness, and he thought now was just the right time to let Berning know.

Bökman typed:

Dear Mr Berning,
In making the accounts of Swedish Match Company for the year 1928 there was created a certain secret reserve by temporarily crediting International Match Corporation's account with $1,135,753.09, being one quarter of the profit made by Swedish Match Company on the sales of certain foreign bonds. International Match Corporation has no claim on this profit which during the current year has been brought back to Swedish Match Company.[46]

In other words, Ivar initially had permitted International Match to claim credit for a quarter of Swedish Match's profits for 1928, but now he was taking those profits back. Easy come, easy go.

Ivar wanted a letter from Ernst & Ernst certifying that these shenanigans were appropriate, and that International Match had no claim to any of these profits. Ivar even suggested an attestation, in his best accounting jargon:

We herewith certify that on December 31st, 1928, the balance of all accounts between International Match Corporation and Swedish Match Company resulted in a debt of Swedish Match Company to International Match Corporation of $520,872.87. We are informed that in the books of Swedish Match Company, as at December 31st, 1928, there is booked a debt of $1,656,625.96 to International Match Corporation and that the difference is caused by Swedish Match having credited International Match Corporation with an amount of $1,135,753.09, corresponding to one quarter of the profit on certain foreign bonds. We herewith certify that, as far as we know, International Match Corporation has no claim on any profit on these bonds, and that the amount given in the books of International Match Corporation is correct.[47]

Ironically, shifting profits away from International Match to save for a rainy day had been Durant's idea initially, and Durant might even have approved of these terms, especially given that the "certification" was followed by the loose qualifier "as far as we know." Yet Berning decided to keep the million-dollar adjustment a secret from Durant. Ivar wanted to move the income away from International Match without Durant's knowledge, and Berning gave him what he wanted.

Ernst & Ernst complied with Ivar's request, and issued the certification privately to Ivar in almost identical language a few days later, even using Ivar's term "as far as we know."[48] At the same time, Ivar wrote to Berning that he had just taken over some interests in the Swedish lumber and pulp industry, and would probably have some new work, and some new fees, for Ernst & Ernst related to these interests.[49]

During 1929, while Ivar's bankers and accountants were scurrying around trying to issue new securities to be traded on the New York Stock Exchange, Ivar was focused on a more precious commodity: his reputation. Ivar had become extremely selective about social engagements. He now spent most of his time either alone or with Krister Littorin and Karin Bökman. He sought out only the most reputable people, leaders who could bolster his already exalted name. Otherwise, he preferred to be by himself.

At the time, two of the most sought-after men anywhere were the newly elected President Hoover and Isaac F. Marcosson, an editor at the *Saturday Evening Post* and one of the world's most widely read journalists. During the next few months, Ivar would meet and charm both of these men.

Marcosson was first. He started a mutual courtship with Ivar on April 15, when he sent a formal letter, on stationery from the Carlton Hotel in London, requesting an interview in Stockholm on June 15.[50] Marcosson included a letter of introduction from Frederic Allen, the Lee Higginson partner and Director of War Savings who had proclaimed in 1922 that Ivar was "a brilliant business head, full of compelling ideas, and a gentleman to boot." Allen's recommendation was even more glowing seven years later.

As Ivar knew, Marcosson was connected to just about every important person in the world, people far more important than Frederic Allen. It was apparent from the tone of Marcosson's letter that he was aware of Ivar's importance. In an exchange of letters through July 1929, these two important men engaged in an extended sniffing exercise, like two big dogs walking the same trail, establishing turf by marking the same spots.

Ivar thanked Marcosson for his letter, but replied that he wasn't sure he could be in Stockholm precisely on June 15. Ivar suggested they meet at "about that time." That wasn't good enough for Marcosson, who responded that in any event he would be delayed in Berlin until June 20; could Ivar meet on June 25? This time, Ivar didn't respond at all. Not one to be jilted, Marcosson wrote back on June 17 that he needed to postpone their meeting for a few weeks so he could interview Ramsay MacDonald, who as the first leader of the Labour Party to be elected Prime Minister of Great Britain had just formed a new minority government. Marcosson thought he might be able to meet Ivar in July, but he hedged, "At least this is as it looks at the moment."[51]

The correspondence trail suggested that Marcosson was the bigger dog, at least on paper. Then, the men finally met, in July 1929.

From the moment the two met, the power balance shifted, just as it had with Donald Durant in 1922. Ivar charmed Marcosson like no foreign leader or movie star ever had. Marcosson found Ivar soft and persuasive in speech, modest and unostentatious in manner. He was utterly without vanity, almost self-effacing. He seldom spoke of himself, and Marcosson found what he said enormously interesting. He loved the tour of the Match Palace, and appreciated its architecture and art, the Milles sculpture, the boardroom panels, and the details throughout.

Marcosson dashed off several handwritten notes to Ivar immediately after the interview. On July 12, he wrote, "I hope you will permit me to thank you again for your generous hospitality. It has been a genuine privilege to meet you in such delightful circumstances and I look forward to seeing you again soon." Marcosson wrote again several times in the next weeks, sending Ivar books they had discussed and suggesting that Ivar sit for another photograph because Marcosson didn't think the first one did him justice. In turn, Ivar sent Marcosson a book of engravings and some old maps of New York and Philadelphia. They promised to meet again, in January in Paris.

Marcosson also provided an introduction to the President. On August 23, he wrote to Ivar,

> I had a long talk yesterday afternoon with President Hoover. After we had finished with reparations and the International Bank, I told him about my visit with you and that I want to take you down to meet him when you are next in America. The President said that he would be delighted to make your acquaintance, so you can now consider this experience in store for you when you come.[52]

Marcosson kept his promise and introduced Ivar to Hoover several weeks later, when Ivar was in Washington, DC. Ivar planned his first visit to the White House carefully. He scripted this meeting as carefully as he had plotted his 1922 *Berengaria* entrance. Hoover was impressed by the breadth of Ivar's knowledge of global finance, the history of monopolies, the current American political scene, and even the individual names of flowers in the White House gardens. Hoover was an engineer, too, and had founded the Zinc Corporation before becoming Commerce Secretary. The men had visited the same places, stayed in the same hotels, eaten at the same restaurants. They shared friends. During the following years, Ivar would become one of the President's most valued advisors.

The markets rose throughout 1929, just as they had since Ivar's 1922 trip to America on *Berengaria*. The 1929 boom was rooted in consumer products companies, especially the chain stores, such as Montgomery Ward, Woolworth, and American Stores, which were attracting hordes of customers.[53] Many companies had followed Ivar's lead, and now had substantial off balance sheet liabilities, inter-company holdings, and complex hybrid securities issues. United Founders Corporation had 320 million dollars invested in related corporations, and even owned thousands of shares of Kreuger & Toll.[54] Goldman Sachs had issued a quarter of a billion dollars of complex new securities in August alone. Lehman Corporation, another investment bank, launched a novel securities offering, which immediately rose by 30 percent.[55]

Wall Street's performance during the summer of 1929 was spectacular. *The New York Times* industrial average rose by 25 percent from May 1 through August 31. Westinghouse was up from $151 to $286; General Electric from $268 to $391; Steel from $165 to $258; Alleghany from $33 to $56. Even United Founders, with its mysterious leverage and subsidiaries, shot from $36 to $68.[56] America's intelligentsia applauded the markets. Bernard Baruch heralded a "great forward movement." Academics praised the wisdom of crowds, including the millions of people trading through the New York Stock Exchange. A Princeton economist questioned whether anyone could "veto the judgment of this intelligent multitude?" Yale professor Irving Fisher remarked that "stock prices have reached what looks like a permanently high plateau."[57]

But then, in September 1929, as Marcosson was finishing his article on Ivar, stocks began to fall, for no apparent reason and gradually at first. Investors and the media hardly noticed the early declines. Everyone assumed the seven-year bull market, including an overall increase of 38 percent during the previous year, would continue. During September, a few stocks held firm, fluctuated, or even went up, as did Ivar's securities, which now amounted to one-fourth of all foreign corporate issues in the United States. But most stocks fell.

Marcosson's lengthy cover story on Ivar was published in the October 12 edition of the *Saturday Evening Post*. It was glowing, a paean from one Renaissance man to another. Marcosson reported details about Ivar's extravagant lifestyle, praised his match business, and argued that monopolies such as Ivar's were of great benefit to society and should be encouraged. He also mentioned Ivar's response to a question about what three things accounted most for his success. The answer, which became emblazoned in the public's memory, was: "One is silence; the second is more silence; while the third is still more silence."[58]

The next week, Ivar was the most talked about person in the United States, even as the markets continued to decline. Marcosson's article ignited the media's interest in Ivar. Journalists from every major publication called and cabled, desperate for interviews. But Ivar remained silent, even when reporters from *Time* said they were putting his face on the cover. He had decided to talk to Marcosson, but he didn't want to bother with anyone else.

The *Time* cover story appeared anyway, even though no one at the magazine had spoken to Ivar. The article concluded with a cribbed quote from Marcosson's interview, the only time Ivar had spoken to a journalist that year. Ivar said,

> There is not a single competitor with sufficient influence upon the different markets to cause us any really serious harm. No market is sufficiently significant to be of importance to us. The reason is that the whole world is our field.[59]

By the time investors read this bold statement, on October 28, the markets would be in a full-blown panic. Ivar's words, like his face on the cover of *Time*, would seem to float above the fray. That week, finally, he would achieve true greatness.

9

A WEEKEND IN GERMANY

As part of the Treaty of Versailles of 1919, the Allies had required that Germany pay billions of dollars of reparations from the world war. But the fragile German economy couldn't handle the burden, and Germany defaulted in 1923. Because of hyperinflation, leading to a dramatic increase in local prices, German currency was virtually worthless by then – a postage stamp had a face value of 50 *billion* marks. According to John Maynard Keynes, the world's leading economist at the time, given the weak financial situation, it would have been impossible for Germany to make all of its reparations payments. The German Weimar Republic could not have printed enough money to meet even one day's interest.

The Dawes Plan, for which Charles G. Dawes, Coolidge's vice president, received the Nobel Peace Prize, was an attempt to ease Germany's burden. In October 1924, the Allies reduced Germany's annual obligations and extended an additional 25-year loan of almost $200 million at 7 percent interest.[1] The initial payments were low, but stepped up rapidly. The central assumption of the Dawes Plan was that Germany would recover quickly enough to support increased payments.

Although the Germany economy improved somewhat, it soon became apparent that the tax revenues Dawes had assumed would materialize to cover the increased payments were not coming. Germany could not meet the stepped-up Dawes Plan payments, any more than it could have met its previous obligations. By 1928, the Dawes Plan was in shambles.

In response, Owen D. Young, the founder of RCA, assembled a group of businessmen, including Jack Morgan. Jack Morgan was no fan of Germany, but he saw the need to participate in negotiations to reset the country's reparation payments. Small American lenders had been financing Germany's obligations under previous plans, and another German default could bankrupt them and precipitate a financial crisis. In August 1929, as Ivar was preparing for his first meeting with President Hoover, the group finalized the Young Plan, which reduced Germany's unconditional obligations to roughly 150 million dollars per year, a fraction of the reparations payments that had been called for in the post-war treaty.

Still, Germany's economy remained weak in 1929. Adolf Hitler had become more than just a minor political figure in the fringe Nazi party, and his 1925 autobiography, *Mein Kampf*, which initially sold poorly, had suddenly hit a nerve of discontent among German nationalists. German officials had become desperate for funding and were no longer looking past the next year. Now, they were just trying to come up with the next 150 million dollar payment, which would be due soon.

During the Young Plan negotiations, Ivar came to Germany to discuss a loan-for-monopoly solution. He had been lobbying German government officials for more than a decade, so they knew him well. Ivar already controlled 70 percent of German match output and he also held interests in several German banks and three-quarters of the German ball-bearing industry. Many German steel plants depended on buying ore from mines Ivar controlled. He was an important figure in Germany, and held a strong negotiating position.[2]

Ivar's first stab at a match monopoly in Germany had failed several years earlier, even after he offered a substantial "side payment" to one official if a monopoly law were passed within a specified time.[3] More recently, though, the balance of negotiating power was shifting. Cheap imports from Russia, which had large timber reserves, had hurt the Germans. Competition among match producers was increasing, and prices were falling. Germany was running out of options.

Finally, as the Young Plan was materializing, the Germans indicated to Ivar that they might be interested in a deal. The Governor of the Reichsbank, Dr Hjalmar Schacht, who had rebuffed Ivar's initial efforts five years earlier, said he needed a loan with a low interest rate. Specifically, he needed 150 million dollars, to make the first Young Plan payments. Most importantly, Dr Schacht said he was open to Ivar's request to take over the German factories, sell matches at higher prices, and keep out Russian imports. Now was the time for Ivar to strike. If he really wanted a monopoly deal with Germany, this was his chance.

Unfortunately, the timing could not have been worse. Global stock markets had declined throughout September, and were continuing to fall in October. Although shares of Ivar's companies were holding firm, the declining market was dampening investors' appetite to buy new securities issues. Ivar's strategy required that he raise money from American investors and then lend that money to a government in exchange for a monopoly. By summer 1929, Ivar's outstanding securities already were massive; by comparison, they had a higher market value than the value of the entire loan portfolios of all of Sweden's banks.[4] But American investors were hurting, and his sources of funds were drying up. As stocks fell it seemed less likely that Ivar would be able to raise the money he would need to fund a German loan.

Nevertheless, Ivar pressed forward. He negotiated with Dr Schacht as if a new securities issue in America would be easy to sell. The markets had fallen before, and the declines were always temporary. Ivar wasn't about to let a few worries at the New York Stock Exchange stop him from closing a once-in-a-lifetime deal. The German loan would be historic. Ivar ignored the faltering markets and marched ahead.

News of negotiations between Ivar and Dr Schacht was published prematurely in the German press in early October,[5] forcing the men to rush through an agreement in principle. It remained unclear whether either side ultimately would sign a fleshed-out contract. Yet because of media leaks, on October 12, 1929, the world knew the basic terms of the deal the men were contemplating.

Ivar would lend the Reich 125 million dollars at a 6 percent interest rate for fifty years. The German government would create a new company to run a match monopoly, which the Germans would control. The government and Ivar would split profits equally. The government would exclude Russian imports and fix the price of ten boxes of matches at 8.5 cents, up from 6 cents.

The agreement still needed to be signed by the finance minister and it had to pass the Reichstag, where there was opposition from industrial groups that exported to Russia and feared reprisals.[6] Ivar wasn't sure he would sign it, either. He told an assistant that "a large loan to the German government would be a substantial burden on us, so that I do not think we should hesitate to break off negotiations unless we can obtain conditions which are clearly in our favour."[7] Ivar wanted to close the German deal, but he wasn't willing to do so at any cost.

Moreover, Ivar didn't have 125 million dollars to lend. As with previous deals, he would need to raise that money from American investors. Donald

Durant had been working on a new securities issue for Ivar – this time, a debenture issue from Kreuger & Toll. But Durant warned Ivar that the markets were slumping, and now was not the time to try to raise such a large amount of money. When Ivar suggested he planned to go ahead with the deal, either in New York or London, Durant warned him to be careful. Durant wrote on October 4 to discourage Ivar from attempting to raise any money:

> Our primary concern is the importance of maintaining the unique good will that you have among investors on both continents. A major financial operation, whether undertaken in America or Europe, would do serious damage to this good will. We hope that we and our friends will have the opportunity of discussing this with you in person, before you make a final decision to go ahead.[8]

Ivar dismissed Durant's concerns, and told Lee Higginson to press ahead. Durant should tell his sales force to inform the firm's clients that a new deal was coming, backed by a German match monopoly. Ivar may still have had doubts, but he didn't want to show his bankers any weakness.

Ivar clearly had impressed the Germans. During the negotiations, he had spent an entire day answering detailed questions in Berlin without once consulting notes or statistics.[9] Dr Schacht, the German central bank governor, had solicited other bankers, including Jack Morgan, who was in Europe for the summer. But Jack was less impressive.

Jack was less interested as well. He saw a German loan deal as too risky, and he put off Dr Schacht while he warned his partners about negotiations with Germany:

> You will remember that our first and only German business was the Dawes Loan, and that was only undertaken at the request of all the allied Governments, our clients. This business is quite different, and the allied Governments are totally indifferent as to who does it, and it would obviously involve us eventually in competing for German business. For my part I should be very reluctant to abandon our position, which we have held for five years, that all and any German business was open to anybody in America who wanted to do it, and that we were not interested in it at all. From what I see of the Germans they are second-rate people, and I would rather have their business done for them by somebody else.[10]

When Jack learned that the "somebody else" was going to be Ivar, the publicity seemed to change his mind. He dispatched his partner, Thomas W. Lamont, to Berlin to discuss a loan with Dr Schacht. Jack also wrote directly to Dr Schacht that

> Assuming a reasonably decent Bond market here and proper terms and prices upon the proposed issue we can see no reason why we should not be able to arrange a Syndicate for the issuance of $50,000,000 or $75,000,000 in this market of the proposed new German Government Reparations Bonds. This you understand is not in any sense a commitment. It is simply a guess prompted in part by our natural co-operative desires.[11]

On October 16 and 17, Jack and Ivar were both in London, but they were moving in different directions. Ivar was on a fast track, preparing to go to Berlin to lobby the legislature to approve a deal with him right away. In contrast, Jack was noncommittal and seemed skeptical that the Germans would approve a deal with anyone, including Ivar.

While Ivar frantically cabled various German politicians to arrange meetings, Jack also replied to cables – of a very different kind. These were messages from Jack's son, Junius, who had just attended a luncheon of their America's Cup syndicate in New York. Junius had sent word of two matters of apparently more significance to Jack Morgan than a German loan.

First, Junius had asked whether his father had any thoughts about what name to call their new boat. The consensus among the America's Cup syndicate members seemed to be that *Aurora* was the best choice, but everyone wanted to be sure Jack was in accord. Did he have any wisdom on this pick, or any new recommendations?

The second matter concerned the plans for the newest version of *Corsair*, the ship Pierpont Morgan had built and rebuilt in sequential models, each larger and more opulent than the last. Jack Morgan scrutinized the plans for the new *Corsair* design and cabled Junius on October 17 with an urgent question:

> Have been over CORSAIR furnishings, etcetera. All I think in good shape. One matter disturbs me a little – there is no way from my room to the deck, without going well forward. Would it be possible make door in place of the after window, of course with raised sill? Should greatly prefer this, if it can

be done without causing too much delay ... In regard to name for our ship, wrote you yesterday suggesting COLUMBIA or SPEEDWELL, but should be quite happy with AURORA, if that appeals to most of them. Father[12]

Junius, apparently oblivious to Ivar's ongoing efforts to close the German loan, immediately cabled back, to the great relief of Jack:

Porter tells me door can be arranged direct from your room to deck if you need it. Present arrangement provides for door from your room into vestibule on port side, which in turn opens direct on deck aft. No delay will be caused by this, as window can be converted into door at any stage in the construction.[13]

As the Morgans corresponded, Ivar quietly rushed to Berlin, obtained the preliminary agreement of finance minister Rudolf Hilferding, and then quickly returned to London. The cables sent during this time by Jack and his emissary, Tom Lamont, suggest that they were unaware that Ivar had achieved this coup, right under their noses. While Jack Morgan was ensuring that he would have a direct bedroom-to-deck path on his new yacht, Ivar had tiptoed into the deal of the century.

On Tuesday, October 22, as Ivar arrived back in London, Tom Lamont sent Jack a note of congratulations, but not on the German loan. There previously had been some question about whether Jack would renew his appointment as president of his alma mater's alumni society. Lamont cabled, "Awfully glad you agreed to be President of Harvard Alumni this year. They are all enormously pleased."[14]

So was Jack, at least for a few days.

Stocks had been up almost 10 billion dollars during the first eight months of 1929, but after the September reversal they were down overall for the year. During the first three weeks of October 1929, stocks continued to plunge. It was a terrible environment for raising money. Corporations were breaking deals, not issuing new securities. Lee Higginson was having an awful month, and Donald Durant was anxious to close Ivar's new securities issue, which would generate one of the handful of investment banking fees anyone would earn during the last quarter of 1929.

When the markets opened on Monday, October 21, so many investors decided to sell that by noon the New York Stock Exchange ticker was a full hour late. Shareholders had to wait until the evening, when the ticker finally caught up, to learn how much their stocks were down. More than 6 million shares were traded, the third highest volume ever. Even after the markets fell again on Tuesday and Wednesday, the experts insisted it was just a blip. National City's Charles Mitchell observed that "the decline had gone too far." Yale's Irving Fisher described the soft markets as just a "shaking out of the lunatic fringe" and insisted that stocks would go higher.[15]

Throughout this time, Ivar appeared entirely without concern. Although he sensed the increasing panic, along with everyone else, he didn't want anyone in New York to see him falter, particularly given the market's decline. He knew markets reflected emotions and perception. In finance, there was no such thing as reality. There was only, as Pierpont Morgan had intimated, what traders thought of a man's character. If everyone saw Ivar as a shining beacon of confidence, his securities would maintain their value, even if the rest of the market crashed. He still could point to Marcosson's article. And in a few days, the *Time* cover with his photo would be out. He needed to keep up a show of confidence, to persuade American investors to buy the newest issue of Kreuger & Toll's securities.

Wednesday was the deadline for that issue, which was being called Kreuger & Toll "American Certificates." American investors had never seen an investment like this one. It was part bond, part preferred stock, and part profit-sharing option. The certificates enabled them to gain exposure to a foreign company that had been paying dividends of 25 percent. It would be backed by the largest private loan to a foreign government in history. Even in a sharply declining market, investors went crazy for this kind of exposure. They promised to buy 28 million dollars of the new securities backed by Kreuger & Toll.

There were two major business stories in *The New York Times* on the morning of October 24, 1929, the day that became known as Black Thursday on Wall Street. The smaller headline was "Warner Bros Deal with Paramount Off." The much-anticipated merger between the two major movie studios, Warner Brothers Pictures, Inc. and Paramount Famous Lasky Corporation, would have created the largest entertainment company in the world. Now, the merger was dead. Bankers everywhere wondered if the seven-year rush of corporate deals during the 1920s might be coming to an end.

But the even bigger news was an announcement of the success of Kreuger & Toll's new issue of American Certificates, which miraculously had closed Wednesday in the midst of the growing panic. A half-page panel next to the Warner–Paramount story described the terms of the innovative deal, which

Lee Higginson had arranged. Each American Certificate of Kreuger & Toll represented a share of the Swedish company's participating debentures. The certificates would be denominated in US dollars but would carry rights related to securities in Swedish kronor. Investors had bought the certificates, even though neither Ivar nor the German government had yet approved a monopoly deal. The media coverage of Ivar had been enough to spur them on.

Notwithstanding Ivar's success, when the markets opened on Thursday, the bottom fell out. Within hours, a record number of shares had traded. Panicked crowds gathered outside the Exchange as share prices collapsed. Rumors spread about brokers jumping from buildings downtown. The New York police commissioner sent a special detail to Wall Street. Eleven well-known speculators killed themselves, and many more were bankrupted.[16]

Just after noon, the New York Stock Exchange closed the gallery, and officials escorted the visitors into the teeming crowds outside. The world's top bankers quickly convened at the offices of J. P. Morgan, down the street at 23 Wall. Jack Morgan was still in London, so Tom Lamont, Jack's senior partner, presided. The bankers decided to pool resources and support the markets. As their buy orders flooded the floor of the Exchange, Lamont met with reporters and blamed "a technical condition of the market."[17] Their support temporarily stopped the free fall, and the ticker, when it finally caught up, showed that stocks had recovered from their midday lows.

Both Jack Morgan and Ivar learned by transcontinental cable of the panic and wild price swings. An assistant reported to Jack that:

At noon today the decline in the Stock Exchange, which for several days has been severe, turned into panic conditions. With no supporting orders whatsoever stocks began to drop many points at a time in a perfectly wild, illogical and uncontrolled manner. We decided to make a sort of faith cure demonstration by purchasing certain pivotal stocks on a scale down, thus attempting to steady the decline.[18]

The New York Stock Exchange announced it would close for the Friday and Saturday trading sessions, and reopen on Monday. The hope was that investors would be calmer then. Littorin cabled to Ivar that:

As you know, the market has for several days shown symptoms of a threatening collapse, and the sales pressure has today reached hectic proportions. Several of the leading shares have fallen by 25–50%, while our shares have kept up reasonably well with a price drop of only 12% during last week in spite of very little support. Banking circles are very nervous, and there is no doubt, as I see it, that our issue comes at a very bad moment, as banks are being hit right and left. The enthusiasm (for our issue) that we had counted on, has been transformed into a feeling of great skepticism.[19]

Perhaps the most intense panic was from members of Lee Higginson's syndicate for the new Kreuger & Toll issue of American Certificates. That syndicate included nearly all of the major banks except Morgan: Brown Brothers, Clark Dodge, Dillon Read, Guaranty, National City, and Union Trust Company. Investors already were reneging on their promises to buy American Certificates. So many purchasers had backed out that more than one-fourth of the issue was now unsold. Now that investors were refusing to pay, these banks would be on the hook. They were stuck with 28 million dollars of American Certificates whose value already had fallen 12 percent, and might fall even more.

Ivar saw the next few days as a crucial turning point. Sentiment was turning, as investors fled from stocks. Opinion easily could turn against him as well. He had learned from dealing with Swedish bankers during the early 1920s that he must preserve the confidence of his supporters. Ivar's bankers had to believe in him, even if the markets were crashing. Even if they believed in nothing else. Ivar had to give Durant and his partners good reason to think Ivar was different.

On Friday, as he reflected on the reports of panic in the United States, Ivar spent several hours composing an extraordinary cable to send to Lee Higginson. He needed to say something to persuade the bankers that, although the American markets were collapsing, everything was just fine in Europe. Ivar would show them that his companies were as strong as ever. They might be worried about America, but they didn't need to worry about him.

This is what he wrote:

I am very sorry that our issue seems to have come at a very unlucky moment. We are very anxious that the syndicate that has taken over ... our debentures will not have reason to regret their action, and we are also anxious not to overload the American market with our paper. We have therefore arranged with a Swedish syndicate to offer to take over, on December 31, 1930, up to half the amount of such debentures as the American syndicate has acquired. This will be done at the acquisition cost to the American syndicate. We expect to receive notice no later than December 15, 1930, of the extent to which the American syndicate wishes to avail themselves of this offer.[20]

This was astonishing news. Ivar was saying he had arranged to guarantee half of the banks' exposure to the American Certificates. If the banks were unable to sell the certificates in one year, Ivar would buy them at cost. In other words, he was giving them the right to "put back" the certificates to Ivar. And he was doing it for free.

Durant couldn't believe what he was reading. Ivar was bailing out not only him and his partners, but several other major American banks. The tone of Ivar's cable was almost casual, as if he couldn't be bothered with such a trifle as millions of dollars worth of unplaced American Certificates. After all, he was about to close the biggest privately organized government loan in history. What was a little panic in New York compared to his blockbuster deal with Germany?

Ivar's offer to give the banks this "put back" right was designed to instill confidence in the bankers, and investors, and to buy time. They did not need to rush to take any dramatic action, even if the markets continued to free fall. They could take a breath. Indeed, Ivar's bailout package gave them the ability to wait more than a year, until the end of 1930. Then, if any bank ultimately had been unable to sell its allotment of Kreuger & Toll Certificates, Ivar would make up the difference in his rescue package by letting the banks put the certificates back to Kreuger & Toll. After Durant read, and then reread, Ivar's cable, he eagerly established a book entry at Lee Higginson for the "Ivar Kreuger Current Account" to keep track of these put backs.[21]

Durant reported Ivar's extraordinary guarantee to members of the syndicate. He described the put back right, "which we believe to be absolutely without precedent, which shows conclusively the breadth of the man."[22] Charles Mitchell, head of National City, told Ivar it was not necessary for him to exercise any put back yet. Mitchell announced that the "industrial condition of the United States is absolutely sound" and that "nothing can arrest the upward movement."[23] Joseph R. Swan, president of the Guaranty Company of New York, heartily agreed. Swan's endorsement reflected the bankers' confidence in Ivar: "He certainly plays up handsomely and, also, I think, wisely."[24] Both National City and Guaranty agreed to hold onto 1 million American Certificates.[25] No need to put them back to Ivar, or to worry about any paper losses. They would sell them to investors when this panic subsided.

Donald Durant was relieved. Given Ivar's guarantee, it seemed that Lee Higginson would take no risk, the members of its syndicate would take no risk, and yet Durant and his firm would pocket a fee of nearly 1.4 million dollars.[26] The entire banking syndicate earned a fee of 2.5 percent. Given losses from the declining markets and the dearth of deals, that fee was indispensable.

Ivar remained cool throughout. He calmly sent Durant a one-sentence cable that was probably the greatest understatement of his life: "I regret very much that our issue seems to have gone at a very unfortunate moment."[27] The put back right could cost Ivar his entire fortune. Essentially, he had given his bankers a put option – the right to sell him American Certificates – until the end of 1930 at a price of 28 dollars. For every dollar the price fell below 28 dollars, Ivar would lose a million dollars. That could amount to a lot more than "regret." For now, though, everyone seemed safe. As Kreuger & Toll's 1929 annual report later would state:

> The issue was announced on October 23, 1929. Although a stock market crisis of exceptional severity hit practically all of the world's financial centres immediately thereafter, it is satisfying to note that the whole issue was rapidly subscribed to, so that the underwriting syndicate did not have to absorb any part of the issue.[28]

Now that Ivar had agreed to guarantee the American Certificates, he faced an even more difficult question that weekend: Should he actually sign the German deal? If he said no, he still could try to salvage his reputation. He could cite the recent market decline as a plausible excuse for him to pull out. And there were good business reasons for him to do so. Although the loan was clearly a good deal for Germany, it wasn't necessarily good for Ivar. Germany's government would lock in a low 6 percent interest rate in an environment of rising rates. But Ivar could do better by lending his money elsewhere. Moreover, given the market collapse, and Ivar's put back obligations, it would be much less risky for Ivar to keep the cash he had just raised in America, instead of sending it to Germany. If Ivar abandoned the German loan, he could use the money he had just raised for Kreuger & Toll as a cushion against further stock price declines. His businesses still were profitable and his companies were in a reasonably solid position, at least relative to everyone else. Saying no to Germany was the prudent course.

But if Ivar said yes, he could make history. He could leave a legacy even more permanent than the turrets at Kalmar Slott, the castle near his childhood home. Ivar Kreuger, a self-made Swede, would become the largest lender to foreign governments. Acting alone, he would replace the Dawes and Young Plans, which had been negotiated over years by several governments and dozens of officials. He would become known forever as a one-man financier to Europe. He, not Jack, would take over Pierpont Morgan's throne as global banker. And, if Germany's economy recovered, Ivar would earn huge profits from his match monopoly there.

Of course, he would be taking incredible risks, especially if the stock market collapse continued. It wasn't even clear that he could raise the entire 125 million dollars to send to Germany; the money he raised by issuing American Certificates covered less than a quarter of that amount. And even if he did raise the money, the German loan would leave little room for error in his business overall. Ivar would receive interest of just 6 percent from Germany, but his dividend obligations would remain as high as 25 percent. Was Ivar confident he could earn enough profit to make up the difference? Was it worth the risk?

The crucial question for Ivar was this: What would the markets do when the New York Stock Exchange opened on Monday? If the markets recovered, he would be able to raise more money, fund the German loan, and continue to pay high dividends. But if the markets continued to crash … Well, he couldn't even think about that. His best guess was that the markets would rise Monday.

On Saturday, Ivar met again with finance minister Hilferding in Berlin and finalized terms. As Ivar held the pen, about to sign the loan documents, he considered the two paths his life might follow as a result of his decision. This audacious deal might be the miracle that would reverse the darkening psychology of investors everywhere. Ivar imagined the buzz spreading about his extraordinary weekend feat. When the New York Stock Exchange opened on Monday, his securities would soar in value. The rising tide of optimism would make it possible for him to raise more cash and shift his personal loan obligation to American investors. Those investors would rescue him and buoy stocks overall. With any luck, by the close of trading Monday, the worst would be over.

That was one possibility Ivar could imagine. The alternative – that the crisis would continue, or even deepen – was unthinkable. He couldn't bear to consider what would happen if the market freefall continued. Then, the German loan would catapult him to ignominy, not fame.

Ivar decided not to spend the evening alone in his apartment at Pariser Platz, as he normally would on a Saturday night in Berlin. Instead, he walked to the Hotel Adlon nearby, and celebrated with a culinary binge at its restaurant. In one meal, Ivar violated every dietary rule he had been obeying for more than a decade: he ate all of his favorite dishes at once, from caviar to rich bouillon to ice cream to chocolate soufflé. Back at his apartment, completely stuffed, he phoned Ingeborg Eberth, his neighbor at Villagatan in Stockholm, and asked her to play the piano for him, as she often did when he was home.[29] Ivar tried to savor the moment, and the brief peace. He had taken the greatest gamble of his career.

Jack Morgan still didn't believe Ivar really would close a deal with Germany. He knew Ivar had been working with German officials for several years, but he never imagined that Ivar would do a deal on his own, or that Germany and Lee Higginson would agree to exclude Morgan from any participation. Morgan partnered with Dillon Read & Co., another bank, which also had been working on a loan arrangement with German officials. Jack had assumed that either there would be no loan at all or that there would be a loan on favorable terms, which Morgan would participate in by taking a piece. Jack and his bankers assumed they had plenty of time given the recent turbulence in the markets.

When Ivar told Donald Durant he had secured a preliminary agreement with Germany, Durant and Lee Higginson decided to refuse to share the loan with anyone, including Morgan. Durant flatly rejected any joint arrangement with Dillon Read, even after Clarence Dillon offered to increase the size of the deal. Dillon proposed to do a 200 million dollar issue together, with 125 million dollars going to Ivar and 75 million dollars going to Dillon Read.[30] But Germany didn't need 200 million dollars. One hundred and twenty-five million dollars was plenty, at least for now, and all of that could come from Ivar.

Lee Higginson sent a "courtesy notice" to Morgan describing the terms of Ivar's deal with the German government.[31] There wasn't any new information, just the same details previously reported in the business papers, along with a note saying that the parties had signed a deal. Jack didn't find that notice very courteous. When he learned that Ivar had closed the loan on his own, and that Morgan wouldn't be part of it, he was furious. He angrily cabled home, "Am just advised by telephone from Gilbert that Dr Schacht informs him that Dillon's proposal has been declined by German Government."[32] Parker Gilbert, one of Morgan's partners, said he was "fully alive to the dangers of the situation" and saw a need for secrecy. Gilbert had called Jack by phone, instead of cabling, "so as to leave no record."[33]

In signing the German loan even as the markets were crashing, Ivar was kicking Jack Morgan when he was down. This wasn't the way proper bankers behaved, particularly when a German loan at a low rate of 6 percent was at risk of losing money. The loan would seriously harm Morgan's business, even if it ultimately hurt Ivar even more. Jack wrote to a colleague:

> I do not see that there is anything else that we can do. I do not want to take any special stand in regard to the way we are being treated, for I think Schacht has been honest in the matter, but that the politicians have been too much for him. It is a horrid mess, isn't it.[34]

On Saturday, as the monopoly agreement was being signed in Berlin, Jack was still in London, still accepting congratulations on the Harvard alumni post, most recently from his son Junius, who had learned the news. In Jack's life, the Harvard post really was a high priority. He responded to Junius, "Thanks very much for your congratulations on my new honor, which is quite impressive. Very well and getting on comfortably, but find myself in the usual rush before sailing."[35]

Many ships were ready to sail that weekend. A crew was putting the finishing touches on Jack's new 3 million dollar yacht, which was being readied in Bath, Maine. In Washington, the US Secretary of Commerce was raising 100,000 dollars of public funds for upkeep of the original *Corsair*, which Morgan had just given to the federal government.[36] Donald Durant, the master mariner, was considering a trip to Europe, though he could not sail right away. And Ivar had booked a cabin on *Majestic*, which would soon leave for New York.

Ivar's greatest triumph was immediately followed by the most spectacular two-day decline in the history of financial markets. The stock market fell 13 percent on Monday, and 12 percent on Tuesday. In two days, stocks lost a quarter of their value. This time, there would be no concerted buying effort from the banks. And this time, there would be no recovery.

October 28 and 29 came to be known as Black Monday and Black Tuesday. Twenty-six million shares traded. In forty-eight hours, a full year of gains was wiped out. Goldman Sachs fell from $60 to $35. White Sewing Machine Company fell from a summer high of $48 to $11. Blue Ridge, an investment company, opened on Monday at $10, but closed on Tuesday at $3. It was the most devastating time in the history of stock markets.[37]

By comparison, Ivar's companies were star performers, buoyed, at least at first, by the news of his deal with Germany. A few days earlier, Durant had worried when the price of International Match debentures declined to $33.50, still in line with the original issue price. Now, like a single stone refusing to roll downhill, that was where the price remained. International Match's debentures hovered above $33, defying the pull of the market's black hole.

Few people, including Jack and Ivar, could predict just how much the markets and the economy would deteriorate. Before he sailed home, Jack cabled,

> So far as we know, there are no houses in serious difficulty. The banking group had supporting orders in at the opening today but after that the market pursued a natural and vigorous course. Buying came in from all quarters, including some excellent European buying. A public statement which John D. Rockefeller, Sr made today, after his people had talked with us, also helped to improve sentiment.[38]

Jack knew that Ivar's 125 million dollar loan would help Germany stave off a financial crisis, pay down its deficit, and carry out promised reforms. The loan wouldn't help the American markets, though, and it already had angered senior Russian officials, who had opposed a deal and said Germany was favoring a foreign private investor at the expense of Russo-German trade relations. In an official communiqué, Russia's trade commissioner in Berlin charged the German government with a "hostile act."

Jack studied the terms of Ivar's German deal. As with all of Ivar's financial deals, this loan had some unique innovations. Ivar gave Germany the option to pay a floating interest rate if rates fell below 6 percent, as well as the right to repay the entire loan early. The loan, and the fifty-year match monopoly, were contingent on Germany's ratification of the Young Plan, which was scheduled to occur in a few months. If the Young Plan wasn't ratified, the deal was invalid. Most importantly, International Match and Swedish Match would pay just 93 cents for each dollar of loan obligation. As with the French loan, Ivar would make extra profit, in this case 7 cents per dollar, if Germany prepaid the loan.[39]

Bankers everywhere focused on Ivar now, as they tried to figure out exactly how he was making enough money to support his massive dividend payments to investors. The hefty discount on the German loan wouldn't generate any cash to help Ivar meet obligations, and the Germans might not repay any principal for decades. The match monopoly might produce profits, but the Germans would keep half.

In addition, Ivar was now obligated to send Germany 50 million dollars by August 30, 1930, and 75 million dollars more by May 29, 1931. The first 50 million dollars would come from International Match; the remaining 75 million dollars would be split between Swedish Match and Kreuger & Toll.[40] Did Ivar have that much money to send to Germany? It certainly didn't show up on the balance sheet of International Match. Given the recent market turmoil, it would be virtually impossible even for Ivar to raise that much cash. Jack wired an assistant that he was "much interested in Kreuger & Toll Company arrangement with German Government."[41] He wasn't alone.

Ivar was determined to preserve investors' faith in him, even as the markets crashed. He suggested to Durant that they encourage investors and support International Match's securities by increasing the promised dividend payments. Ivar left it to Durant to decide when to increase the dividend, and by how much. He felt that if Durant made the decision, Durant and Lee Higginson would feel more confident about International Match. On November 5, Ivar cabled Durant, "I feel that present conditions make it particularly desirable to increase the dividend now. Kindly therefore take such steps as are necessary to have the increased dividend declared at the moment you consider to be the right one."[42] Three weeks later, at Durant's instruction, International Match increased its annual dividend from $3.20 to $4 per share.[43]

Ivar and Karin Bökman publicized the German deal by sending copies of the agreement to everyone Ivar knew.[44] Isaac Marcosson also helped. After chaperoning Ivar's first meeting with President Hoover, as he had promised, he wrote about how both the President and Ivar benefited from the interaction.[45] Ivar thanked Marcosson for the continuing good words. He wrote, "I find your article a brilliant piece of work and feel greatly flattered over the contents of same."[46]

November 1929 was full of surprises. Just seventeen days after the crash, *The Kiss* opened in New York. The movie, one of the last silent movies in an era of talkies, was not expected to do well. Yet it was a box office smash. Millions of Americans went to see Greta Garbo's "silent swan song," not to mention that kiss.[48] Garbo's popularity soared, and she became widely known as the "Woman of Mystery."[49]

Many investors were destroyed, but others prospered. It wasn't obvious that the stock market decline would have any real impact, and some commentators maintained it was merely a blip. According to the Harvard Economic Society, "A severe depression like that of 1920–21 is outside the range of probability. We are not facing protracted liquidation." Financier Bernard Baruch sent a cable to British former Chancellor of the Exchequer Winston Churchill on November 15 noting, "Financial storm definitely passed."[47]

Given the support of increased dividends and good publicity, the crash didn't immediately hurt Ivar's companies. It took time for crashes to ripple through financial businesses, particularly when those businesses were complex. Although the prices of securities had collapsed, most of the actual losses based on those securities would not be disclosed for several months. Likewise, even after the October crash, Ivar's businesses sustained their value for several months. The persistently high value of Ivar's securities might not reflect economic reality. But it was taking many people, even expert commentators, a long time to learn the truth.

If Ivar could continue to raise enough money, he could meet his obligations and support his companies, perhaps for long enough to weather the aftermath of the crash. The problem was that the market for raising new funds was dry. Ivar could have decided to cut his dividends, instead of raising them, so that he could afford to make payments for a longer period of time. However, such a decision would have forced him to swallow his pride, and it might have raised suspicions. Ivar preferred to do the opposite: increase dividends and gamble that he would be able to get enough money soon enough to pay them. Everything hinged on the continuing ability of Ivar's companies to pay high dividends.

The Young Plan was signed in Paris on January 29, 1930, and the German parliament passed the monopoly law the same day, confirming the validity of Ivar's loan, and his obligation to deliver 50 million dollars in a few months.[50] Instead of backing down, Ivar continued to increase his companies' obligations. Ivar agreed to another deal with the government of Poland in 1930, promising to lend it 32 million dollars to keep his monopoly there. The odds of Ivar raising enough cash to satisfy all of these obligations seemed slim.

After the crash, Krister Littorin and Karin Bökman, the two people who were closest to Ivar and saw him the most, began noticing some disturbing changes in his personality. Increasingly, it seemed, the pressure to raise more money and meet his company's increasing obligations was splitting Ivar in two.

One version of Ivar spent more time alone, either locked in his Silence Room or behind the closed doors of hotel rooms throughout the world. Even when Karin Bökman traveled with Ivar, she might not see him for days. He spent hours memorizing new financial data and economic statistics. He seemed determined to jam all of this information into his brain, presumably so he could impress the world's leaders with his command of the fragile markets.

But a different version of Ivar was suddenly more sociable than ever. He met periodically with President Hoover, and dined with the prime ministers of leading nations.[51] He addressed the Bond Club at its monthly lunch, where he impressed everyone by citing bond yields from memory. He delivered major lectures, including a widely publicized address in Chicago advocating that "What the world hopes from the great creditor countries is no altruism, but only enlightened selfishness."[52]

Ivar continued to charm young women, even while traveling with Karin Bökman.[53] For example, when Ivar sailed *Majestic*, shortly after the October crash, he beguiled one passenger, Katharine von Rosenberg, with what she called a "charming vegetable dinner." She found it memorable and offered to "reciprocate if we will ever be at the same time in the same city," perhaps at one of the hotels he recommended, the Meurice or the Crillon.[54]

However, if a social occasion did not suit Ivar's purposes, or he was not in the mood, he could be rude. He refused to attend the Queen of Sweden's funeral because he considered the place offered him in the procession inadequate in view of his international standing.[55] And when Miss Wilma Waite – who, like Katharine von Rosenberg, met Ivar on *Majestic* – asked not only if he would suggest a time and place for them to meet, but added a question about whether he "might be interested in purchase of ninety eight thousand acres pine land in Florida partly owned by our family," Ivar's response was brusque: "Regret not interested in pineland in Florida."[56]

Ivar seems to have understood what was happening to his mind, because he increasingly worried about spending time in person with the people who mattered most to his business, particularly Donald Durant and A.D. Berning. After a brief stay in New York, he left for Europe and avoided these two men for months. Instead, he maintained his relationships through periodic letters and cables. Throughout 1930, nearly all of his dealings with Durant and Berning, including major business decisions, were done in writing, not in person.

For example, instead of pressing Durant in person with his plan to increase

Kreuger & Toll's dividend – just as they had increased the annual payments by International Match – Ivar merely reported in a letter "a strong feeling with our directors for increasing the Kreuger & Toll dividend to thirty percent."[57] Durant gave Ivar written authorization to sign for him on behalf of Kreuger & Toll, but did so without any in person discussion. [58] The closest Ivar came to a real personal touch with Durant was handwriting some of his letters. In one note, about the Peruvian monopoly, Ivar's handwriting was in a sprawling and flowery cursive, with large loops at the bottom of his "y"s and "p"s.[59]

In early 1930, Donald Durant reported that Ivar's put back guarantee of the Kreuger & Toll American Certificates, one of Ivar's chanciest moves, seemed to be working. More investors had purchased the Certificates, although the banks still held millions of dollars' worth. Durant reported that "since October 24th, 1929, the day of the start of the panic, to date the number of holders of American Certificates has increased by 3,645, or in other words, an advance of over 20%."[60] That was good news to Ivar, but not good enough.

Ivar paid Berning even less attention than he paid Durant. When Berning sent Ivar queries about International Match's most recent financial statements, he received a letter indicating that Ivar was away and could not respond. When Berning requested details about the German loan, Ivar eventually responded that "I would not like you to give details of the item. I do not want the definite figure of our holdings in Germany to be known at present and I therefore suggest that you group our German holdings with our holdings in some other country and call them Sundry Investments."[61]

The fact that Ivar was rarely available created problems for both Durant and Berning, particularly when American investors pressed them for details about International Match. After several unsuccessful attempts to contact Ivar, they drafted a short memorandum to send to investors, essentially explaining that many of International Match's financial details couldn't be released for political reasons. In the draft, the two men wrote,

A large part of the corporation's activities are carried on under special concessions or monopolies. In many cases, it is quite in order for such arrangements to be publicly known. In others, however, the political situation is such that it would be most detrimental to both the corporation's interest and also to that of the country involved if these relationships were known to exist. The corporation has therefore used the greatest care and bided the time when it will be proper and in order to announce publicly its position in various countries. It is for this reason that an itemized statement of the countries involved under the items of "ADVANCES FOR INVEST-MENT IN MATCH CONCESSIONS" and "ADVANCES TO GOVERN-MENTS" has never publicly been made. Its relationship with France, Poland, Hungary, Roumania and other countries, and more recently with Germany, has of course been published. There are other countries, however, where conditions do not permit the corporation at this time to disclose its relationship, but there is little doubt that these conditions will change in times as they have in other instances.[62]

Durant and Berning sent this draft to Ivar, but heard nothing for six weeks. When Ivar finally dictated a response to Karin Bökman, he was breezy, noting only that the memorandum was "excellent." He wrote, "I expect to come to America during the month of March and hope then to have the pleasure of seeing you."[63] But when Berning arranged a meeting time in March, Ivar abruptly cancelled his travel plans.[64]

Investors might have wanted to see something more than a generic description of "Sundry Investments," but Ivar was unwilling to give anyone more than a half-page of detail about the sources of International Match's income. Ivar confirmed that there were roughly thirty companies consolidated with International Match, but wouldn't say more than that.[65]

The questions about how Ivar actually made so much money persisted when International Match reported "earnings" from 1929 of 21 million dollars, and Swedish Match reported 15 million dollars. Some of those "earnings" for one company were really just dividends paid by the other company. Those weren't real earnings; they were just movements of cash from one pocket to the other. Still, even excluding those payments, the total reported earnings of Ivar's two match companies was in the range of 30 million dollars.[66]

Many bankers and investors questioned these numbers. Total world consumption of matches was about 40 billion boxes. Ivar's factories produced roughly two-thirds of all matches, and the public paid an average price of perhaps one-half cent per box. Basic math suggested that Ivar's total annual revenue from match sales throughout the world would have been less than 150 million dollars. How much profit could Ivar earn on that revenue? Profit margins on matches, even with a monopoly, were narrow. Raw materials were costly and there also were shipping expenses, taxes, duties, and sales costs. Could Ivar really earn 30 million dollars from revenue of 150 million dollars? That was a wide profit margin of 20 percent.

According to one banker who asked Ivar this question, Ivar readily admitted that only about half of his companies' profits were from the match business. The rest, Ivar said, were from speculation.[67] But even if Ivar was making large profits from speculation, so that his match companies actually had made 30 million dollars, that amount still wouldn't be nearly enough. Ivar needed to come up with 50 million dollars for the first installment due on the German loan in August. Unless one of his bets paid off quickly, he wouldn't be able to pay Germany. If Ivar breached that agreement, his reputation, and his businesses, would be destroyed.

He needed a rescue, and it came just in time.

10

ONE LAST CHANCE

When French Prime Minister Raymond Poincaré retired in late July 1929, citing health concerns, he was replaced by Aristide Briand, then the Minister of Foreign Affairs. Briand was a close friend of Poincaré. In the closeted world of French politics, he already had succeeded Poincaré once as prime minister, in 1913. This time, Briand wouldn't last as long (indeed, he would predecease Poincaré, coincidentally in March 1932, just as Ivar was sailing from America to Europe for the last time).

The French economy was thriving, and one of Briand's first acts was to repay the 75 million dollar loan his good friend Poincaré had arranged with Ivar. Recall that Ivar had structured the deal with Poincaré at a discount, so that the French received just 70 million dollars upfront, even though the government promised to repay Ivar 75 million dollars. If the French prepaid their loan, Ivar would receive the cash years earlier than he had planned. Ivar wanted that 5 million dollars as soon as possible.

For months, Ivar had been hanging by a financial thread. Now, an early payment of 5 million dollars from France would keep him from falling. Most importantly, money from France would give Ivar enough cash to make his first installment on the German loan.

Incredibly, the French committed to repay the 75 million dollars by April 1930, just before Ivar's first payment to Germany was due. That payment would give Ivar enough cash to cover his obligation to Germany. Either Ivar had negotiated a sweetheart rescue deal with Prime Minister Briand, or he was incredibly lucky. One commentator called it "manna from Heaven."[1]

Ivar immediately wired 50 million dollars of France's money to Germany.

He then transferred $23,733,152 to his Lichtenstein subsidiary, Continental. As usual, he left virtually nothing for International Match.

Time reported these payments with skepticism. The magazine was embarrassed by its glowing cover story about Ivar during the same week as the market crash, and it now highlighted concerns from investors about what Ivar was doing with France's early repayment. *Time* scoffed at Ivar's simple response that his funds would now be earning 6 percent from Germany instead of 5 percent from France.[2]

Yet most investors were unfazed by *Time*'s new doubts, especially when Ivar announced plans to use some of the remaining funds for new loan-for-monopoly deals that year. In fact, Ivar would add Bolivia, Bulgaria, the city state of Danzig, Guatemala, Lithuania, Turkey, and Yugoslavia to his portfolio of match monopolies during 1930.[3] Those deals led McNeel's, the well-regarded investment analysts, to issue a confidential bulletin recommending Ivar's securities as "sound" with "possibilities of appreciation."[4]

Privately, Ivar was concerned that the 1929 crash might have damaged his business prospects irreparably. He couldn't cover double-digit dividends with 6 percent payments from Germany. And if the market overall continued to plummet, eventually the prices of his securities would be hit hard. Ivar could not continue to raise money during a financial crisis. Although Ivar projected confidence in his public dealings, he began spending more and more time alone in his Silence Room, worrying that he had made a mistake with the German loan. He needed to find a way to survive at least one more year, and pray that then the market's downward tide would turn. Ivar crossed his fingers, and announced an increase of Kreuger & Toll's dividend, from 25 to 30 percent.

When Ivar turned fifty years old, on March 2, 1930, he could have retreated to the Match Palace to retire comfortably. He certainly had plenty of money, and accolades. He had just received an honorary doctorate from Syracuse University, where he had built the Archbold Stadium. He played a prominent role in the annual Nobel Prize ceremonies. He met regularly with foreign leaders. Apart from the recent turnabout at *Time*, he was still a media darling. He could spend his days advising policymakers, and on social or philanthropic endeavors.

Yet not long after his fiftieth birthday, Ivar planned to begin a renewed and relentless push to secure another match monopoly – this time in Italy. Ivar asked Sweden's King Gustav to help him by pulling some political strings, to get Ivar back in touch with the senior Italian officials who would be responsible for any monopoly deal. Italy was the only major European country left to do a deal with Ivar. Spain had balked and, like the United States, Britain would not grant him a monopoly for antitrust reasons.

Ivar had been involved in negotiations in Italy off and on since 1923, just after he first raised money in America. At the time, the Italian government had just dissolved its public monopoly and formed a syndicate to handle domestic match sales. Ivar owned more than 30 percent of the largest Italian match company, Fabbriche Riunite di Fiammiferi (FRF), as well as several smaller Italian match factories.[5] During the fall of 1928, Ivar approached the Italian government through an Italian intermediary to propose a 75 million dollar loan in exchange for a match monopoly, but the government wasn't interested.

One barrier to a loan had been Thomas Lamont, Jack Morgan's partner, who for many years had been doing clandestine work for the fascist regime, in addition to pitching banking deals. An Italian deal would have been particularly galling for J. P. Morgan & Co. Pierpont Morgan had been a major figure in Italy, and the government had honored him in 1904 for finding and returning a cope stolen from the cathedral of Ascoli Piceno. A few years later, after the papacy had lost money on poor investments, Pope Pius X remarked, "What a pity I did not think of asking Mr Morgan to give us some advice about our finances!"[6] After that, the papacy hired Morgan for advice on the purchase of US stocks.

Jack Morgan was obviously angry when he began hearing rumors, initiated by Ivar, that Italy might do a deal with International Match. Ivar told people the deal must be kept secret because the funds were for Italy's military use. When he visited New York, he told some people about a deal with "Y Country." By the time Ivar told Durant that he was working on a "great Italian coup," all of Lee Higginson already had heard the story.

King Gustav put Ivar in touch with an Italian count, who arranged a meeting with the two key men, other than Mussolini, who would need to agree to a deal. Ivar began a flurry of correspondence with these two men. As usual, Ivar was highly persuasive, and they expressed some interest, notwithstanding their Morgan ties. By the time the three finally met for formal negotiations in October 1930, Ivar had decided to put all of his chips on Italy.

One of the men was Antonio Mosconi, the Italian minister of finance and Mussolini's leading finance advisor. The other was Giovanni Boselli, general manager of the government's monopoly grants.[7] After a few months, they were close to a deal, and were talking about specific terms, including how much money would be lent and what interest rate would be charged.

Ivar had met Mussolini only once, three years earlier. Nothing had come of that meeting but, now that talks with his deputies were progressing, Mussolini agreed to meet with Ivar again. Even though Mussolini insisted that the details of their meeting were to be kept entirely secret, the prospect of a meeting was enough to sustain Ivar's hope that Italy would be the pathbreaking new deal he needed to revive investor interest, raise more money, and buoy his securities. America might be plunging into depression, but Ivar was sustained by rays of hope from his three new Italian friends, Mosconi, Boselli, and Mussolini.

Ivar told Littorin and Bökman he was leaving to do some business in Hungary that he could not discuss. He traveled alone and didn't give any details about when he would return. A colleague, who saw him before the trip, remarked, "I had never heard him be so secretive about anything."[8]

Instead of going to Hungary, though, Ivar entered Italy from the north and headed straight to Florence. The details of Ivar's trip to Italy were later hotly disputed.[9] Ivar's colleagues claimed he indeed had closed a secret deal with the Italians after meetings with all three men. The Italians later admitted they had needed funds, and confirmed that some meetings had occurred, but said they couldn't reach terms with Ivar. A letter emerged years later, signed by Giovanni Boselli and dated December 23, 1930, which stated that "we do not wish to continue the negotiations. These are therefore terminated."[10] Mussolini denied taking any money from Ivar. He said they had met, but had never reached an agreement. Other observers said Ivar secretly had loaned Mussolini some money, but not in any amount approaching the value of the French or German loans. The truth would never be known.

What was absolutely clear, however, was that when Ivar returned from this trip to Italy, he did something so surprising that no one ever would understand it or be able to explain why he did it. Ivar previously had fudged numbers in his financial statements, just as he had cheated on exams as a child. He had exaggerated profits to smooth reported income. He had avoided reporting liabilities. He had kept investors in the dark about important details. All of those actions might have been questionable, but they never rose to the level of outright fraud. Mostly, Ivar had been skirting the edges of legal rules, to preserve his own flexibility.

What Ivar did next was different.

When Ivar returned from Italy, he locked himself in the Silence Room. He finally emerged and frenetically reported to a few colleagues that he had been engaged in widespread clandestine negotiations throughout Europe. He mentioned so many deals that they could not keep track of where he had been, where he was going, or which transactions might be next.

Then, he left the Match Palace, saying he was late for an important meeting. He walked to the offices of a Stockholm firm that previously had printed stock certificates for his companies. Ivar told the assistant director of the firm that he needed help with what he said was a top secret project. The man was not to tell anyone about the order Ivar was about to place.

Ivar then asked the man to lithograph forty-two Italian government bills. Ivar showed the man an actual bill and described how he wanted the finished product to appear. He wanted the bills to bear the same coat of arms imprint as official Italian government treasury bills, as well as the title "Italian Monopoly Administration." He wanted them to state "six percent treasury bills with interest payable at Barclay's Bank, Ltd, in London." Below that statement would be the words "Rome 15 August 1930" and "General Director" on a signature line. In the lower left corner, it should read, "Guaranted [sic] as to principal and interest by the Kingdom of Italy" along with the words "Minister of Finance" and another signature line.[11]

Ivar went over each of these details, to be sure the bills would look exactly like a real Italian treasury bill. Then, after he had placed this order, he went home to his apartment at Villagatan. He walked past the Carl Milles statue and stopped in to see Ingeborg Eberth next door. Although he rarely played any music, this time he tried a few improvisations on her grand piano.[12] In his own flat, he patted the heel of the small wooden bear on the lowest banister of the handrail. He ate some fruit. He went back out for his nightly walk. He tried to fall into the patterns of his normal life, the habits he had followed before this trip to Italy changed everything. But inside his fantastical genius mind, something profound had changed. He would never be the same.

While Ivar was away on what appeared to be a trip to Hungary, A.D. Berning had decided to come to Stockholm unannounced, to check on the Swedish audit of Ivar's companies. Berning was the last person Ivar wanted to see, and he certainly wasn't in the mood to answer any accounting questions. When he learned Berning was in town he arranged an elaborate series of excuses to avoid a meeting. Karin Bökman, Ivar's assistant, told Berning that Ivar was not seeing anyone; even she was unable to get any time with him.[13] Ivar managed to dodge Berning throughout his stay. Then, the moment Berning left Sweden, Ivar inundated him with increasingly bizarre written requests.

For example, he cabled Berning that he wanted to change the recorded cost of the German loan on International Match's financial statements. He wanted it to be listed at 83 cents per dollar rather than the actual cost of 93 cents. Then, Ivar wanted to take that extra 10 cents and record it as ownership of shares in the German monopoly.

This accounting switch made no sense: the cost of the loan *was* 93 cents per dollar, whereas any profits from the German monopoly would flow in over time. Ivar apparently wanted to use the reduction in the cost of the German loan to hide profits on the French loan. Perhaps Ivar thought it unseemly to report that he had made 5 million dollars from the French government. Perhaps he just wanted to save those profits for a future date, or move them somewhere else. In any event, he wrote to Berning that, "If this is done I think the five million dollars profit on the French bonds will suffice to cover the shrinkage in the value of the German government bonds."[14]

Other cables from Ivar were simply impenetrable. Here is an example, which one can only imagine Berning trying to decipher:

> Major changes in Continental's portfolio since first of year are that eighty thousand shares in Kreutoll were sold in May with profit of approximately three million dollars. Part of the proceeds of this sale has been used to pay off the debt to Swedish Match Company and the remaining part has been lent to Swedish Match Company. Of the forty million dollars obtained by Continental in April part has been used to pay for German bonds taken over by International Match and about five million dollars have up to now been paid on Turkish business. The balance is temporarily debited Swedish Match Company until end of year when different assets will be taken over by Continental or International Match from Swedish Match Company.[15]

The only response to this kind of cable was: What? Didn't Ivar understand that these companies were separate? He couldn't just move shares, sales, cash, and assets among Kreuger & Toll, Swedish Match, International Match, and Continental. Or perhaps he could. These were either the requests of someone who was blatantly ignoring basic business and accounting principles or someone who was spewing gibberish and had simply gone mad.

When Ivar's lithographer sent the forty-two printed Italian bills, Ivar copied the names "G. Boselli" above "General Director" and "A. Mosconi" above "Minister of Finance" on each of them. Although Ivar had claimed as a child to be skilled at forgeries, his forged signatures on these bills were extremely crude. He even misspelled Boselli several times.

Ivar locked all of the signed bills in the private safe in his office at the Match Palace, along with a draft of an Italian match contract. According to the terms of the contract locked in the safe, Ivar was to acquire a 90 percent stake in Italy's match business in exchange for a loan.[16] The amount of the loan was left blank.

Why would Ivar forge the Italian treasury bills, which now sat unseen in his safe? Did he think the bills might help him raise money in America, by convincing key people that there was proof of an Italian deal? Did he believe the bills would assuage his bankers, who were worried he might not be able to repay his companies' loans? Or did he plan to use the bills to justify entries on his financial statements for 1930, which were about to be closed? Ivar often had included projections of future profits in the income statements he sent to his accountants, both Berning and Wendler. Were the fake bills support for a claim of profits from Italy in 1930?

In late 1930, only Ivar and the assistant manager of the lithography firm knew enough even to ask such questions.

More than a year earlier, during the crash, Ivar had pledged to buy any American Certificates of Kreuger & Toll the syndicate members could not sell for the original purchase price of $28. Now, the due date of the put back right was approaching. During the first six months after the October crash, the prices of Ivar's securities had held reasonably steady and the number of holders of American Certificates actually increased by more than 20 percent.[17] But later in 1930, the prices began to fall.

Near the end of December 1930, several of the banks exercised their put back rights. They requested that Ivar buy a total of 157,036 American Certificates at the issue price of $28, or just under $4.4 million dollars.[18] Donald Durant was in Paris when he got the news that the banks were putting back the certificates.[19] His reaction, on behalf of Ivar, was disbelief and desperation. Durant wanted to do everything possible to avoid the put back.[20] Durant sent word that Ivar soon would be obligated to pay the syndicate members, and he insisted on meeting with Ivar, who also was in Paris at the time.

Ivar couldn't dodge Durant, as he had Berning. Instead, he used the meeting to persuade Durant that everything was fine. Ivar's companies had never been more solid, and this put back obligation was nothing more than a minor nuisance. Ivar simply asked Durant how much money he should send, and said he would send it right away. He seized the in-person meeting as an opportunity to show Durant that his businesses still were doing so well that a 4.4 million dollar payment was a mere trifle.

Ivar rounded the put back obligation up to 5 million dollars and wired that amount to Lee Higginson's account at the Federal Reserve Bank of New York later that day.[21] Ivar said Lee Higg could hold onto the extra 600,000 dollars. He didn't need it right then.

At the same time, Ivar asked Durant to raise yet another 50 million dollars for International Match. Ivar said he planned to use the proceeds from the new issue to repay some of his outstanding debts to Oscar Rydbeck's bank, the Swedish Credit Bank. Interestingly, Ivar also owned 10 percent of Rydbeck's bank. There was a saying that if you owed the bank a thousand dollars, the bank owns you, but if you owed the bank a million dollars, you owned the bank. In Ivar's case, this statement was not just figurative; it was true. He planned to use this new money, in part, to repay himself.

As for a new securities issue, Durant initially said Lee Higginson couldn't possibly do a deal for Ivar, given the declining markets and the lack of detail in International Match's financial statements. Durant's major sticking point seemed to be the fact that International Match's balance sheet included an entry for "marketable securities" in the amount of 77 million dollars with no other description. When Durant asked Berning for help getting details about this entry, Berning bristled. Berning insisted that investors would not object to the missing detail; to the contrary, even given the depressed markets, they were delighted to have another opportunity to invest in Ivar's company.[22] Berning didn't understand why Durant was being such an obstacle.

Berning also prepared what he called a "little memorandum" on those marketable securities. The little memorandum was designed to be seen by Lee Higginson, but not any investors. Berning wrote to Ivar that "This seems to be the only item on which any question would arise and we hope you will agree with the manner in which the matter has been handled."[23] Ivar liked Berning's work. He replied that, "I find the memorandum prepared by you regarding the $77,000,000 security item excellent."[24]

The specific problem Berning addressed was that "marketable securities" included 50 million dollars of bonds from the German deal. There were numerous questions about where those bonds were and what they were worth. Many of Ivar's impenetrable cables to Berning had involved this issue.[25]

In January 1931, Durant finally relented and Lee Higginson agreed to do a deal for International Match, notwithstanding the remaining questions about the company's financial statements. The new issue was in the form of gold debentures, the safest investment International Match had offered investors. The deal resembled the company's first American issue, from 1923.

This time, International Match sold 50 million dollars of ten-year gold debentures at 96 percent of par, to raise a total of $46,125,000. The prospectus said the money was to be used "for investments in Portugal, Norway, Denmark, Poland and Colombia, as well as for the purchase of a match factory in Turkey and/or Turkish and German Bonds."[26] Some of the money would be used to pay down the loan to Rydbeck's bank in Stockholm. In fact, more than half of the money went straight to Continental, Ivar's still somewhat secret subsidiary in Vaduz.

Ivar's bookkeeper and former Kalmar schoolmate Sigurd Hennig was especially perplexed by all this activity. Hennig couldn't figure out how to add up Ivar's income for 1930. Neither could Anton Wendler, Ivar's Swedish auditor. Ivar had transferred funds among his companies frequently throughout the year, and he now seemed to owe Kreuger & Toll the equivalent of about 100 million dollars. Ivar told Hennig he owned numerous other assets that weren't listed on the books yet, including a gold mine at Boliden, and more than 11 million dollars of investments in two American companies, Diamond Match Company and Ohio Match Company. Ivar told him, "There must be something wrong here, Hennig. The money can't have run away, can it?"[27]

When Hennig persisted in questioning some French bonds that appeared to be deposited in a Dutch bank Hennig did not recognize, Ivar finally exploded, "That bank is a good bank. Is this a conspiracy against me? Have you all joined in an attack against me?"[28] Ivar told Hennig and Wendler that, if they had to know, the missing entries were made up for by an Italian deal he had been negotiating. It was top secret. Mussolini had insisted no one should know.

Ivar said he would show the Italian contract and treasury bills to Wendler, and let him decide if they bridged the gap. Ivar no longer trusted Hennig, and would not permit him to see the bills. Wendler went to the Match Palace, entered Ivar's office, and watched as Ivar unlocked the safe and removed a contract. The contract amount was no longer blank. The amount written there was 21 million pounds, triple the missing value. There seemed to be that amount of Italian bills there as well, also signed by the relevant government officials. These bills appeared to represent Ivar's claims on the Italian government, and they were more than enough to cover any discrepancies.

Wendler apparently was satisfied. He told Hennig to make an extra entry on Kreuger & Toll's 1930 financial statements for 7 million pounds. Given that the value of the Italian treasury bills was triple that amount, there remained a 14 million pound cushion for Kreuger & Toll to use during the following year.

Oscar Rydbeck had heard rumors about Kreuger & Toll's deficit, and he also confronted Ivar. Ivar explained that there was no trouble; if there had been, why would Ivar have repaid part of Rydbeck's bank loan? Ivar told his banker in confidence that he had just made one of the biggest deals of his life. In fact, Ivar said, he would need another 35 million dollar loan by April 1931 to cover this secret deal. With the Swedish government's backing, Rydbeck arranged for a small additional loan. That money bought Ivar time until his next dividend payment was due in July. Once again, he had only a few months to raise enough cash, to keep his world from collapsing, and he just narrowly made the deadline.

By now the strain on Ivar was obvious to all of his colleagues and friends. He drank more alcohol than ever before, and he smoked constantly. He spent increasing amounts of time locked in the Silence Room. One assistant who saw Ivar in April 1931 in Paris described him as alternating between moods of depression and mania:

Kreuger was even more depressed than when I saw him the last time in March. It was difficult for him to hide his agitation in my presence, and he completely lost his usual self-control as soon as he thought himself alone. Pacing nervously back and forth in the room, speaking loudly to himself, smoking one cigarette after the other and always ready to rush to the phone, he seemed like a person who was not quite in his right mind. It was terrible to hear his restless steps in the quiet apartment and the sound of his talking to some invisible enemy. As soon as I entered the room he none the less regained control over himself and now seemed calm and collected.[29]

Meanwhile, A.D. Berning continued to help Ivar with positive spin. Berning included in International Match's financial statements substantial gains from various subsidiaries,[30] including Swedish Pulp Company, a significant subsidiary that had generated some skepticism among American bankers.[31] But because Berning and Ernst & Ernst vouched for the profits of Ivar's subsidiaries, those bankers had no way to dispute the accuracy of the financial statements.

With Berning's help, Ivar's reputation in the international markets remained solid. He was still able to borrow money. One major bank, Paribas, wrote in a May 1931 credit report that "Kreuger & Toll enjoys the best reputation and unlimited credit."[32]

By this time, Ivar had fooled just about everyone: the world's smartest bankers and accountants, leading journalists and politicians, and millions of investors in America and throughout Europe. Bluffing these people, and winning, was exhilarating in a way. But Ivar's sources of funds were running out. Now, to get the money he needed to survive, Ivar would need to confront the one bank he had not yet been able to fool: J. P. Morgan & Co.

Ivar had first started buying shares of L. M. Ericsson Telephone Company in 1927, based on A.D. Berning's recommendation. Berning had envisioned a global merger between L. M. Ericsson and International Telephone & Telegraph, known as IT&T.[33] Ivar understood the synergies such a global conglomerate would enjoy. He told a friend, "The telephone, as far as I am concerned, has the same qualities as matches. With the arrangement and management of telephone organizations, I can get State concessions and monopolies just as I can with my little wooden soldiers."[34]

Within a few years, Ivar had acquired control of Ericsson and put Oscar Rydbeck and other friendly directors on Ericsson's board. Ivar then used his control to get something he needed even more than a worldwide telephone monopoly: cash. Ericsson had paid 8 million dollars for part of the German loan and issued 25 million kronor of 5.5 percent debentures in June 1931.[35] After a year under Ivar, Ericsson was hardly the same company. It now had much more debt and was losing money. Still, it had a strong market share, and was an attractive takeover candidate.

Before the 1929 crash, Sosthenes Behn, the president of IT&T, had proposed a merger of his company and Ericsson.[36] At first, Ivar had rejected a deal with IT&T. In part, Ivar wanted to wait to cement control of Ericsson. But Ivar also was skittish about dealing with IT&T, which was represented by J. P. Morgan & Co. Ivar was busy taking over Morgan's lending role in Europe, and the last thing he wanted was to give Morgan's bankers any insight into his business. Two Morgan partners sat on IT&T's board of directors, and Ivar knew they would be digging for information.

In May 1931, though, Ivar succumbed and told Sosthenes Behn he was prepared to discuss a deal. Ivar also sent Berning a coded telegram saying he would "appreciate your getting together as much information as possible about international telephone and telegraph corporation."[37] If Behn thought Ivar might be desperate, he held his tongue. The men agreed to meet in New York, after Ivar stopped in Washington to discuss world affairs once again with President Hoover.

In New York, Ivar met first with Donald Durant. He told Durant about IT&T and, more importantly, the Italian deal, which Ivar insisted Durant must keep secret and refer to only as a deal with "Country X."[38] Ivar informed Durant that, although he appreciated all of Lee Higginson's hard work on his behalf, Ivar would represent himself in the negotiations with Morgan and IT&T.

The talks were to be held at IT&T's headquarters. Ivar stopped by his New York office, which he almost never visited, to prepare. Even after the crash, everything seemed to be in place, including, he was pleased to see, all of the eighteenth-century furniture he had chosen: twin walnut Queen Anne side chairs with a matching lowboy, a William and Mary folding card table with three mahogany and leather Hepplewhite armchairs, and two mahogany desks with inlaid drawer fronts, floral marquetry, and bun feet.[39] It was quiet and formal, just like his apartment at Villagatan in Stockholm. Since the crash, the influences of his wild Norwegian friend Anders Jordahl had become more muted.

During the discussions at IT&T, Ivar sat on one side of the table alone, while Sosthenes Behn sat on the other, flanked by a dozen men, including IT&T's directors and the Morgan partners. Occasionally Ivar would ask a question about IT&T and one of the men from the other side would leave the room for an hour to get an answer. But when someone from IT&T asked a question, Ivar always stayed put and answered from memory.

Ivar's performance during these talks was enormously impressive, and he held forth on a tapestry of topics. According to one source, every night Ivar would stuff his memory with details about some obscure matter, such as Hungarian financial statistics, and the next day he would ensure that the topic came up and then would recite every memorized detail. Someone from IT&T would check the facts, in the hope they could confront Ivar the next day with an exaggeration, but everything Ivar said was correct, to the penny.[40] Later, when Ivar cited precise income figures for one of his companies from memory, it seemed more certain that the men from IT&T were hearing the truth.

Ivar also employed to great advantage the tactic he had used during the luncheon speech he gave to Lee Higginson's partners nearly a decade earlier. When the men from IT&T asked an important question, Ivar would take an uncomfortably long pause, sometimes as much as several minutes, before saying a word in response. According to one person who attended the negotiations, Ivar would

> slowly take out a cigarette, tap the end of it on the table for several minutes, slowly light it, then twirl it around in his fingers and squeeze the tobacco out of the unlit end before he finally tore the end off or crunched the cigarette out. The whole process might take five minutes or more, and then he might repeat it. Nine times out of ten, someone else would break the silence by saying something that would somehow modify the type of answer Kreuger gave. His poise was tremendous.[41]

On June 18, after two weeks of long pauses, Ivar and Behn finally reached agreement.[42] Ericsson would deposit 600,000 shares with Swedish banks in the name of IT&T, and IT&T would write a check for 11 million dollars to Kreuger & Toll.[43] Ivar also agreed that, during the upcoming year, accountants from Price, Waterhouse & Co., the firm that had discovered inaccuracies in Ivar's financial statements during his earlier run-in with Diamond Match, could perform an audit of Ivar's companies in Europe. In fact, Ivar would have agreed to just about anything, as long as IT&T gave him the 11 million dollars upfront. He needed the money right away.

IT&T's check cleared just in time for Ivar to meet the payments due on one of Kreuger & Toll's participating debentures on July 1. Meanwhile, Price Waterhouse's accountants would not come to Sweden until early next year. Ivar still had a few months.

Donald Durant was becoming more of a problem for Ivar. He asked for an annual report that was "more complete than usual" along with a "supplemental memorandum in typewritten form to be used in the greatest confidence by the Guaranty, the City, and possibly by some insurance companies and investment trusts."[44] Durant said other bankers were pestering him every few days to get more details from Ivar. They wanted to send their own men to Sweden.

Even Joseph Swan, the head of Guaranty, who had praised Ivar's put back deal in 1929, was concerned. Durant wrote to Ivar,

> The other day Joe Swan came in with rather a long face and with your report in his hand and said he was a little afraid the situation was getting too big. His attitude intrigued me a good deal because generally Joe Swan has been

very bullish about your securities and has always had an opportunity to talk to you when you are here and I believe has been to see you in Sweden.[45]

Durant told Ivar "I may be over suspicious,"[46] but he still needed some comfort in the form of more details. For example, Durant still did not know the answer to an earlier question about whether Ivar was including unrealized "mark-to-market" profits from his trading activities in International Match's income.[47] Durant's concern was that Ivar could exaggerate the gains from investments the company held but had not yet sold.

Ivar struggled to address Durant's concerns. He began by agreeing to pay Lee Higginson an additional 300,000 dollars a year as a "financial advisor" fee, in addition to the other fees he had been paying. He also tried to use a more personal touch with Durant, and even began signing his notes "Ivar" instead of "Kreuger."

Durant's wedding engagement was a timely opportunity for Ivar to try to restore his credibility. In May, Durant sent Ivar a handwritten note:

Dear Ivar,
I want you to know in advance and for the moment confidentially that I am engaged to Miss Alice Stowell whom I think you have met. We plan to be very quietly married some fine day in the next month.
Sincerely,
Donald.
Have told Krister.

Ivar sent a basket of orchids to Durant's apartment, on East 74th Street, and Donald, Alice, and Ivar had dinner together the next evening.[48]

Ivar must have impressed the new couple. Alice sent a glowing thank you note, and Durant followed up with a letter to let Ivar know he heard "that you called on Mr Hoover while here and that Mr Hoover's recent plan for the improvement of the world is really a creature of your brain."[49] But Ivar's kind gestures and public service didn't stamp out Durant's suspicions. There were too many coincidences. International Match's reported net income was always just enough to pay its dividends. The company had needed 2.35 million dollars to pay dividends each quarter during 1930 and 1931, and its quarterly net income had ranged from 2.36 million dollars to 2.4 million dollars.[50]

International Match earned most of its profits from interest charges on loans to its subsidiaries, particularly Garanta and Continental.[51] Nearly half of International Match's dividend payments were covered by interest on the 17 million dollars "owed to it by Garanta," and still charged at a rate of 24 percent. International Match also had claims of 74.7 million dollars on Continental, apparently related to Italian, Polish, and Spanish loans. The fact that the subsidiaries' interest payments almost precisely matched International Match's earnings couldn't be a fluke.

For some banks, such as National City, these coincidences were too much, and they stopped dealing in Ivar's securities entirely. The other banks collectively sent Durant a seven-page memorandum asking for a "break-down of the balance sheet items" of International Match, Swedish Match, and Kreuger & Toll.[52] Durant reported to Ivar that the banks' request for more information was "of the greatest importance and is rather charged with dynamite."[53]

Yet Ivar ignored the request for two months. When he finally responded, he apologized for the delay, and for the "fall in our securities," and blamed "the constant propaganda which is carried on against our concern. There is hardly one day when there is not a new rumor ... of such a nature as to frighten the investors."[54] Ivar blamed short-term speculation by short sellers – traders who borrowed and sold securities, betting on a decline in prices.

To assuage Durant and the directors of International Match, Ivar sent them a confidential memorandum claiming that International Match's assets included a 17.5 million dollar loan to Poland, a 30 million dollar loan to Italy, a 27.8 million dollar loan to Spain, and a 9.5 million dollar investment in the Diamond Match Company.[55] Ivar cited extensive details about his holdings throughout Europe: two companies in Norway, one in Denmark, and a new match concession in Poland. He also said that Continental owned two companies in Finland, a factory in Estonia, and controlling interests in match factories and other companies in Austria, Czechoslovakia, Latvia, and, most significantly, Italy and Spain. The directors had never seen any documents establishing this ownership. Durant called the memorandum "particularly interesting."[56] The other bankers were surprised by all of the assets in Italy and Spain. No one could tell whether any of Ivar's claims were true.

The memorandum was enough to persuade Ivar's bankers to agree to one last loan. If International Match actually held all of those assets, it was still a relatively low risk proposition. On August 27, 1931, Donald Durant announced that he had formed a syndicate with National City, Bankers Trust, Continental Commercial of Chicago, and Union Trust of Pittsburgh and arranged for a six-month unsecured loan. Payment of 4 million dollars, the full principal amount, would be due on February 27, 1932.[57]

By fall 1931, Berning decided to try to verify all of the numbers Ivar was sending him. Apparently, he finally had become concerned that Ivar's companies couldn't afford to continue to pay high dividends.[58] When he asked Ivar for more information, Ivar rebuffed him at first, saying he "would like to postpone as long as possible."[59] After several inquiries, Ivar reluctantly permitted Berning to return to Stockholm in late 1931 to inspect all of the documents supporting Anton Wendler's Swedish audit.

During that visit, Berning went through several inches of paper for each subsidiary for each year, hundreds of pages that set forth minutiae for each of Ivar's companies. For example, Wendler's dossier on International Match as of December 31, 1930, showed 145.6 million dollars of assets, 56.7 million dollars of "Inter-Company Accounts," and 32.5 million dollars of "Investment in Constituent Companies." There was a mass of supporting detail for each category.[60]

Berning also saw the complete list of International Match subsidiaries, which included many companies he had never even heard of. As Berning ran through the subsidiaries of International Match, which itself was a subsidiary of Swedish Match, he saw a few companies he recognized, such as Continental and Vulcan Match, an American firm. But he hadn't realized that many of International Match's subsidiaries, including Continental, also had subsidiaries. Did their subsidiaries have subsidiaries, too? It was like a corporate family tree from hell, and it extended into obscurity. Here was a partial list:

Continental Investment A.G. and Subsidiaries
Vulcan Match Company, Inc.
Philippine Match Company Ltd
American Turkish Investment Corporation
Compania Mexicana de Cerillos y Fosforos, S.A. and Subsidiary
Handels Kompagniet "Hafnia" A.S. and Subsidiaries
Finska Elektrokemiska A.B.
Nitedals Taend-stikfabrik and Bryn Och Halden Taendstik-fabriker
Drvorez-Barska Tvornica Vrbovsko and Subsidiary.
Bjorneborgs Tandsticks-Fabriks A.B.
"Drava" Zundwaren-Fabrik A.G. and Subsidiary ...

It went on. Details for each subsidiary were included, along with the percentage ownership by International Match. Most of them were 100 percent owned by International Match; the exceptions were Bjorneborgs and "Drava" – whatever those were.

The precision in the financial statements was staggering. Everything seemed official, too. The parcels for each subsidiary were sealed in orange wax with Anton Wendler's signature. Berning worried that when he returned to New York, everyone would ask him one obvious question: Why hadn't he looked through all of this before? He copied down as much detail as he could, and packed his pages of notes to bring home.

Even after Berning finished his document review, Ivar refused to meet in person. Instead, Ivar went to the Grand Hotel and the men communicated through a bizarre room-to-room colloquy, handwriting notes on hotel stationery and passing them back and forth using a messenger.[61]

Just as before, when Berning finally left Stockholm, Ivar immediately sent him cables with important information and requests. One cable to Berning's first-class cabin on *Mauretania* explained that there were numerous mistakes in Anton Wendler's documents. Ivar said he would come to New York to explain everything in a few weeks. Berning hastily responded:

> your message received will hold all papers for your disposal if there is anything I can do in preparation for your arrival regarding telephone or any other special newyork matters which we discussed I would be glad if you will advise me.[62]

Ivar asked Berning to destroy the documents he was taking to New York, and it appears that Berning did.

During the second half of 1931, Ivar's securities plummeted in value, so that they were worth only about a fifth as much in December as they had been in June. The decline weighed on Ivar. He complained to Durant that he and his companies "have been the subject of a deceitful press campaign from ... some twenty black-mailing papers who continually attack our securities."[63] Ivar became increasingly paranoid about short sellers, and he personally bought large volumes of his companies' securities, in an effort to prop up the price. As the short selling of Ivar's companies increased during late 1931, he became increasingly frustrated and ultimately published the following statement:

> On account of the latest fall in the prices of Aktiebolaget Kreuger & Toll debentures and of shares in the companies belonging to that group, I would

like to state that nothing has transpired in these companies that could justify this fall in price. In my opinion, this fall is due to recent developments in European money markets, and to the market situation in general. It must be remembered that the shares and debentures of Aktiebolaget Kreuger & Toll and Swedish Match have a wider international distribution than any other listed securities in the world. It is therefore only natural, that these securities are the first to be used to raise liquid funds abroad. This situation has been utilized by an internationally organized short selling syndicate, which has not hesitated to spread unfounded rumours about the group.[64]

The level of anxiety about Ivar increased during late 1931, as these rumors spread. Some analysts and banks expressed skepticism about Ivar's companies; others said they were near collapse. One major bank, Credit Suisse, declared Ivar a "very dangerous person" and said it would not lend to any of his companies without a guarantee that the money would not be available to Ivar personally.[65] Rydbeck and Svenska Handelsbanken continued to stand behind Ivar, but Rydbeck was increasingly skeptical as well. He had tried to persuade Ivar to cancel his dividends on Kreuger & Toll, with no success. However, Ivar finally conceded that he could not afford to pay shareholders of Swedish Match. He sent them a notice that was alarming in both substance and startlingly vague form:

> The industrial and commercial activities of the Swedish Match Company have produced about the same results for the first half of 1931 as for the similar period the previous year ... The sharp fall in the prices of various government loans that have occurred lately may make it necessary for a large part of the company's profit to be used for write-offs on these securities. With due consideration to this possibility, and bearing in mind the uncertainty of the current state of affairs, the board considers that greater consideration must be given to the liquidity of the company than would otherwise be the case, and has accordingly decided to postpone its final decision regarding the payment of an interim dividend for 1931 until the world economic situation has become somewhat more settled.[66]

The obvious message to investors everywhere who had depended on Ivar was that they had made a mistake. The dividends they were expecting from Swedish Match would not be coming soon, or possibly ever. The subtext to this message was even more alarming: perhaps the rumors about Ivar were true.

Ivar spent late November and early December alone in London and Paris, trying to avoid questions, particularly from Durant and Berning. Even Ivar's friends rarely saw him; Oscar Rydbeck thought Ivar had withdrawn almost entirely from personal relations. Ivar said, "I have no time to bother with people, and besides I want to avoid being influenced by their wrong ideas."[67]

Yet when Ivar was forced to see someone, he couldn't help turning on the charm, insisting all was fine, and even trying to convince them to invest in his companies. During a medical check-up, he persuaded his Paris physician to invest 113,000 dollars in International Match.[68] But most of time he avoided all human contact.

Ivar apparently didn't give up on a deal with Italy, or perhaps Spain, even though he couldn't bear to do the work in person. He assigned Ernst August Hoffman, the loyal ex-bank clerk who had helped him with Continental, to handle what Ivar claimed were ongoing secret negotiations with the Italian government. According to Ivar, Hoffman was in Italy during November "urgently attending important conferences."[69]

Some of Ivar's securities, which had been as high as $863 before the crash, had fallen to half of that in August and then plummeted to nearly $100 by October.[70] Ivar was clearly depressed about the market's loss of confidence. Krister Littorin tried to comfort him. He wrote, "While markets have been particularly bad this week and generally feeling blue I for some unaccountable reason have been unable to shake off a feeling all week that we are approaching a turn or at least a good rest. If we could only stop printing of the newspapers in the world for six months we would get somewhere."[71]

By now, Ivar had delegated most of his day-to-day responsibilities to Littorin, who kept tabs on the markets and monitored their investments in various securities.[72] Littorin met with senior government officials, including the Governor of the Bank of England.[73] When Oscar Rydbeck returned from America even more nervous than before, Littorin came to Rydbeck's bank with Ivar and ran the meeting.[74] Littorin also stepped into Ivar's negotiating shoes: he handled talks with Hungary regarding its 8 million dollar loan, 3 million dollars of which was overdue.[75] He also took over discussions about Ivar's involvement in the American match business.[76]

By Thanksgiving 1931, Durant was begging Ivar to come to New York. He desperately cabled, "Presume you will bring with you figures of all three companies as uptodate and detailed as possible."[77] Durant had seen a report made to National City by a person described as a "good friend who was recently in Sweden," suggesting that Ivar had been scrambling to pay his debts and effectively had been bailed out by Oscar Rydbeck's bank.[78]

Ivar wasn't at the Match Palace, but Krister Littorin intercepted Durant's telegram. Littorin was concerned about Ivar's mental health, and decided not to push Durant's requests too hard. The last time the two ex-classmates had seen each other, a few days earlier, Ivar had frantically demanded that Littorin find an obscure quote from Abraham Lincoln about government borrowing and currency inflation. Then, Ivar abruptly left town.[79] Littorin finally found Ivar locked in his favorite room at the Savoy Hotel in London. With Littorin's help, Ivar responded to Durant that the accusations about a bailout were false, and replied that, "As a matter of fact no Swedish private bank has had to find any money at all for this purpose as I got the money needed from the National Bank."[80]

In fact, the directors of Rydbeck's bank, which *had* bailed out Ivar, were increasingly concerned. They held a private meeting to discuss their largest customer, and asked Rydbeck to have a serious talk with Ivar. But when Rydbeck approached Ivar, everything seemed fine. Ivar said he would be happy to share any details, but didn't have time right then because he was dashing off to Paris for a meeting with British Prime Minister Ramsay MacDonald, German Chancellor Heinrich Brüning, and French Council President Pierre Laval. They had asked him to come advise them about the ongoing financial crisis.[81] Rydbeck must have felt embarrassed to be pushing his pedestrian concerns on such an important man.

Durant, on the other hand, was undeterred. He tried various tactics to get information from Ivar, claiming a large shareholder of Kreuger & Toll thought the share price might be too low,[82] and even sending messages in code, with a separate translation key.[83] Speculators had heard the rumors about Ivar, and were increasing their short sales, which was further depressing the prices of Ivar's companies' securities.

Meanwhile, the sporadic answers Ivar sent to Durant kept changing, and the numbers were inconsistent. First, Ivar would send a set of financial statements; then he would cable "updates" to account for previous errors. These responses were not comforting the partners of Lee Higginson. One cable, which Ivar sent to George Murnane, one of Durant's partners, was particularly unnerving. Ivar wrote, "Naturally the division of the assets between Swedish Match and International Match is somewhat arbitrary but during all these years in any such division we have always carefully guarded that the interests of International Match have in the first line been taken care of and the interests of Swedish Match have always been put in the second place."[84] Why would anyone believe Swedish Match would agree to take "second place" behind the American interests?

The Lee Higginson partners were especially puzzled by International Match's entries for "Deposits with Affiliated Companies" and "Additional Investments." Ivar explained to Murnane that these lines included "assets which logically should be owned by International Match and which are intended ultimately to be owned by that company but which for very strong reasons for the time being rather ought to be carried in the books of Swedish Match Company."[85] With every such word, Ivar's reputation fell. Assets either were owned or not owned. There was no in between. Ivar's latest missives suggested that International Match didn't have any real assets or earnings; instead, the company depended entirely on Ivar's promises.

Ivar repeatedly mentioned "Boliden" in his correspondence with Lee Higginson. The Boliden Mining Company was Ivar's secret treasure and his last hope. Few people knew about the Boliden gold mines, which had been discovered in 1924, in the Norlaand district of Sweden, and were reputed to have the third-largest gold deposits in the world, along with rich veins of silver and other precious metals. Ivar estimated that the gold mines alone would generate more than 8 million dollars a year. He had bought 80 percent of Boliden through Rydbeck's bank for 14 million dollars in 1929, and had tried to sell an interest in Boliden only once, to the Guggenheim family. When the Guggenheims decided not to buy, Ivar maintained his stake, which he determined to keep confidential until it became clear how much precious metal was there.[86]

By the end of 1931, Ivar had known he would need to use his interest in Boliden to raise cash. He went to the Riksbank, Sweden's central bank, in October 1931 and asked for a loan of 40 million kronor (about 10 million dollars). They said yes, but only if he would pledge his Boliden shares as security. Ivar said he was willing to do that but, because of his interlocking accounts, the transfer of shares would be difficult.

Oscar Rydbeck's bank already held the Boliden shares, as security for a different loan. Ivar was sure he could persuade Rydbeck to take German bonds – his only other major asset, from the 1929 Germany deal – as security in place of the Boliden shares. However, International Match held the German bonds. Ivar didn't dare ask anyone in America if they would let him substitute some other asset for the German bonds. They already were asking too many questions about Ivar's intermingled accounts.

Fortunately, Ivar previously had insisted that International Match's German bonds be held outside the United States, at the Deutsche Union Bank in Berlin, and the directors had given him the right to put the bonds there back in 1924. There was the solution. Ivar ordered that bank to transfer the bonds to the Nederlandish Bank, the small Copenhagen bank Ivar controlled. Nederlandish then listed the German bonds in the name of Rydbeck's bank. That switch persuaded Rydbeck to release the Boliden shares to the Riksbank for Ivar's loan. It was a complex quadruple play – German bank to Dutch bank to Swedish bank to Swedish central bank – that secured a 10 million dollar last-gasp loan for Ivar.

What was International Match left with? Ivar needed something of value to give his American company in exchange for the German bonds. Should he use the forged Italian treasury bills? Ivar decided he didn't dare send them to Deutsche Union Bank, to replace the German bonds. Instead, he kept them at the Match Palace, and sent some other bonds, including some real Italian bills he held. Now, Rydbeck's bank held the German bonds, the Riksbank held the Boliden shares, and International Match was left with a potpourri of assets, along with the hope that some day the German bonds would be returned.[87]

On November 23, 1931, Ivar left Stockholm for the last time with the final 10 million dollars he could squeeze from his home country. He had emerged from solitude, once again seemingly energized and hopeful. Ivar saw Ingeborg Eberth, his neighbor at Villagatan, for a concluding visit.[88] She played a few songs on the piano, and found Ivar to be "the same quiet, calm man as always."[89]

Even Sigurd Hennig, the accountant who thought he had discovered a great fraud at Kreuger & Toll, believed Ivar was back on track. Ivar showed Hennig the most recent balance sheet for the company, and explained how the value of the Boliden mines more than made up for any shortcomings elsewhere. Ivar said, "You see, Hennig, the holes are not as big as you seem to think."[90] Ivar also wrote to assure Durant about the "loan against the shares in the Boliden Mine as collateral. These shares as you may know are owned by me privately."[91]

Ivar stopped in Paris for a few weeks, to check on the construction of his new apartment there, and then sailed to New York on *Bremen*, another of his favorite luxury liners. On board, he received an optimistic cable from Krister Littorin, who was worried about Ivar's mood swings, and wanted to encourage positive thoughts. Littorin wrote, "Unbelievable change in sentiment ... rapidly rising market with good volume."[92] The facts told a different story: Ivar's famous B Shares, the ones with 1/1000 of a vote, had risen as high as 449 but now were trading below 100.

Ivar arrived just before Christmas, and the New York papers reported his arrival with the usual fanfare. That day, on the floor of the New York Stock Exchange, Kreuger & Toll shares were the only securities among the fifteen most actively traded to close with a gain. The *Herald Tribune* reported on Ivar's business in America: "It is also expected that he will confer with officials of the International Telephone & Telegraph Company in regard to the IT&T-Ericsson Telephone deal."[93]

11

COMING BACK TO AMERICA

Ivar spent the holidays in New York, and then toured the country in what could be described as either a victory lap or a farewell trip. He saw his friend President Hoover in Washington, and publicly reassured Hoover and the American people about the problems in Europe.[1] He traveled to Chicago, the city where he had found his first job by posing as an architect, and then went on to Boston and Philadelphia. During this trip, he gave rousing speeches to brokers about the future of his companies, and claimed earnings were down just 10 percent from 1930.

Ivar had tried to persuade Kreuger & Toll's board to issue a report announcing high profits, and promising to continue to pay dividends, but Oscar Rydbeck balked. Although Ivar was chairman of the board, the increasingly cautious Rydbeck held some influence among the Swedish directors. They couldn't understand how Ivar could make claims about the company's finances in early January; the accounting books still wouldn't be closed for months. They also didn't understand how Kreuger & Toll could raise enough cash to pay dividends.

Given this dissent, Ivar issued a Kreuger & Toll report under his own name only, explaining that "Stockholm is always interfering with the wording of my statements."[2] The new report estimated net profits for 1931 at 21 million dollars, down from 32.7 million dollars the previous year, but still substantial. Ivar also announced that Kreuger & Toll had acquired Boliden, "one of the largest and richest gold mines in the world."[3] The report bolstered his sales pitches to brokers, some of whom spread word that Ivar's securities were a buy.

Back in New York, Ivar sought to raise more funds backed by Boliden shares. He hoped that no one in America would discover the fact that he already had pledged the Boliden shares to the Swedish central bank for the 10 million dollar loan. But Ivar's efforts failed well before he got to any discussion about whether Boliden shares would be adequate collateral. Increasingly, opinion was turning against Ivar.

Durant still stood behind Ivar and International Match; he had no choice. But he told Ivar there was no chance of another issue on the New York Stock Exchange, or probably anywhere else. America was deep in an economic depression and no one was buying shares of any kind. Simply put, Durant would not be able to raise any more money for International Match. After Durant told Ivar no, Ivar called on Sune Schéle, a Swedish stockbroker in New York who had been Ivar's director of operations in India. Ivar asked about listing the shares of a new company backed by Boliden shares on the Curb Exchange, the place Ivar's first gold debentures had been listed in 1923. But no matter how far Ivar stepped down the prestige ladder, everyone said no. The Americans seemed to be done with investing in Ivar.

Ivar met with Jordahl, his risk-loving Norwegian friend, and they decided to try gambling on stocks to generate some cash to sustain Ivar's companies for a few more months. They didn't want anyone to trace the trades to Ivar or Jordahl; that would lead to even more vicious rumors. They considered trading through Alexis Aminoff, the young Swede who managed Ivar's business in New York, but Aminoff's office was near Lee Higginson's and they worried he might be discovered. Ivar thought for a moment, and then realized he had the perfect surrogate trader, particularly given the season. It was Christmas in New York. Time for Santa Claus.

Sune Schéle introduced Ivar to a well-known New York broker, and Ivar told the man he had a wealthy friend who wanted to speculate on the Curb Exchange. The trades would be executed through Hirsch Lilienthal and Barr Cohen, two other US brokers. Ivar would send 50,000 shares of Kreuger & Toll as collateral for whatever this man wanted to buy. Ivar said the man's name was Karl Lange.

The broker made a few calls and found that a man called Lange was listed as the operator of a restaurant in Stockholm. He was described as stocky, with a white beard. The broker immediately phoned Durant, who called Ivar.

"Ivar, do you know a man named Karl Lange? Is he a responsible fellow?" Durant asked. Durant was losing faith in Ivar's companies, but he apparently wasn't as suspicious about Ivar's Swedish friends. After Ivar vouched for Lange, Durant informed the broker that "you have nothing to worry about."[4]

The day after Christmas, Ivar sent a cable to Krister Littorin:

Please have Lange deposit 50,000 American certificates in favor of Hirsch Lilienthal and 50,000 in favor of Barr Cohen and Company and ask Lange to send separate telegrams to each of them to deliver them to Schéle. Have explained to Donald that Lange got a credit against them. Please telegraph Schéle.[5]

Lange immediately sent instructions from Stockholm to the two brokers. He said he wanted to use all of the money to buy Kreuger & Toll shares. With Lange's purchases, Ivar could prop up the shares of Kreuger & Toll in the United States. The Americans would see the purchases as a surge in demand for Ivar's shares.

But the brokers saw through the scheme immediately and called the bluff. They responded that Lange was welcome to buy any shares he liked – that is, any shares except those of companies Ivar controlled. When Lange didn't place any orders, the brokers returned the collateral. Kreuger & Toll shares continued to plummet in value.[6]

In early 1932, several men from Price Waterhouse arrived in Stockholm to inspect Ericsson's earnings, as Ivar had agreed they could during his negotiations with IT&T, the talks that had led IT&T to give him a check for 11 million dollars. It didn't take the accountants long to find discrepancies. Ivar had represented that Ericsson had 6 million dollars of "cash in hand and in banks." Price Waterhouse discovered that the Swedish term for this entry translated as "cash, bankers and on deposit." The difference was crucial. Ericsson didn't actually have 6 million dollars of cash; instead, that cash was "on deposit" at Kreuger & Toll. Ericsson had some German government bonds as security, but those had declined in value and were hardly the same as cash.

The IT&T directors called on their bankers from J. P. Morgan. There was no question what Morgan would say, particularly given the previous tensions between Jack Morgan and Ivar. As Morgan recommended, the directors of IT&T immediately sought to rescind the contract with Ivar. They wanted IT&T's 11 million dollars back, and they jumped at the chance to return the Ericsson shares, which had declined in value since June.

On Tuesday, February 16, Ivar begged Littorin to come up with some money. He wrote,

Arrangements I thought would produce amount necessary for acceptance credit fell through. It is vital avoid default tomorrow. This should be made clear to banks. If absolutely impossible have funds telegraphed tomorrow then company should cable a statement explaining delay and stating that money will be wired following day. If nothing is possible then wish company to cable a statement explaining how it proposes to meet the obligations.[7]

Littorin managed to persuade a few banks to extend a brief credit line. But the fact that International Match would survive another few days didn't sway anyone from Price Waterhouse, J. P. Morgan, or IT&T. On Friday, February 19, 1932, Sosthenes Behn met with Ivar in New York to deliver the bad news: their deal was off. Behn wanted his 11 million dollars.

If Ivar was upset, he didn't show it. With his best poker face, he responded calmly that it was merely a translation error. The German bonds were there in place of the cash temporarily; Ericsson had a short-term loan to Kreuger & Toll, and would soon receive the cash back. Didn't the IT&T directors also see that Ivar had personally guaranteed Ericsson's obligations? Ivar insisted that there was nothing to worry about. Nevertheless, he said he would rescind the agreement if that was what IT&T wanted.

It was. Sosthenes Behn accepted a written satisfaction from Ivar promising to repay IT&T 11 million dollars in cash before September.[8]

Ivar obviously didn't have 11 million dollars. Nor did he have a chance of raising any more money. In four days, Swedish Match would need to repay a 2 million dollar loan. Then, more interest payments would come due. Without a miracle, Ivar's companies soon would be in default.

That weekend, Ivar acted like a man who didn't think his businesses would survive. He frantically cabled relatives in Sweden, instructing them as to how to divide various securities among the members of his family. He wired Krister Littorin to arrange delivery of millions of dollars of debentures to Anders Jordahl, presumably so Ivar would have something of value to distribute to friends in the United States.[9]

As Ivar sent these telegraphs continuously for hours, he resembled the energetic and focused man who had amazed the passengers peering into *Berengaria*'s radio shack back in 1922. Then, during his first trip to woo Lee Higginson in New York, he had merely been pretending, putting on a carefully planned show. But now, Ivar's actions were not planned. This was no act; this mania was real.

Ivar seriously contemplated suicide during this time.[10] One visitor said he noticed a shotgun in an umbrella stand at Ivar's Park Avenue apartment. Ivar sent Karin Bökman a letter with three 10,000-dollar banknotes, and wrote that because his business prospects were not good he wanted to leave her something "while he still had the opportunity" – he ended the letter, "Goodbye and thank you."[11] Ivar refused all visitors, saying he was tired and ill. At one point, his housekeeper saw him muttering financial figures incoherently and persuaded him to lie down.

By Sunday, February 21, Ivar was a wreck.

Durant heard the bad news about IT&T, but had been unable to reach Ivar. That afternoon, he finally decided to visit Ivar at his apartment. The 4 million dollar loan he had arranged for Ivar six months earlier would be due in a few days. Durant wanted a witness, so he asked George Murnane, who also knew about the failed Ericsson–IT&T deal, to join him. Durant waited for Murnane to attend Sunday church services, and then they walked to the southeast corner of 74th Street and Park Avenue. They paused in front of 791 Park, Ivar's building. The sturdy two-story base and arched windows hid what was crumbling inside.

Durant and Murnane rode the elevator to the ten-room penthouse. Ivar had bought the apartment in 1927, around the time of the French deal, and he had spent every fall there since then. The roof garden was one of the quietest spots in the city, due to a high brick parapet and a copse of willow trees Ivar had planted. The novelist Edna Ferber, who would take over the apartment in a few months, called it an "unbelievable country house in the sky."[12]

A servant led them to the right. Durant had remembered the dining room as being very bright, with a silver chandelier and red lights in the cornices. But everything was dark now. Silver plate was stacked on a long, wide sideboard, near where the Prince of Sweden had once stood during a party. The paintings by Dutch masters – Van Ruysdael, Van der Werff, Brueghel, and even a small self-portrait by Rembrandt, works that Douglas Fairbanks, Greta Garbo, and Mary Pickford had once admired – hung in shadow. Ivar's gramophone, which had entertained so many world leaders, was silent.

Durant and Murnane entered the library and walked past Ivar's large writing desk and the bookcases filled with some of his letters and his collection of volumes on Napoleon. A small adjacent alcove, with no windows, contained Ivar's collection of Rembrandt etchings, the third largest in the world. On one wall of the library was a Rubens painting of some satyrs. On the ceiling was a painting on silk, which could be lit from above. But this painting, too, was dark.

The men found Ivar seated in a corner of the library facing Park Avenue, on a slightly raised platform near a curved bench with a view of the skyline.[13] Although it was midday, he was wearing yellow silk pajamas and a purple silk dressing gown. Murnane described the scene:

> We found him in a terrible state. He was almost unrecognizable as he sat huddled in a chair in front of the fireplace. He talked in jumps, with his hand to his head, and then paused for minutes at a time. It seemed unreasonable to discuss anything with him. "I'm so tired that I just can't seem to get down to anything," he said. He was in a very nervous state. That is what alarmed us so – it was not like him.[14]

Durant called Ivar's doctor, Joseph Wheelright, a respected physician who also had several Morgan partners as patients. Ivar managed to dictate a cable to Littorin, which Durant sent.[15] Otherwise, Ivar was silent. Durant and Murnane went out to the garden to wait until the doctor arrived.

During earlier visits, Durant had walked with Ivar along the flagstone path that wound through the rock garden and among the fountains and willow trees. The path wasn't long, but it was a unique spot for the east side of Manhattan. Ivar had enjoyed being able to stroll past many of his favorite plantings without leaving the building. He knew the scientific names for every one: a grape arbor thirty feet long, an eighteen-inch circumference peach tree, espaliered apple trees, rhododendrons, wisteria, ivy, roses, lilac bushes, iris, forsythia, strawberry plants, and rhubarb. Edna Ferber later remarked, with surprise, that the trees actually "bore fruit in this bizarre Eden."[16]

Durant and Murnane nervously discussed what might happen if Ivar didn't recover. How had Lee Higg become so exposed to one man? Were they ruined? As the two men walked back on the garden path, they had no answers. The golden heads of the jonquils would not emerge for a few months. The plants were as quiet as Ivar had been.

Inside, Dr Wheelright diagnosed cardiac fatigue. He prescribed some sedatives and said Ivar should rest. During the next three days, Ivar would cycle through episodes of mania and depression. When the drugs were working, he would simply sit and stare into space. But when the medication wore off, he would stand and shout, "I'm losing my mind, I can't remember, I can't think." He placed dozens of emergency telephone calls. He imagined knocks at the door. He answered the phone even though it hadn't rung. He sent cables to imagined addresses in Amsterdam, Berlin, Paris, Stockholm, and Warsaw.[17]

And then he collapsed. His New York assistant, Alexis Aminoff, who visited one evening, described Ivar as "a deplorable sight."[18]

While Ivar suffered in New York, Krister Littorin and Sigurd Hennig rummaged for funds in Stockholm. They went to banks, the finance ministry, and the Riksbank, but everyone wanted fresh collateral before they would lend more money. That evening the men went to the Match Palace to search for something of value to pledge. At first, they found nothing in Ivar's office. Then, Littorin noticed that Ivar's safe, which he had thought was just for show, was closed and locked. Ivar had entrusted his assistant, Karin Bökman, with the combination, so Littorin called Miss Bökman to open it.

Inside the safe, Littorin found three envelopes filled with Italian treasury bills. He couldn't believe it. Hennig was astonished, too. These bills resolved everything! Why hadn't Ivar mentioned them before? The bills were not pledged, so they could be used as collateral for a loan. Littorin added up the face amounts of the treasury bills. They were worth about 100 million dollars, much more than they needed. It seemed that Ivar, and they, were saved.

Littorin grabbed one of the working phones on Ivar's desk and called the prime minister of Sweden, Carl Gustav Ekman. Ivar had supported Ekman with a large political donation. Now, it was time for the Prime Minister to return the favor. Ekman was delighted to hear about the Italian bills, and said the government would provide enough support for the necessary loans. With that promise, a few Swedish banks were willing to lend Ivar enough money to survive until March. Littorin signed loan documents with the Swedish Central Bank that weekend, so that they would send Lee Higginson 1.2 million dollars by Monday morning.[19]

Littorin cabled the good news to Ivar, who was relieved, at least at first. However, as a condition for the new loans, the bankers had demanded that Ivar come to Europe to meet them, explain his companies' financial status in detail, and answer all of their questions. Ivar saw that it would be almost impossible to avoid the meeting. He needed to prepare some compelling answers during the next two weeks. Perhaps the Italian bills would be enough.

Meanwhile, Littorin began to prepare for the bankers' questions. On Thursday, February 25, Littorin relayed to Ivar that "Country X" – presumably Italy – was the solution to the problem of the missing German bonds, the ones Ivar had transferred out of International Match's account in order to free the Boliden shares for a loan. Littorin said the German "bonds have been exchanged against corresponding value of securities from country X. We have not advised New York yet as we wanted to await your arrival before definitely formulating minutes of the meeting."[20]

The 4 million dollar loan Lee Higginson had arranged six months earlier would be due in two days. In an apparent moment of clarity, Ivar told George Murnane, the Lee Higginson partner, that he secretly owned 350,000 shares of Diamond Match, the American match company, and could pledge those shares as collateral. Ivar also said he was expecting payments from Spain soon. With those promises, and some additional collateral, Lee Higginson and its syndicate agreed to extend their 4 million dollar loan for another three months.[21] They didn't have much of a choice.

When Berning learned about Ivar's promises and the Germany-for-Country X swap, his response was meek.[22] Berning timidly wrote to Ivar about some technical accounting problems of Swedish Pulp Company, in the hope he could secure a meeting to discuss more important issues. Berning said, "I do not know whether or not you wish to discuss this while you are here in New York. If you care to do so and have the time, I would be pleased to be available at your convenience. Otherwise, I will await your further wishes."[23] When Ivar didn't respond, Berning went to Ivar's apartment, but was turned away.[24] Berning knew he was running out of options, but he also saw that, if Ivar's companies collapsed, every finger would point at him.

After two more days, a combination of Dr Wheelright's sedatives, some rest, and the continuation of what apparently passed as good news from Littorin led Ivar to recover. Ivar finally called Rydbeck and agreed to meet with all of his bankers on March 12. Littorin was "glad to learn from Oscar that you are prepared meet him in Paris. Also happy over cable from Donald that you have recovered from your illness and feel fit again."[25]

Littorin sent his final cable to Ivar in New York on March 2, 1932, exactly fifty-two years after Ivar had been born in Kalmar. Littorin wrote, simply, "All good wishes for your birthday."[26]

Before sailing for New York, Ivar had called Isaac Marcosson and arranged for a last round of interviews, this time at Marcosson's apartment.[27] This was Ivar's last shot at preserving a legacy, and he once again chose Marcosson as his exclusive conduit.

Since the snub by *Time*, Ivar had become even more isolated and refused nearly all contact with the media. Before his breakdown, he had given a talk at the Bankers Club, but when the *Wall Street Journal* asked to publish the talk in its entirety, Ivar said no.[28] Likewise, when Karl Bickel, the president of

United Press, learned that Ivar was in New York, he wrote begging for Ivar's "reactions to the present situation." Bickel had met several times with President Hoover, and he praised Ivar's prescience on issues "you saw clearly months before most of them at the capital began to dimly comprehend."[29] But again, Ivar refused the interview. Ivar would rely entirely on Marcosson.

The man who arrived at Marcosson's apartment at 119 East 19th Street bore little resemblance to the real Ivar, if there still was such a thing. Marcosson didn't know Ivar well enough to see how much his behavior was out of character.[30]

Previously, Ivar had rarely smoked, unless he thought it would serve some social purpose. Now, he smoked before, during, and after lunch, putting down a half-finished cigarette and then lighting a fresh one. Although Ivar generally didn't eat much food or drink alcohol, particularly at lunch, he demonstrated a hearty appetite for Mrs Marcosson's cooking. She made a heavy cheese and bacon dish, and, instead of nibbling at the edges as he typically would, Ivar devoured his portion and asked for an extra helping, along with a large pewter mug of beer. After he ate the second portion, he rushed to the kitchen to congratulate Mrs Marcosson on the dish. They decided to call it Soufflé à la Kreuger. Ivar returned to the apartment for five more interviews, and five more lunches, and she served their special dish each time.

Ivar had always been a charming guest, and he put on an urbane show for the Marcossons. But anyone who knew him well would have seen a new person. One of Ivar's most consistent traits since childhood had been that he rarely laughed. Yet now he was suddenly a comedian, relaying humorous anecdotes throughout the day and cackling after the punch lines. When the Marcossons invited Nigel Bruce, the English actor, to one of the lunches, Ivar and Bruce traded jokes for hours.

Throughout the interviews with Marcosson, Ivar was prolific with detail about his businesses. One of the first things he told Marcosson was, "I am no Stinnes," referring to Hugo Stinnes, the German industrialist and politician who owned thousands of companies and manufacturing plants. Ivar said, "The Stinnes *Konzern* was a jumble of unrelated properties without unified direction. What I have acquired bears directly on match production and distribution."[31]

According to Ivar, by 1932 he had 225 subsidiaries. He had operations in every civilized country except Russia, and he manufactured three-quarters of the world's matches. Ivar had secured match monopolies in twenty-four countries. During seven years, he had loaned almost 300 million dollars to

European governments. Ivar's loans had helped borrower governments repair their countries. The Romanian government stabilized its currency after the world war. The Latvian government purchased food and essentials, including seed grain. The Estonian government built railroads. The Greek government repatriated thousands of refugees. The French government moored its currency to a fixed exchange rate, to prevent a repeat of the cycle of depreciation and hyperinflation that had hit Germany a few years earlier.

Although Ivar insisted he was no Stinnes, his organization extended well beyond matches. Marcosson was convinced that Ivar had a unique vision, a flair for organization, and an uncanny sense of salesmanship in many new businesses. Ivar's phone company, Ericsson, had factories in a dozen countries and monopoly concessions in five. Ivar's mining company, Boliden, controlled the Swedish output of precious metals and ore. Ivar also owned a fifth of the Grängesberg iron mines in central Sweden. His sulphite company, Swedish Pulp, was the largest producer of that compound. Ivar also owned banks in Paris, Warsaw, Berlin, and Amsterdam, as well as newspapers, office buildings, apartment houses, and film companies throughout the world.

Ivar insisted he had no ambition to become the richest man in the world. Indeed, Marcosson said Ivar expressed the utmost contempt for personal wealth and told him, "Money, as such, means nothing to me. I cannot tell you how much I am worth – I don't care."[32] Oscar Rydbeck, the Swedish banker, had claimed Ivar was the third richest man in the world, but Ivar neither confirmed nor denied it.[33] It simply didn't matter.

When Ivar finally said goodbye, Marcosson didn't notice anything unusual. He didn't see any inconsistencies in Ivar's personality. When friends later asked about Ivar's behavior during the interviews, Marcosson replied, "Except for the fact that he smoked more cigarettes than usual he was the same serene, impassive Kreuger that I had known in the years before." Marcosson couldn't believe Ivar had just been ill, or that he had considered suicide. According to Marcosson, Ivar "always gave the impression of not having a nerve in his physical make-up. It was inconceivable therefore that he could have succumbed to a sudden crack-up and, in tabloid parlance, ended it all."[34]

When Ivar left, Marcosson immediately began drafting his article on Ivar for the *Saturday Evening Post*. The article was scheduled to appear in a few weeks. It would describe their six lunch meetings, Ivar's last social engagements in America, and his final attempt to set forth his case. The bulk of the words would be Ivar's, not Marcosson's. Ivar would hold forth on foreign policy, the lessons of the depression, and a range of macroeconomic issues. At the end of the article, Marcosson would quote Ivar saying, "I feel hopeful regarding the immediate future."[35]

Shortly after his last interview with Isaac Marcosson, Ivar withdrew 60,000 dollars of cash from his American bank accounts and left New York on the *Ile de France*.[36] Alexis Aminoff rode with him to the dock in a taxi. They stopped at a news stand where Ivar bought ten copies of the *Saturday Evening Post* for a nickel each. Perhaps Ivar was in a confused state, and thought Marcosson's article already would be in print. But it was much too early. Aminoff paid the $2.20 cab fare and said goodbye.[37]

For Ivar, the trip across the Atlantic was simultaneously liberating and imprisoning. He shared Greta Garbo's views of ocean travel: "The sea is wonderful. Nowhere does one feel so free! At the same time one is caught – there is no escape. Then, in port, one is free to go, and the sense of freedom is gone."[38] Ivar certainly was caught. His escape hatches had closed. As the *Ile de France* left port, and he watched Manhattan recede, Ivar must have understood that he was trapped. When he arrived in Europe, there would not be very many places to go.

The boat was full of bankers, including Durant, and the mood on board generally was bleak. The stock market had been falling for more than two years. Thirteen million Americans were unemployed. Concerns about global terrorism were high, and there recently had been several attempts to assassinate important leaders of international finance. Finally, Jack Morgan's paranoia was justified. Two friends of Tom Lamont, Morgan's partner, had been shot dead in recent months, allegedly by Japanese nationalists who were responding to speculation against the yen.

The bankers on board were suspicious of Ivar, and kept close tabs on him. One Belgian banker closely followed and reported on Ivar's moods. Morgan's legal advisor also was a passenger on the *Ile de France*, accompanied by four Morgan "detectives."[39]

These men watched Ivar vacillate during the trip. One moment he was brooding in his cabin, mumbling nonsense to Donald Durant. An hour later he was dancing with Sonja Henie, a 13-old Norwegian girl who had just won the gold medal in women's skating at the Lake Placid Olympics. Ivar spent several hours each day on the deck shooting skeet, staring blankly as the shattered clays disappeared into the waves below.[40] But he also spent hours discussing financial matters with prominent business people and economists, including Bernard Baruch and the British academic Sir Arthur Salter.[41] At one point, he cabled Karin Bökman that his thoughts of suicide had arisen only temporarily and were now gone. Yet hours later, he sent his brother-in-law instructions to go to his apartment to retrieve some shares Ivar claimed belonged to his father and should be returned to him right away.

Although A.D. Berning had wanted to sail to Europe, his partners at Ernst & Ernst said he was needed in New York, so he tracked Ivar from there. The Ernsts were concerned about how the problems at Ivar's companies might affect their firm. While Ivar was aboard *Ile de France*, Berning sent invoice #14400 from Ernst & Ernst to Swedish Match in Stockholm. Berning included an item in the amount of $12,750 for services in "making detailed survey of accounting organization and procedure of subsidiary companies of SVENSKA CELLULOSA A.B.," one of Ivar's subsidiaries. Berning also requested reimbursement of $5,992.92 of cash expenses. It was the largest invoice Berning had ever sent Ivar. Berning must have wondered whether Ivar would be able to pay any of the money he owed Ernst & Ernst.

Ivar reached Paris at 11 a.m. on the morning of March 11, 1932, and took a taxi to his apartment at 5 Avenue Victor Emmanuel III.[42] He walked up the three flights of stairs, and greeted Jeannette Barrault, his housekeeper of four years. She thought Ivar looked worn and tired.

Krister Littorin was waiting inside. Littorin had just arrived in Paris that morning. Several of Ivar's assistants would join them soon, including Karin Bökman, Ivar's bookkeeper Sigurd Hennig, and his Swedish accountant Anton Wendler. Littorin put his arm around Ivar's shoulder, and exclaimed, "By Jove, it's nice to see you again after all this time, Ivar."[43] Ivar nodded softly, and they sat in the kitchen to have lunch.

Littorin warned Ivar that the Swedish government was investigating his personal and business finances. While Ivar had been in New York, Swedish officials had procured search warrants and collected many of Ivar's important documents. Auditors already were scouring the books of Kreuger & Toll and Swedish Match. Most importantly, Littorin told Ivar, the authorities were asking questions about "those Italian bonds."

When Littorin mentioned the Italian bonds, Ivar merely stared into the distance. He hardly moved when Bökman, Hennig, and Wendler arrived to brief him on the investigation. They had been responding to various warrants and requests, particularly to questions about the Italian treasury bills Littorin and Hennig had found in the Match Palace safe just a few days earlier.

Ivar was obviously exhausted, so they treated him gently. Hennig was the first to mention the Italian treasury bills. He said they didn't understand the details about the treasury bills, and asked Ivar for some specifics: "Has interest on these bills ever been paid? To which accounts was it credited?"[44]

Ivar seemed far away. He remained silent for several minutes, and then mumbled that the Italian bills were locked in a safe in Stockholm. Finally, he answered, as if he was repeating rehearsed lines from a play: "Yes, I collected the payments and credited the dividend account myself. Everything is in order." Then he got up to leave the room.

When Ivar returned, a few minutes later, Hennig asked, "Why is it that these bills were never stamped?"

Ivar again rose and left the room without saying a word. Hennig whispered to his colleagues, "There is a lot here that I cannot understand." Ivar paced the hall a few times. He didn't want to be the next one to speak.

Hennig continued to press Ivar for answers. "But where did the 400 million kronor come from which you paid Italy for these bills?" Again, Ivar was silent. Hennig couldn't take the suspense any more. He recalled Ivar's childhood schemes – stealing exam answers, forging signatures – and feared the worst.

Hennig stood and finally asked the question everyone had been avoiding. "I say, Ivar, are these Italian bills genuine?"

Ivar's face took on a tortured expression during a painfully long pause. He then stared at his former classmate and answered, "Yes, they are genuine."

It was now shortly before 4 p.m., and they all left the apartment together. Littorin and Ivar had an appointment with Oscar Rydbeck at the Hôtel Meurice, the spot he had recommended to Katharine von Rosenberg, the woman he had dined with on *Majestic* several years earlier. The concierge greeted Ivar on his way out, and immediately saw that something was wrong. Ivar usually pressed a 10 franc note into her hand, and, if her children were there, patted them on their heads. Today, Ivar walked right past, staring blankly, saying nothing. Instead of hailing a taxi, as he usually did, Ivar walked toward the Seine.[45] Krister Littorin quietly followed.

Oscar Rydbeck got straight to business. He wanted to discuss Ivar's mounting debts, and he made it clear that the Swedish Credit Bank couldn't lend him any more money.[46] When Rydbeck asked if Ivar could raise money to repay his Swedish bankers by pledging the Italian treasury bills as collateral, Ivar responded that he already had promised not to pledge them.

Rydbeck suggested, "Can't we do a deal with the Italian government? Couldn't we resell them the bills at a discount?"

Ivar replied, "Yes, maybe, but it will take time. I will go to Italy to see about it, but first I want to return home to Stockholm for a while."

Rydbeck emphasized that Ivar needed to do a new monopoly deal soon. Rydbeck's bank, and his career, depended on it. He invited the men to stay for dinner, but Ivar said he was tired and wanted to go to bed early. He had some important letters to write and needed to phone New York.

As they walked outside, Littorin also suggested they have dinner, but Ivar refused. He told Littorin, "Come by early tomorrow morning so we can talk before the meeting." Ivar's bankers were scheduled to meet at the Hôtel du Rhin at 11 a.m. The two men said goodbye at about six o'clock.

12

DEATH IN THE AIR

Later that evening, a man in a black overcoat appeared at Gastine-Rennette, a firearms shop at 39 Avenue Victor Emmanuel III, a few steps south of the Champs-Elysées.[1] He pushed open the door, stepped in from the Paris fog, and said he wanted to buy a gun.[2]

Antoine Bervillier, the 70-year-old clerk, didn't recognize the man, at least not at first. Bervillier was accustomed to selling guns at night to shady characters, most of whom didn't want to be recognized. The man in the overcoat seemed to be just another customer, nothing out of the ordinary. Besides, the wizened Bervillier had learned long ago not to ask too many questions.

The man asked to see pistols, but when Bervillier brought some out, he shook his head, insisting that he needed something bigger. "*Plus gros, plus gros,*" he repeated as Bervillier showed him pistol after pistol.[3]

Finally, Bervillier brought out the most powerful semi-automatic he had, a new 9 mm service pistol the French military had just commissioned from John Browning. He called it GP, for *Grande Puissance*. Ultimately, ninety-three nations would adopt a version of this weapon for military sidearm issue.[4] But back in March 1932, the Browning was more of an experiment, an extravagant weapon not many people had seen, or could afford.

Bervillier clicked the safety catch and released the firing mechanism. He showed the man how a new cartridge would automatically settle into the chamber, in case a second shot was needed. Given the Browning's muscle, that wasn't likely.

The man weighed the gun in his hands, and admired its heft. It was expensive, modern, and powerful. For his purposes, it was perfect.

French law required an official record of the purchase. As the man instructed, the clerk wrote down his information. The man spelled the name, instead of saying it: "I-V-A-R K-R-E-U-G-E-R."

"*Was it possible?*" Bervillier must have thought. "*The incredible Ivar Kreuger?*" Just fifty-two years old, Ivar was among the most distinguished and influential men in the world. Stocks and bonds of his companies were the most widely held securities in America, and the world.[5] He was known globally as one of the handful of savvy businessmen who had survived, and maybe even profited from, the 1929 crash. He was the leading lender to Europe who had helped France's economy recover.

Ivar was a celebrity, too. Photos of Ivar had been published in virtually every major magazine and newspaper. *Vanity Fair* was begging him to sit for a shoot with Edward Steichen, the renowned photographer. A full-length feature movie, *The Match King*, based on Ivar's life, would be released in a few months. A short film of him motorboating with Mary Pickford and Douglas Fairbanks was already being shown in theaters – the 1930s version of a movie preview – along with news clips about the tensions in Germany and the declining global economy. *The Match King* would depict Ivar's life as the American dream. But even before the movie was out, many people already knew much of the story.

If Bervillier read the local papers, he would have known that Ivar had just arrived from New York on the *Ile de France*. But he could not have possibly imagined how much trouble Ivar was in. If Bervillier had known any of the details, he might not have sold a gun to this man. He might not have obliged when the man asked for four boxes of cartridges, twenty-five per box. But the old clerk, and the world, were still in the dark. Bervillier took the cash, and watched the man hide the purchases within the folds of his overcoat, walk out the door, and turn south, away from the Champs-Elysées. He was headed toward Ivar Kreuger's apartment, at 5 Avenue Victor Emmanuel III, a block away.

According to the concierge at Ivar's building, he received two visitors during the late evening: a man who did not stay long, and a young woman who did. One version of the facts put John C. Brown, a Morgan employee, at Ivar's apartment late that night. It is unclear what Brown would have done, except to tell Ivar his fate was sealed. According to another, perhaps consistent, version, a Finnish girl who occasionally accompanied Ivar on his European trips visited him at an even later hour and spent the night. She was about the age Ivar's first love had been when she died, more than thirty years earlier.

The next morning, Krister Littorin arrived around 9:30 a.m., and found Ivar dressed, but looking even more tired than he had the previous afternoon. According to Littorin, Ivar mentioned the Finnish girl, who had just left. Ivar and Littorin had switched roles since engineering school. Back then, Ivar had been awkward with women. His lines about the latest performance at the Stockholm Opera House or Royal Swedish Ballet caused them to yawn or run away. Today, he said the same things and they jumped into his bed. No woman ever poked fun at Ivar's obsession with flowers, or even mentioned his stunted left index finger. Now, Littorin was the cautious sidekick, and Ivar was the ladies' man.

Littorin later testified that the two men talked about the future. Ivar spoke in Swedish, rather than English, as he typically did with Littorin. Ivar assured Littorin that he had rested enough, and was prepared for the important meeting. Ivar didn't say whether he had made any decisions about the future.

Littorin asked about a forecast Ivar had given to Lee Higginson, whose partners wanted to know if Ivar's companies had as much cash now as he had predicted they would. Ivar responded softly that, "It was probably not a good idea to give them this forecast." Littorin tried to assure Ivar. He said, "Whatever you have done, whatever you may have said and whatever you may have written, you must realize that you are surrounded by friends who wish you well and who want to help you put things right."[6]

After forty-five minutes, Karin Bökman arrived. Ivar said he needed her to take some dictation. Littorin reminded Ivar that many of his good friends and colleagues, including some of the most powerful bankers in the world, would be waiting at the Hotel du Rhin. Ivar replied, "Krister, I may be about ten minutes late. I have some other people to see first." Littorin said Ivar shouldn't keep them waiting too long, and Ivar promised to do his best.[7]

At 10:45 a.m., Miss Bökman left for the Hotel du Rhin with a thick envelope Ivar had just pressed into her hand. According to Bökman, Ivar's final words to her had been that she should pack her bags and go directly to Stockholm, where he would try to meet her. She thought about the suicide note Ivar had sent from New York just a week earlier. None of this made any sense.

A few minutes after she embraced her boss for the last time, just as the meeting at the Hotel du Rhin was about to begin, a telegram boy was seen making a delivery to 5 Avenue Victor Emmanuel III. This boy was the last person to report seeing Ivar Kreuger alive.

In a suite at the Hotel du Rhin, a dozen anxious men were pacing the floor.

Krister Littorin assured everyone that Ivar would be there soon, but Oscar Rydbeck and Donald Durant were concerned. The men whispered when they spoke, as if they were concerned someone outside the door might hear the truth about Ivar. Some of them referred to Ivar as "Oak," a code name. It was the first time they could remember him being late.

Littorin tried to calm the men by mentioning that, after the meeting at the Hotel du Rhin, he and Ivar were planning to visit the new offices Ivar was building for his French businesses, a slightly smaller version of the Match Palace. The original façade of his building was a "Monument National," and could not be altered, but inside Ivar was constructing a massive modern complex, stretching down the Rue du Faubourg St Honoré. Cases of colored wood from Sweden had been sent for the panels and walls, but had not yet been unpacked. Ivar was to have a flat on the top floor, with the roof divided between a winter and a summer garden.[8] Surely, Ivar would not be planning such an extravagant construction project if he were in serious financial distress?

Karin Bökman arrived at the hotel and waited in the vestibule. She had no news for the men, but confirmed that Ivar should be on the way. As she sat, she must have wondered what Ivar would do. Should she worry? Should she leave now for Stockholm? She felt the envelope from Ivar in her bag, still unaware that it contained stacks of crisp Swedish bills.

Back on Wall Street, the lights were just going on at the New York Stock Exchange, and traders were preparing for the Saturday morning trading session. American Certificates of Kreuger & Toll were worth about $5 each, well below their initial value of $28, but a decent price given the market's doldrums, the wave of recent skepticism about Ivar, and the increased short selling of his securities. No one on the Exchange floor was supposed to know about the meeting taking place in Paris. Yet during the previous two days, selling of Kreuger & Toll securities inexplicably had increased. The spike in trading was suspicious. Apparently, someone was making a very large bet that the prices of the company's securities soon would plummet.

After another half an hour, Krister Littorin phoned Ivar's apartment. There was no answer. The men speculated that Ivar must be stuck in traffic – Aristide Briand, the French prime minister, had died a few days earlier, and the funeral procession was moving near Ivar's apartment, clogging the streets. Littorin continued to phone, off and on, for another hour. The men grew more nervous. Littorin said Ivar's housekeeper, Jeannette, was probably out shopping and should be back soon.

Finally, at about one o'clock, Jeannette answered the phone, sounding

DEATH IN THE AIR | 197

winded from the stairs. She said Ivar was still in bed. She had been planning to straighten his bedroom when she returned from shopping, but when she opened the door, she saw him lying in bed. Littorin asked her to call the hotel when Ivar was awake.

Ivar had seemed tired that morning, so a nap was not out of the question. Still, Jeannette's story seemed odd. Littorin suggested to the men that he and Karin Bökman take a taxi to Victor Emmanuel III, to check on Ivar. No one at the meeting questioned them, or suggested that someone else go. It seemed perfectly natural that two of Ivar's closest friends would be the ones to do it. Besides, the men were too concerned about the financial implications of Ivar's absence to notice any suspicious behavior by Littorin or Bökman. They agreed to wait at the du Rhin.

The taxi ride along the Seine was painfully slow. The early afternoon sky had turned a darker gray, and the wind was howling for the Briand cortège. All of Paris was sad, and death was in the air.

When they arrived at Victor Emmanuel III, Littorin ran up the stairs and into the apartment. He opened the bedroom door and stood at the same spot where he had greeted Ivar a few hours earlier. As his eyes adjusted to the dark bedroom, he could just make out a silhouette on the left side of the double bed, a tall body covered by white sheets, lying still. A neat dispatch case was next to the baseboard, along with a cane. The apartment typically smelled of wild flowers or roses, but not now.

Littorin used a low voice, in case the man was asleep. He whispered the name of his long-time friend and boss.

"Ivar, Ivar."

The body did not move.

It was after one o'clock, but the curtains were drawn and the bedroom was damp and dark, like a wine cellar. Even with the door ajar Littorin could hardly see.

He glanced back at the two women waiting for him to enter. Jeannette Barrault, who had been at the vestibule when they arrived, now stood aside, indicating that he should go in alone. Karin Bökman waited for Littorin to make the first move, as she typically did. Littorin whispered, "He must be sleeping." The women turned their heads away as he approached the body.

The details and evidence of their next steps, and the hurried investigation that followed, would be scrutinized and debated for decades. In several crucial respects, testimonies about the events would be in conflict.[9]

Littorin entered the bedroom and saw the man lying flat on his back, with his coat and waistcoat unbuttoned and pulled to the left. According to Littorin's testimony, he immediately recognized the man as Ivar. Littorin said the man held a pistol, a Browning 9 mm, in his left hand in what he later called a "cramped grip." There was blood on his left wrist. Littorin saw a red stain on the man's shirt and what appeared to be a hole in his chest, directly in line with the heart. Littorin shouted, *"Il ne dort pas, il est mort!"* ("He's not sleeping, he's dead!")

At this point, the two women rushed into the room. Both later testified that they did not remember the placement of the gun clearly, but believed it was on the bed next to the man's open left hand. They also said they recognized him as Ivar. All three of them insisted they did not touch the body.

On the bedside table were three sealed personal notes, addressed in what Littorin said was Ivar's handwriting.[10] The notes lay next to a copy of the novel *The Single Front*, by the Russian Jewish writer Ilya Ehrenburg, about an industrialist named Olsson who eerily resembled Ivar. Like Ivar, Olsson owned match factories throughout the world, and was known as "The Match King." At the end of the novel, Olsson died of a heart attack in a Paris apartment.

Littorin grabbed the notes. One was addressed to Ivar's sister Britta, who later insisted that its contents remain private. Another included instructions to Sune Schéle, the New York broker who had helped Ivar try to buy shares through Karl Lange, the Santa Claus lookalike. Ivar wrote that Schéle should close some accounts, and included 10,000 dollars of cash.

The third note was the only one bearing that day's date.[11] It was addressed, in English, to Littorin, who opened it and read it aloud, in a shaking voice:

12 March 1932

Dear Krister,
I have made such a mess of things that I believe this to be the most satisfactory solution for everybody concerned. Please take care of these two letters also see that two letters which were sent a couple of days ago by Jordahl to me at 5 Avenue Victor Emmanuel are returned to Jordahl. The letters were sent by Majestic. Goodbye now and thanks.
I.K.

Karin Bökman sobbed as Littorin dropped the note. He had worked with Ivar for thirty years, and now his friend was gone. Instead of ending with

"Kreuger," as Ivar typically signed his messages to Littorin, this note was signed "I.K." – with two fat dots.

Instead of calling the police right away, Littorin and Bökman rushed back to the Hotel du Rhin to tell the bankers their story: that Ivar Kreuger had committed suicide. Ivar's death confirmed everyone's worst fears about the man and his finances. The investment bankers from Lee Higginson, which had sponsored Ivar for a decade, were dismayed. Soon, Lee Higg, one of the most prestigious investment banks of the era, would file for bankruptcy and the partners would be ruined, all because they had bet the venerable firm on a self-made man. George Murnane, the senior partner, later told investigators what he thought when he heard the news: "I suddenly knew we had all been idiots."[12]

In New York, the markets were still open, so everyone promised to keep quiet until the close, to avoid another crash. They knew Ivar's suicide would trigger a panic, and no one wanted to repeat the black days of October 1929.

But Durant, and perhaps others, couldn't resist. Right away, a cable arrived at Lee Higginson's Wall Street office warning: "For partners only Oak died very suddenly today not public yet please say nothing until announced here."[13] Shortly thereafter, on the New York Stock Exchange, there was a surge of orders to sell securities of Ivar's companies. Most of these orders were anonymous, but they originated in Paris. Someone was betting that Ivar's shares soon would collapse.

In recent sessions, Kreuger & Toll had been the most active security traded on the New York Stock Exchange. On Saturday, trading was even heavier; Kreuger & Toll accounted for 25 percent of the Exchange's volume, and that was before word of Ivar's death had leaked.[14] Eager investors in the United States, ignorant of the news and still believing in the Match King, had gobbled up shares from the short sellers. By the close of trading that day, the price of Kreuger & Toll securities had actually risen, by 37 cents.

After an hour, Karin Bökman finally went, alone, to the Faubourg St Honoré police station. Teary-eyed, she told her version of the day's events, and concluded that Ivar had shot himself. An examiner rushed to the scene, found the body semi-warm, and hurriedly noted that "death appears to have occurred by suicide with a firearm."[15]

One of the officers was surprised by the precision of the single wound, in the exact center of the man's heart, and estimated that a person attempting suicide would have had only a one in 10,000 chance of such a precise hit. Still, the investigation was brief: no one examined the gun for fingerprints or noticed whether the body had a stunted left index finger. The police never even asked which hand Ivar had favored. They placed Ivar's note to Krister Littorin under seal, where it would remain for twenty-three years.[16]

As the shocking news spread the next day, the world mourned Ivar Kreuger's death. The London *Daily Express* reported that the sky seemed to darken and "the same thoughts came to men as when Caesar died." Families gathered around their radios to hear John Maynard Keynes, the famous economist, eulogize Kreuger as "perhaps the greatest constructive business intelligence of his age." The London *Times* wrote that Ivar "was the victim of a world-condition affecting and afflicting every industrialist and every financier in greater or less degree." The *New Statesman* called him "a very Puritan of finance."[17]

When the New York Stock Exchange finally opened on Monday, share-holders panicked, just as Ivar's colleagues had feared. Ivar had visited the gallery of the Exchange more than thirty years before, as an immigrant just off the boat with only a hundred dollars and no job. He had dreamed that one day his shares would be traded there. Now, the famed Exchange ticker could not keep pace with the number of trades in shares of Ivar's companies, even on a delay. When the ticker finally caught up, it recorded the largest single trade in the history of the markets: a sale of 673,800 American Certificates of Kreuger & Toll.[18] By the end of the day, those securities – still among the most widely held in the world – were worth just pennies.

13

GREATNESS?

During the next two weeks, public sentiment about Ivar flipped. Journalists drew hasty conclusions about him based on preliminary assessments of available evidence. The abruptly revised view, that the Match King had perpetrated the greatest financial fraud in history, quickly became cemented in the public mind. The world now saw an epic betrayal: a villain, not a hero; a schemer, not a planner; a destroyer, not a builder. Ivar became the Judas of the financial markets.

Ivar's sisters flew from Stockholm to bring the body home, where it was cremated after a brief public viewing of a casket with a glass cutout for the face.[1] King Gustaf cut short a holiday on the French Riviera to be in Stockholm for the funeral. Gustav Vasa chapel was filled with lilies of the valley, one of Ivar's favorite flowers.[2] Authorities read Ivar's final will and testament from 1930, which contained just one provision: a bequest of 1 million kronor to Ingeborg Eberth, his neighbor at Villagatan in Stockholm. Ivar also had given her 65,000 dollars of debentures before he died, but those were now worthless.[3] Eberth told reporters she "never had an inkling of what was coming" and insisted that Ivar's "memory is sacred to me and I am not going to give it away."[4] Still, she added, she knew quite a lot about Ivar and was planning to write a book about him.[5]

She wasn't the only one.

Ivar's companies suffered a similar fate to the body, as panicked selling reduced them to dust. The remaining directors of International Match met hurriedly, and decided not to pay the dividend that was coming due.[6] On March 25, less than two weeks after the public learned of Ivar's death, investigators from Price Waterhouse declared that his companies were insolvent. The Swedish committee investigating Kreuger & Toll concluded that its 1930 balance sheet "grossly misrepresented the true financial position of the company."[7] When formal charges were read in the Second Chamber of the Riksdag, just before midnight on April 5, they seemed indisputable. Investigators estimated the loss at 2 billion kronor, more than Sweden's national debt.[8]

The accountants were comfortable reaching such sweeping preliminary conclusions because they found abundant evidence that Ivar had treated his companies and subsidiaries as personal assets. He had wired millions of dollars among secret subsidiaries and arranged for dubious intercompany transactions. The details were too complex to unravel, but that didn't give the accountants pause. Although they hadn't yet figured out where all of the money had gone, they nevertheless concluded that Ivar's businesses were a massive fraud.

But these early reports of financial manipulations were not the death knell of Ivar's companies and reputation. Nor was it the reported suicide, although that certainly led many people to suspect the worst. Instead, the nails in Ivar's coffin were the Italian treasury bills. Those forged bills crystallized the public's view of Ivar in a way that explanations of intermingled accounts, offshore subsidiaries, and off balance sheet liabilities never would.

At first, it was difficult for some people to accept Ivar as a fraud. He had helped central Europe avert financial crisis. He had restored the financial morale of France and Germany. He was a friend and advisor to government leaders, including President Hoover. Even Isaac Marcosson couldn't accept the public's about-face on Ivar – until he read about those Italian treasury bills.

The forged Italian treasury bills galvanized opinion against Ivar. The media replayed the investigation over and over. The public accounts repeated the same facts. First, investigators found the bills soon after they impounded the Match Palace. Then, Sweden's foreign minister, Johannes Hellner, flew to Rome to show the bills to Mussolini. Hellner asked Mussolini the question everyone had been asking since the news broke: "Did Ivar Kreuger lend your government money in exchange for a monopoly on the manufacture and sale of matches within Italy?"[9]

Mussolini said he and Ivar had discussed a loan twice, in 1927 and again in 1930, but they could not agree on terms. He examined the Italian bills and said they were clearly forged. Mussolini ordered his assistants to bring out other state documents with the signatures of Mosconi and Boselli. The shapes and sizes of the letters didn't match. Moreover, although Mosconi usually placed a comma after his name and didn't sign with his first initial, the bills were signed "A. Mosconi" with no comma. Boselli's name was misspelled on several bills. Mosconi, Boselli, and Mussolini all signed statements that the bills were forgeries. They said they had never seen them before.

When Hellner reported these answers to the public, Ivar's good name was destroyed. Copies of both the bills and the statements attesting they were forged appeared in every major newspaper and magazine. Reports also spread that Ivar had ordered 150 sacks of waste paper to be recycled before he shot himself. The police found nearly 2,000 of Ivar's personal letters and cables inside those sacks.[10] People could only imagine what secrets were buried there.

Millions of investors saw for themselves that Ivar was a crook, just like Charles Ponzi. The only difference between the two men was scale: Ivar had raised fifty times more money and lasted ten times as long.

The investigation of Ivar's companies spread to the United States, where congressional hearings led many legislators to advocate federal requirements that companies obtain audits and disclose material facts.[11] Ivar's friend Herbert Hoover had been swept from office, and Franklin D. Roosevelt, the new president, favored dramatic legislative intervention. With a boost from Ivar, securities reform quickly became part of the agenda.

Ivar and his companies became a centerpiece in the government's inquiry. Members of Congress were especially skeptical of Ivar's bankers, and demanded to know what they knew and when they knew it. The forged Italian treasury bills hung over the debates, and legislators cited Ivar's collapse as a prime example of what must never happen again.

The Senators were particularly tough on Donald Durant, and wanted to know why he had not done more as a director of Ivar's companies. Investigators expressed dismay at Durant's testimony that he had never attended a board meeting as a director of Kreuger & Toll.[12] They also questioned why Durant had notified his firm so quickly about Ivar's death, even while he insisted that others keep the news quiet until the trading session in New York had ended. Had Lee Higginson sold securities based on Durant's advance word? This questioning became intense, and culminated in a "Who's Who" colloquy of prominent American lawyers, with Judge Joseph M. Proskauer, Durant's counsel, trying to amplify one of Durant's responses to a question from Senator Thomas Gore, only to be rebuked by Senator Peter Norbeck that, "We are not going to let a visitor who has come into the room, and who has not been called upon, take part in the hearing."[13] Durant must have been grateful that Proskauer deflected some of the heat.

A.D. Berning also testified, and once again people got his name wrong, as Ivar often had. (Even *The New York Times* called him "Birning."[14]) Berning previously had worried that investors would point fingers at him, given his lack of attention to the details of Ivar's companies. But Ivar was not there to contradict him, so Berning aggressively defended his role. He skillfully navigated the questions, and, this time, his role switched from lackey to champion. Berning could forgive the *Times*'s spelling when the newspaper labeled him the "Man Who Trapped Kreuger."[15] The investigators saw Berning as one of their kind, the cat in an international cat-and-mouse chase, the one man who finally uncovered Ivar's massive fraud, an epic con that left Ivar with no escape.[16] They didn't hear anything about Ernst & Ernst's consulting fees or the Bernings' extravagant trips to Europe. They never questioned Mrs Berning.

Members of Congress ignored the inconvenient facts about Berning's conflicts of interest and duplicity. Instead, they called Berning an exemplar. America needed to give men like Berning a more prominent role. Congress needed to require that every company have a proper audit from an American audit firm. Berning blamed his failure to catch Ivar earlier on the auditors in Sweden, and everyone saw the wisdom in pointing fingers abroad.

With the public clamoring for Congress to act, legislators first took aim at the New York Stock Exchange, particularly its willingness to list unaudited companies. Representative La Guardia of New York claimed that American investors "could not have been swindled out of their money had it not been either for the carelessness, indifference or connivance of the New York Stock Exchange."[17] The Exchange tried to fend off legislation by voluntarily requiring newly listed companies to agree to future audits; when that wasn't enough, it agreed to require audits before granting listings.[18] But neither move satisfied the public, or Congress. The era of laissez-faire self-regulation was over.

Both President Roosevelt and Felix Frankfurter, the House of Representatives legal counsel (and later a Supreme Court justice), cited Ivar and Samuel Insull in pressing for new laws. Although legislators referred to Insull's companies, his schemes were smaller and generated less publicity than Ivar's; they were geographically limited to the Midwest, and involved neither Wall Street nor New York bankers. Moreover, Insull ultimately was acquitted of alleged financial crimes whereas Ivar would never be acquitted of anything. Insull was an important part of the debate, but Ivar was the man members of

Congress had in mind as they thought about who the new securities laws must stop.

Opponents of the new laws argued that Congress should not react to a case as unusual and spectacular as Ivar's, because it was unlikely to be repeated. George O. May, one of the lead accountants from Price Waterhouse, testified that Ivar was "a quite different phenomenon, to my mind. This is an absolutely unique case, and I think for that reason there is danger in legislating for it because I do not suppose there has been anything to compare with it since the South Sea Bubble."[19]

But public sentiment ultimately prevailed over industry lobbyists, and the new Securities Act of 1933 became law in May. It was an amalgam of provisions that had been on the back burner since the world war, but finally drew support after the collapse of Ivar's companies. The new law was designed to prevent what Senator George Norris had said Ivar's schemes achieved: "deceit and trickery and debauchery with which men of great wealth are trying to accumulate millions more [from] the contributions of the pennies of the poor."[20] The Securities Act required that companies register securities before selling them. Public companies had to disclose material facts, including many matters that companies such as International Match had not disclosed. Congress also included a key provision directed at uniformity of accounting principles. General Accepted Accounting Principles, or GAAP, arose out of this law.

A year later, Congress passed the Securities Exchange Act, a related law that created the Securities Exchange Commission and gave American shareholders the right to sue companies for fraud. That right – one of the most important and controversial provisions in American law – also had roots in the public reaction to Ivar's collapse. A major article in the *Accounting Review* concluded that Ivar's collapse was "probably the strongest activating force ... the dynamic incident that focused attention on the evils possible under the holding-subsidiary form of corporate enterprise."[21]

The 1929 crash was not the impetus for the securities laws of 1933 and 1934. Instead, those laws are more accurately described as encapsulating a political reaction to a single bullet and to one man, who was labeled during congressional debates as "the greatest swindler in all history."[22]

This reaction was not surprising, given the publicity and public debate about Ivar at the time. The crash had occurred in 1929, four years earlier, but several life spans in political terms. When Congress began to discuss the securities laws, the debate began with Ivar, not the crash. The Committee Report for the Securities Act of 1933 included more than 250 pages on Ivar, and congressional hearing reports also focused on Ivar.

Whatever one thought of the 1930s securities laws, it was undeniable that they were a reaction to Ivar. The United States developed its system of securities regulation in response to the public's reaction to the collapse of Ivar's companies. Simply put, without Ivar Kreuger, modern securities regulation and litigation would not exist.

At the five-year anniversary of Ivar's reported suicide, one commentator reflected that Ivar's enduring legacy to society was not the loan-for-monopoly concept or off balance sheet financing. It wasn't the vote-light B Shares or complex derivatives issued by offshore subsidiaries or even landmark buildings such as the Match Palace. Instead, this author noted,

> from the record of falsehood and betrayal with which Kreuger besmirched the very pillars of finance in the leading countries of the world has come, particularly in the United States, the erection of new safeguards for investors. In our Securities Act are to be found preventives whose origin is to be traced definitely to the Kreuger experiences.[23]

The legislative debates about Ivar brought closure. During the middle of the Great Depression, most people accepted the simple story that Ivar was a villain who used forgery and financial shenanigans to scam investors out of their hard-earned money. Few people could spare the time or resources to probe further. Fifty-seven factfinding reports from Price Waterhouse,[24] and the firm's 67-volume final report,[25] were too voluminous. For most people, Price Waterhouse's punch line was enough: Ivar's companies were a "confidence" game, which worked only because Ivar had "autocratic powers," "unquestioning obedience of officials," and "complete secrecy."[26] This triple threat – power, obedience, and secrecy – was lethal, and, in Price Waterhouse's view, Ivar could not have continued to inspire confidence without them. Investors who had purchased securities of Ivar's companies really didn't want the details anyway. For them, it was enough to know their investments were worthless.

Lee Higginson got a different kind of closure. In 1932, the partners who reflected on the demise of their firm must have wondered what would have happened if they had followed the conservative advice of their founder, Henry Higginson. What if they had hired a Harvard graduate instead of Donald Durant? What if they had passed over Durant for partnership, and instead promoted yet another blood relative? What if they had been more skeptical of Ivar at first, as Jack Morgan had been? What if they hadn't entrusted so much of their firm's capital and reputation to one self-made man?

Unfortunately, the partners would have to ponder these questions at different firms or in different businesses. In the aftermath of the collapse of International Match, Lee Higginson entered liquidation proceedings. The bank's stakes in Ivar's securities were worthless. Its liabilities were too great, and Lee Higg's most important asset – its reputation – was trash. In 1936, the partners sold their remaining claims to the United States bankruptcy trustee for one dollar.[27]

Thus, the generally accepted account of Ivar Kreuger became a straightforward one. He was an evil man, a slippery schemer who defrauded investors in a massive pyramid scheme, crudely forged some Italian treasury bills, brought down one of America's leading banks, and then, seeing a dead end, shot himself in the heart.

The truth, as in most big financial stories, is far more complicated.

During the four months between the reports of Ivar's suicide and Lee Higginson's liquidation, the firm's partners insisted, contrary to the investigators' conclusions, that Ivar's companies were solvent.[28] According to Lee Higginson, Price Waterhouse was wrong. International Match had taken a major financial hit, but it was no Ponzi scheme.

On March 17, Lee Higginson sent a letter to holders of Ivar's securities, saying, "Upon the announcement of Mr Kreuger's death, we immediately endeavored to secure information as to the present condition of Kreuger & Toll Company, International Match Corporation and their affiliated companies."[29] In that letter, and several follow-on statements, Lee Higginson highlighted the valuable assets still held by Kreuger & Toll and International Match: government monopoly concessions and loans; investments in other companies, including Swedish Match, Swedish Pulp, Grängesberg (the iron ore company), L. M. Ericsson, and various real estate and banking companies; and a sprawling trading operation with investments throughout the world.[30]

The firm publicized Ivar's most recent annual reports, which, though cursory, included more information than many New York Stock Exchange traded companies. According to Lee Higginson, Kreuger & Toll had a net worth of more than 272 million dollars, five times the value of the Kreuger & Toll securities traded in the market. Indeed, Kreuger & Toll's most recent annual net earnings were $3 per American Certificate, more than the value of a Certificate in the market.[31]

Lee Higg's partners admitted that Ivar's accounting had been sloppy, and they couldn't defend the forged Italian bills. But they insisted that Ivar's core business had been perfectly legitimate. His directors had given him authority to transfer assets among companies as he saw fit.[32] His financial statements were deliberately vague, but no one could accuse him of lying about details – there were no details. Investors who bought his securities got roughly the same amount of information about Ivar's companies as they got from anyone else. That is, nothing. If they bought anyway, whose fault was that?

Of course, Ivar's corporate assets weren't worth as much as they had been before the 1929 crash. And it undoubtedly would be difficult to unravel the strands of financial claims Ivar had woven into his complicated multi-company tapestry. But there was value there, somewhere. A lot of value. It just took some digging to find it.

Although it appeared at first that Ivar's massive fraud left behind minimal assets, as the bankruptcy trustee began to dig, value popped up everywhere. The bankruptcy process was complicated, and there was a feeding frenzy to get at Ivar's remaining assets, most of which were in Sweden. That disadvantaged International Match, which was subject to bankruptcy proceedings in the United States. It also hurt Kreuger & Toll, which held a secondary claim to many assets, behind Swedish Match. Although International Match and Kreuger & Toll ultimately did not survive, holders of their securities did receive some value.

Moreover, Swedish Match, which held Ivar's most valuable assets, recovered. In 1936, Swedish Match filed with the new Securities and Exchange Commission to issue yet another round of securities, including B Shares, the innovative class of common shares Ivar had invented and given just 1/1000 of a vote.[33] Far from being the empty shell some people thought, Ivar's primary company, Swedish Match, survived the scandal[34] and maintained a substantial share of the global match market.[35] The Wallenbergs, a prominent Swedish family, bought a major stake in the company, and Jacob Wallenberg, Sr, served as Swedish Match's chairman until 1973. Swedish Match changed its name a few times and acquired dozens of companies. It branched into new business, including paper and packaging, waste combustion, and even bowling halls.[36] Today, the company has refocused on tobacco products, including environmentally friendly disposable lighters and matches, and it employs more than 12,000 people in eleven countries.[37] It is once again called Swedish Match.

Although the newspapers said Ivar's other assets were worthless, they were clearly wrong about that as well. The Boliden mine paid half a million dollars every month,[38] Swedish Pulp had nearly 5 million acres of forest, Grängesberg was the biggest iron producer in Europe, and Ivar's real estate subsidiaries held eighty-seven buildings in Stockholm alone.[39] Ivar's private apartments in Berlin, Paris, New York, and Stockholm were in high demand. Within a month of his reported suicide, real estate brokers in New York were swarming his Park Avenue penthouse, which was ultimately sold to the writer Edna Ferber.[40]

Ivar's biggest claims had been for interest payments from foreign governments, including 3.75 million dollars every six months from Germany.[41] Many of these claims, including those on the German government, continued to pay interest, precisely as Ivar had envisioned. The Nazis left Ivar's agreement in place when they came to power, and the German government regularly made loan payments, even during the Second World War. After the war, the occupied powers tried to dissolve Germany's match monopoly, but the Rome Treaty of 1952 protected it from conversion and extended the repayment schedule to 1983. Not only was Ivar's greatest monopoly legitimate, but it continued in force for more than fifty years after his reported suicide.[42]

One reason the holders of International Match securities did not realize much value from Ivar's assets was that so much was sold at fire sale prices. This was particularly true of Ivar's personal assets, including his priceless art collection. Art historians said one of Ivar's most significant achievements, and his most valuable property, was the beautiful Match Palace.[43] But that building was in Stockholm and generated no value for International Match.

The bidding for Ivar's personal assets drew bargain hunters and collectors. Two of Ivar's expensive speedboats, which he had shown off to Greta Garbo and Mary Pickford, went for just 162 dollars and 180 dollars. A wealthy brewer bought one of Ivar's expansive vacation homes for a mere 8,750 dollars.[44] Even ordinary kitchen kettles and steel scissors engraved with Ivar's name were popular.[45]

Reporters had been skeptical of Ivar's claim to own 350,000 Diamond Match shares (nearly half of the American match company), in part because such a significant purchase would have raised antitrust concerns in the United States. But it soon emerged that indeed Ivar had owned those shares.[46] He had purchased them indirectly through a front company in March 1930 and they were still worth more than the 4 million dollar loan they backed. The discovery of the Diamond Match shares led some people to question whether Ivar really was the massive fraudster he had been portrayed as.

As the truth emerged about Ivar's dealings with the Italian government, it appeared that he might even have had claims on the Italian match business – and not merely because the bills he forged would fetch some novelty value at auction. In fact, investigators found evidence that Ivar *had* done a deal with the Italian government. It was possible that Ivar actually had secretly loaned Italy money, only to have Mussolini renege after his death. But no one was willing to confront Mussolini about this, and Ivar wasn't talking.

Ivar clearly had interests in and contracts with some Italian match factories. It was undisputed that he had met with one of Mussolini's assistants in Florence on October 18, 1930, and with Mussolini himself after that.[47] At the time of those meetings, the Italians had been desperate for cash, particularly after Jack Morgan's 100 million dollar loan became due.

The Italian government made a show of fury about the forged Italian treasury bills. But some commentators thought it protested too much. A note from the Italian finance minister Boselli, whose name was forged on the Italian bills, appeared only after Ivar's reported suicide, and some argued that it sounded like it was written in 1932, not 1930. Boselli wrote to Ivar, in full:

> Dear Sir,
> I note that you prefer to wait on account of the present economic situation. With regard to this, and also with regard to the tendentious and lying prattle which has been caused, I am compelled to inform you that we do not wish to continue negotiations. They are hereby concluded.[48]

The Italians claimed that Ivar had rejected the possibility of a loan when his cash reserves, depleted after the 1929 crash, dwindled so low that he would be fortunate to have enough money to pay the second installment on the German loan. According to the Italian government, when Boselli learned that Ivar would have to postpone the loan, it was Ivar who became offended and canceled the deal.

That explanation was dubious. Ivar frequently had committed to government loans when he didn't have the money. Why wouldn't he do the same for Italy, particularly when he was claiming to his accountants and bankers that he was working on an Italian loan? Might Ivar have secured an Italian loan-for-monopoly deal, which Mussolini opportunistically rejected? The forgeries obviously were illicit, but they were so crude that it seemed unlikely Ivar, or anyone, would think they would pass more than casual scrutiny. Perhaps Ivar made the forgeries after he learned that Italy planned to back out of a deal, thereby destroying his ability to raise more money? Given Ivar's fragile mental state, either version of the story was possible.

Of course, even according to the version offered by Ivar's supporters, he still committed fraud. There was no good explanation for the Italian bills, and no exculpation. Forging government signatures was inexcusable, particularly in the amateurish fashion Ivar did it. The point of looking at all of the evidence is not to acquit Ivar of that crime, but to note that his motivation for the forgeries might have been more complex than people thought at the time. The fact that Ivar lied to prop up his business at the end does not mean that Ivar had been lying continuously from the beginning.

Whatever the truth about Italy, International Match turned out not to be the empty shell many reporters had imagined. Progress was slow, but within two years, the trustee had collected more than 1 million dollars after expenses.[49] The next year, the company resumed paying dividends, and even obtained a refund from the US Treasury Department for taxes paid on fictitious earnings.[50] In October 1936, the trustee sent more than 15,000 checks to investors – about 10 million dollars overall, or 15 cents for every dollar they invested.[51] And those checks were just the first installments.

The International Match trustee also collected money from lawsuits. The first suits, against the directors for negligence, were mostly for show. The trustee demanded 35.8 million dollars from Donald Durant, 31.4 million dollars from Percy Rockefeller, and 36.3 million dollars from Frederic Allen,[52] but even if the trustee could prove a case, these men were financially devastated and in no position to pay. They held worthless securities that they had purchased for nearly 8 million dollars; they could not afford any damages.[53] Lee Higginson, which was declared insolvent, paid just 30,000 dollars to settle claims. But International Match's other bankers agreed to pay 765,000 dollars, a historic amount, particularly given the limited rights and remedies available to holders of securities at the time.[54] That money went to holders of International Match securities.

The final report of the International Match bankruptcy was filed in 1945, after the Second World War.[55] Between 1923 and 1931, investors had bought $154 million of International Match securities.[56] Ultimately, after thirteen years of digging, the trustee recovered 32 cents for each dollar.[57] Including the value lost from the fire sale of Ivar's assets, the total value of International Match after Ivar's reported suicide was about half of the amount investors originally had paid Ivar. That was a massive loss, but it wasn't that much worse than the average return during that time period, which included the 1929 crash and the depression. The markets had lost a quarter of their value in two days during October 1929, when Ivar's securities held firm. The collapse of International Match didn't cost investors nearly as much as Price Waterhouse initially suggested it would.

Kreuger & Toll investors did even better. By late 1937, investors in Kreuger & Toll had received more than half of their money back,[58] including a 23 percent dividend.[59] After Kreuger & Toll declared its last dividend, the trustee ordered the cremation of all of its American Certificates, the innovative securities Ivar had introduced just a few years earlier. Given the huge dividends Kreuger & Toll had paid before 1932, someone who held the securities continuously actually outperformed most other investors.

Of course, the lawyers did much better than the investors. Lawyers for the trustee charged more than 100,000 dollars per year.[60] Most of New York's leading lawyers, including Samuel Untermyer, who famously had elicited Pierpont Morgan's remarks about the importance of character during earlier congressional hearings,[61] earned large fees from the disputes about Ivar's remaining assets.

One reason the lawyers made so much money was that the allegations about Ivar's schemes turned out not to be as clear as Price Waterhouse and the public initially had believed. For example, although International Match did not disclose the names of its offshore subsidiaries to investors, it did note that one of its primary assets was a 75 million dollar credit with one subsidiary, which turned out to be Continental Investment, in Liechtenstein. A 15 million dollar credit with another subsidiary turned out to be to Garanta, in Holland. Those companies were secret, but real. It took many billable hours for the lawyers to uncover the facts about Continental and Garanta.

If Ivar had been around, these facts would have made it difficult to sustain a case against him. Everyone, including International Match's accountants, bankers, and directors, originally had agreed that these two subsidiaries would pay interest to International Match on a sliding scale determined exclusively at Ivar's discretion. These parties all wanted Ivar to have discretion so International Match did not receive more than the funds necessary to cover its dividends.[62] That was basic tax planning, and it was transparent. International Match's income really had been up to Ivar, and that was no mystery. Although investors complained at the end, the truth was that they hadn't had much of a claim from the beginning, based on their own agreement.

And where was the fraud at International Match? Ivar had transferred 50 million dollars of German bonds held by International Match to a bank he controlled to use as collateral for a loan. But he had replaced those bonds with substitute collateral, and the directors of International Match had given him the right to make such a transfer. Ivar had claimed to have deals with Italy and Spain, when he apparently did not. But he made those representations in 1931, after he already had finished raising money in America.[63] The selling prospectuses for his American securities had never mentioned Italy or Spain. The Italian treasury bills looked bad, and they were obviously forgeries. But they didn't affect International Match.

One should not conclude from this revisionist history that Ivar was a saint. He was not. Nor was he forthcoming in his dealings with investors, accountants, and bankers. However, given the rules of the game at the time, it is difficult to say that much of what Ivar did was illegal. That shouldn't be surprising. Ivar had an acute sense of where the legal boundaries fell, and he observed them carefully.

As is the case for many business people, Ivar walked a line between sharp business practices and maintaining an ethical reputation. The simple conclusion that Ivar was a crook is neither accurate nor useful. Like most great financiers, he has a more complicated story. The lesson of Ivar Kreuger is not that his businesses were illegal. It is that they were alegal.

Financial scandals are complicated and their investigations typically lead to the search for a human face: John Law of the Mississippi Scheme, Robert Harley of the South Sea Bubble, Michael Milken of Drexel Burnham Lambert, Jeff Skilling of Enron, or Bernard Madoff. Ivar Kreuger became the face of the International Match scandal, but he should not have been the only target. Overeager investors, sloppy auditors, and pushover directors also bear much of the blame. Holders of Ivar's securities didn't demand more detailed information about his businesses. Ivar's auditors accepted his word as truth even when facts suggested otherwise. His directors did virtually nothing except cash their annual stipends.

If these people had scrutinized Ivar's financial statements during the mid-1920s, they might have constrained the exponential growth of his capital raising. If they had simply demanded to know how Ivar could pay 25 percent dividends while receiving 8 percent interest on government loans, they might have generated enough skepticism to dampen the meteoric rise in the prices of his securities. But no one wanted to question Ivar on the way up, and his investors, auditors, and directors remained silent.

As is the case in many financial scandals, other so-called gatekeepers also were culpable. Ivar's bankers at Lee Higginson asked some questions, but too few and too late; that venerable bank collapsed as a result. Regulators and exchanges, including the New York Stock Exchange, backed down from any serious inquiry about the soundness of Ivar's companies. Securities analysts and journalists didn't probe Ivar's slim financial reports. Without constant adoring support from the media, Ivar might not have acquired such a lustrous reputation.

Undoubtedly, Ivar Kreuger should be held accountable for the collapse of his companies. But in the typical rush to pin blame for a financial scandal on one human being, he wrongly and unfairly came to bear sole responsibility. The truth is that there is plenty of blame to go around.

Few of the people Ivar touched had happy endings. The list of his 15,000-plus creditors ran for 200 pages and included such mainstays as Harvard College and the Chase Securities Corporation.[64] The bankruptcy estate repaid some of these creditors, but most of them ended up losing money.

Krister Littorin and Karin Bökman were devastated by the passing of their dear friend, and were traumatized by their role in what seemed to be a massive fraud. They quietly disappeared into anonymity in Sweden. Torsten Kreuger was sentenced to three and a half years at hard labor for falsifying financial statements, although he was released after a year.[65] He spent the rest of his life trying, and failing, to repair his family's reputation.

Ivar's accountants suffered little punishment. Sigurd Hennig, Ivar's bookkeeper and childhood friend, was arrested, but acquitted.[66] Anton Wendler, Ivar's Swedish accountant, was jailed for a short time for failing to detect false statements in Garanta's balance sheet, including the apparently inflated value of some of Ericsson's assets.[67]

A.D. Berning was praised, not punished. After his fifteen minutes of fame before Congress, Berning returned to Ernst & Ernst and his Greenwich Village home, where his only accomplishment of note was to be elected a director of the Madison Square Boys Club.[68] He retired in 1956, and for his remaining twenty-four years remained a member of the Sleepy Hollow Country Club, where one can imagine him meticulously filling in golf scorecards with neatly crossed sevens.

Anders Jordahl, Ivar's once-wild Norwegian sidekick, escaped to Canada, but eventually was brought back and filed for bankruptcy. Jordahl and his new wife, Mary, were embroiled for years in lawsuits related to Ivar's American business. When they moved the contents of a safe deposit box in New York to a bank in New Jersey,[69] the trustee demanded access and took the case to the United States Supreme Court. The trustee won, but when the box was opened it contained just a handful of shares, blank papers, and an empty envelope.[70] Jordahl later told the trustee Ivar had been "very close-mouthed and told him nothing except immediate matters in which he was directly concerned."[71]

Donald Durant refused to believe Ivar had killed himself, and he would not use the word suicide in describing Ivar's death. He sold his mansion on 89th and West End, and moved into a smaller midtown apartment.[72] He took a job at Cassett & Co., a small investment house, but resigned a year later and went into business for himself. He led an undistinguished and brief life, and died at the age of fifty-three on the northbound platform of the Hanover Square subway station in New York. The cause of death was reported as a heart attack.[73]

The Stockholm police questioned Ernst August Hoffman, the ex-clerk Ivar had hired as president of Continental, but he was released. Karl Lange, the Santa Claus lookalike who had "audited" Garanta, didn't fare as well. The day after International Match was put into receivership, the Swedish police arrested Lange. He was charged with assisting Ivar in falsifying financial statements.[74]

It emerged that Oscar Rydbeck, whose bank Ivar still owed 120 million kronor, had known that Ivar used Lange as a "nominee" to make and receive payments.[75] Rydbeck avoided prison, but his reputation was destroyed, particularly when investigators learned that he had permitted Ivar to transfer assets at will among his companies.[76] Rydbeck lost even more credibility when he tried to explain that "I now know that I was considered necessary in many respects, yet I was never a real friend."[77]

The public trustees of Kreuger & Toll didn't spare Ivar's 80-year-old father, Ernst August.[78] They sued him within months of Ivar's reported suicide, even though he had limited assets. Ivar's mother, Jenny, remained in good health; at the age of 77, she was nearly as strong as Ernst August.[79] She insisted, "My son was a good man. It is too terrible. I cannot believe it."[80]

Government leaders, past and present, were tainted by revelations about their dealings with Ivar. Investigators tracked down former Spanish King Alfonso, in exile in Paris, who categorically denied any deal with Ivar; Primo de Rivera did not comment.[81] Rumors swirled that Ivar had bribed Adolf Hitler, who called the allegations "stinking lies."[82] A 10,000 dollar check from Ivar brought down the Prime Minister of Sweden, Carl Gustav Ekman, the leader who had arranged last-minute financing for Ivar when Krister Littorin first called him about the Italian bills. When investigators discovered Ekman had cashed the check from Ivar, which was made out to "bearer," the Prime Minister initially denied receiving it. But the next day, facing indisputable evidence that this "bearer" was him, and that witnesses saw him cash the check, Ekman agreed to repay the money and resign.[83]

Meanwhile, Ivar's junior employees were running off with whatever cash they could find. Just as Eric Landgren was found to have abused his expense account a decade earlier, Alexis Aminoff, Ivar's New York assistant, was interrogated about club dues and other expenses.[84] Investigators went through Aminoff's gold-embossed red leather book of meticulously documented official accounts,[85] but they didn't find his brown paper bag stuffed with "special accounts," including thousands of dollars of checks to "Myself," and receipts for personal expenses such as cloth hangers and dental floss.[86] Aminoff apparently milked Ivar's New York bank accounts until he closed them on June 29, 1932, with a final withdrawal of $124.72.[87]

Other than Durant, the directors of Ivar's companies escaped without much scrutiny. International Match's directors had served on an average of twenty corporate boards. Percy Rockefeller led the pack with nearly seventy, but even Donald Durant had been on eight boards.[88] Although Durant was criticized and called to testify on numerous occasions, Percy Rockefeller emerged unscathed. He avoided the bankruptcy trustee by saying he was confined to his bed with a stomach disorder and would give testimony as soon as his doctor permitted.[89] He probably really was sick, given that he still held 19,200 participating preferred shares of International Match, and 17,000 shares of Kreuger & Toll.[90]

A few of Ivar's critics profited from the aftermath. W. A. Fairburn, Ivar's adversary from Diamond Match, made a profit of nearly 8 million dollars by repurchasing the 350,000 Diamond Match shares Ivar had bought through some banks just two years earlier.[91] Professor William Z. Ripley, the Harvard economist who had warned about non-voting shares and inadequate disclosure years earlier, became an advisor to the committee of investors in the bankruptcy proceedings.[92] J. P. Morgan & Co. regained its stature as the world's leading lender.

Greta Garbo had remained Ivar's friend until the end. Witnesses gave accounts of seeing Greta and Ivar together on numerous occasions before Ivar's reported suicide. Even after Garbo became a star, Ivar had remained her personal and business advisor. She was always thrilled to see him, and he loved being around another Swede of modest background who had become "somebody."[93] Ivar also appreciated the fact that, although Garbo was famous, she still preferred to be incognito and refused interviews even more than he did. Ivar reportedly said Garbo was his "only true friend in America." [94]

Ivar didn't have a chance to advise Garbo as she renegotiated her contract with MGM, just after his reported suicide. MGM finally capitulated and promised her 250,000 dollars a film, an amount that gave Cole Porter the lyric, "You're the top! You're Garbo's salary."[95] She was happy with the money, but still upset about the reports of Ivar's suicide, and she boarded *Gripsholm* for Sweden on July 29.[96]

Garbo spent several weeks on an island in the Stockholm archipelago, mostly alone or in the company of a handful of family and friends. The press reported that "she continues her Hollywood-style seclusion in Sweden, which the Swedes find puzzling and at variance with the old out-going Garbo who used to go out to clubs."[97] Although there were rumors that Garbo had lost a fortune when Ivar's companies collapsed, she actually held just a few shares.[98] Perhaps Ivar had suggested she sell before that fateful day in March 1932. Ivar didn't leave Garbo any parting gifts, but when the bankruptcy trustee auctioned a castle and an island Ivar owned, Garbo purchased both.[99] She would spend many weeks on that island, as alone as Ivar had been.

The film industry, always one of Ivar's favorite albeit unprofitable investments, benefited somewhat from his downfall. In late 1932, *The Match King* premiered, starring Warren William in the role of Paul Kroll, a fictionalized and one-dimensional version of the real Ivar Kreuger. The movie became a box office hit and an instant classic. The revised screenplay of *The Match King* was considerably different from the paean to Ivar the film producers had originally envisioned. The final cut was surprisingly true to the latest facts, including the loan-for-monopoly deals and the Italian treasury bill forgeries, and was compelling enough to survive as long as Swedish Match has. The film remains an occasional late-night feature on television, and recently was recommended by *The New York Times*, along with a note that Mr William played the Ivar Kreuger role with "bite and conviction."[100] Like Ivar's life, the movie did not have a happy ending.

14

CODA

Much has changed since that foggy night in Paris. Europe realigned after a second world war, and the French renamed Ivar's street Avenue Franklin Delano Roosevelt, to show allegiance to the United States over Italy and its former king. New leaders and their businesses paved over the memories of Ivar Kreuger. In 1932, the notion that Ivar's incredible story might slip from public memory would have seemed ludicrous. Yet that is precisely what happened.

As memories faded, several authors tried to reinterpret the facts in various ways, some more plausible than others. The most common refrain was that Ivar, like Charles Ponzi, was simply a crook. This view was bolstered by rumors that spread during 1932 of Ivar's misdeeds as a child and young adult. One classmate came forward to declare that Ivar had been a "young man completely lacking in principle, who cheated whenever he thought he could do it without being caught."[1] Others recalled how he had pocketed stones he did not know during a crystallography minerals exam, or copied a model steam engine instead of building one from scratch.[2] Yet another reflected, "It wasn't that he cheated more than any of us, he just did it better."[3]

One of the most widely told stories was about how Ivar had first come to America, fresh out of engineering school, with a couple of job references and a hundred dollars in cash. After two months, he had burned through the cash and was eating from garbage cans. Then, a knock on the door changed his life. Ivar shared a room with an architect, who had just moved out. One night, a client came by to check on plans for a small house he had commissioned from the architect. Ivar quickly lied and claimed he had taken over the plans, which would be finished the next day. The man was delighted by Ivar's finished work, and paid him 50 dollars, more than he had earned since arriving in America.

As the story went, the success of this scheme energized Ivar, and showed him that he could succeed only through lies and schemes. Then, the rest of Ivar's life became one scheme after another.

That story was attractive to some people, especially the victims of Ivar's collapse. But it was too simple. It ignored the real wealth Ivar created throughout his career, and the real businesses he established, not only in matches, but in telecommunications, mining, commodities, and film. It ignored Ivar's financial innovations, and the crucial fact that his companies paid double-digit dividends for more than two decades before they collapsed. In contrast, Charles Ponzi's scheme lasted just a few months.

Other writers, primarily in Sweden, had a radically different perspective. To them, Ivar was a national hero, a brilliant man whose competitors abused him, profited from his demise, and then destroyed his good reputation. Swedish artists in particular came quickly to Ivar's defense. The Swedish writer Siegred Siewerts staged a sympathetic drama about Ivar in the Stockholm Royal Theater. *A Panic*, a film that sought to rehabilitate opinion about Ivar, premiered in Copenhagen in 1939.[4]

Most notably, Torsten Kreuger became convinced his brother was murdered. He wrote a book, *The Truth About Ivar Kreuger*, which set forth criticisms ranging from credible evidence of the mistakes made by investigators to more dubious speculations about Ivar's death. Torsten also funded attempts by others to exonerate his brother, in part because he lacked the credibility to make the case on his own. After the reports about Ivar's schemes and Torsten's year in prison, the Kreuger family name no longer commanded much authority. Torsten's book, published in 1968, was not well received.

More recently, some researchers in Sweden have cited evidence that lends some support for Torsten's theory that Ivar was murdered, or at least raises serious questions about the evidence pointing to suicide. For example, the French police never found a spent cartridge, or an exit hole. Forensic evidence of the clean entry suggested the wound might have been caused by a sharp object, not a gun. The body was cremated quickly, before the autopsy ordered by the Swedish government and requested by Kreuger's family could be performed. There even was a report that one doctor who examined the body suggested the man had been murdered.[5]

A few researchers also have cited conflicting evidence about what the three key witnesses, Krister Littorin, Karin Bökman, and Jeannette Barrault, found in Ivar's apartment. They claim the French police ignored a basic fact that echoes a Sherlock Holmes story: Ivar was right-handed.

Recall Krister Littorin's testimony that when they found the body the left hand still clutched the pistol in a "cramped grip." According to the other two witnesses, Bökman and Barrault, their best recollection was that gun was on the bed at the left of the body, level with the leg, and that the arms lay stretched out limply along the sides of the corpse.[6]

If the pistol was in Ivar's left hand in a cramped grip, was the evidence at the scene doctored? Did someone move the gun? It would have been virtually impossible for any right-handed person to shoot himself in the center of the heart with a powerful Browning 9 mm pistol, and then end up holding the gun in a cramped grip in his left hand. This would have been particularly true of a man, like Ivar, whose left index finger was stunted from a childhood accident.

Perhaps Littorin misremembered the facts or someone moved the gun. Perhaps Ivar actually shot himself with his left hand, instead of his right. Perhaps the gun was not in Ivar's hand at all when he was found, but instead had slipped across his body after he fired, to his left side. That placement would tend to suggest that Ivar had held the gun in his right hand and fired it; then, the gun kicked back and landed on the bed to his left.

The murder theorists also point to the disappearance of three suitcases the French police found in Ivar's apartment. Apparently, the police turned the suitcases over to the Swedish Embassy, which sealed all three and left them with Karin Bökman to transport to Stockholm. The suitcases were never seen again.

Apparently, an attorney representing Oscar Rydbeck and other bankers broke the seals and took papers from the suitcases, including Ivar's diaries. According to one view, when these men later discovered that the diaries contained evidence of murder, they burned them. This view remains popular throughout Scandinavia, where *The Burned Diaries of Ivar Kreuger* is a long-standing art and film project.[7]

Although the crime scene and any physical evidence are long gone, and therefore one cannot definitively rule out murder, it seems unlikely that anyone would have had the motive or opportunity to kill Ivar. Throughout midday on March 12, 1932, most of the people who were about to be financially decimated by Ivar's collapse, including Donald Durant, Oscar Rydbeck, and several other bankers, were at the Hotel du Rhin. A.D. Berning was in New York. Ivar's Swedish accountants were in Stockholm.

Who might have killed Ivar? The only people with access to Ivar during the narrow window of time available for a murder were Krister Littorin, Karin Bökman, Jeannette Barrault, and the telegram delivery boy. (The Finnish girl left in the early morning, and Morgan's man, John Brown, was only there earlier, if at all.) Littorin and Bökman wouldn't likely have killed their dear friend, and Barrault had always been a loyal housekeeper. The police questioned all three of them, and no one suspected foul play. If the telegram boy had been a hired assassin, he would not likely have returned voluntarily to tell investigators the details of his few minutes with Ivar.

The concierge remained at her post during the hour or so from the time the delivery boy left until the time Jeannette Barrault returned, and she said there were no other visitors during this time. It is possible that someone slipped past the concierge and entered Ivar's apartment after Barrault left to go shopping. Who might it have been?

Some have suggested the killer was hired by Jack Morgan, who had come to despise Ivar for usurping his role as the leading international financier, for excluding his bank from important deals, and for winning business from European governments, particularly France and Germany, that previously had hired only J. P. Morgan & Co. Numerous witnesses had heard Jack Morgan disparage Ivar. Of course, Jack wouldn't have done the deed himself, and he wasn't in Paris then in any event.[8] Moreover, if Jack had decided to have someone kill Ivar, Jack likely would have wanted to wait until after the crucial meeting on March 12, when the bankers planned to ask Ivar to explain the forged Italian treasury bills and the German bond switch. There would have been plenty of time for murder after that.

Although some of the French police officers acted like Keystone Cops at the scene, particularly given the high-profile nature of the case, they likely would have pursued any viable murder leads, particularly one involving a Morgan, simply out of self-interest. Perhaps the leads went dark because Ivar was murdered so stealthily. Perhaps someone managed to persuade Ivar, at gunpoint, to write faked goodbye notes to his sister, Sune Schéle, and Littorin. But a more sensible conclusion is that Ivar was not murdered. Although a few writers have punched holes in the story that Ivar committed suicide, there are more and bigger holes in the murder theory. Murder seems plausible only through the cloud of hindsight.

One final, highly speculative version of the facts about Ivar is the "escape theory," the notion that Ivar didn't die on March 12, 1932, but instead planned an elaborate escape and disappeared, leaving behind a trail of fabricated evidence of nervous breakdown and suicide. Investigators actually pursued this theory for a year. It was widely publicized in the media, and much discussed among people who had followed Ivar's life. The French police carefully considered the escape theory, in an attempt to overcome criticism of how they had handled the initial inquiry. However, as with the murder theory, every lead came to a dead end. As *The New York Times* reported on March 19, 1933, just over a year after the reports of Ivar's death, French investigators rejected the escape theory and concluded that the body found at Victor Emmanuel III was indeed Ivar's.[9]

Still, the theory deserves a mention, if only because Ivar's spectacular story merits at least the remote possibility of an even more spectacular ending. Certainly Ivar, having constructed Potemkin companies, could imagine a clever getaway. He knew there was no other way out, as he was unable to raise new funds. He had the time and resources to find a lookalike, and then enlist help from someone utterly trustworthy.

The escape story goes something like this. First, suppose that, beginning with the 1929 crash, Ivar knew his companies were destined for collapse. He hadn't intentionally concocted a pyramid scheme, as Price Waterhouse and the bankruptcy trustees later concluded. Instead, he had been too casual in his accounting and had become overextended by borrowing too much money, and paying out too much in dividends. When the market for new funds dried up in late 1929, Ivar must have known he would not be able to sustain those high dividend payments for long.

When he faced the precipice in October 1929, he decided to take the path of gambling on the German loan. But then the markets crashed, and he knew he was ruined. Eventually, falling securities prices would prevent him from raising enough money to pay his increasing obligations. There was no way out.

After the 1929 crash, Ivar had more than two years to ponder every conceivable alternative. He was well read in outlandish schemes; he already had mimicked one, the South Sea Bubble, in his European deal making. He knew how panics destroyed businesses, especially those that had exaggerated their profits. Ivar feared death and was obsessed with preserving his health. He had millions of dollars hidden in various offshore accounts. And he would not have been the first financier, or the last, to consider escape.

Much of the evidence that Ivar's supporters say points to murder could instead be proof of Kreuger-as-Houdini. Suppose, supporters of the escape theory say, Ivar bought a corpse in a Paris morgue, where he could have found a credible body double for a small sum.[10] He might even have arranged for the body to have a stunted left index finger. Suppose he then bought the Browning 9 mm and staged a suicide scene, but inadvertently placed the gun in his poor victim's left hand, as a right-handed person looking down on a body might do. Several observers at Ivar's funeral insisted that the body on display did not resemble him.

Or suppose the body Littorin and Bökman "found" at Ivar's apartment was a dummy. Witnesses said the face in the glass section of the casket appeared to be that of a wax doll. A pallbearer reported that he had never carried a coffin as light as Ivar's, nor had he ever smelled so much wax at a cremation.[11]

The French police relied heavily on testimony from Krister Littorin and Karin Bökman. But what if the two of them were involved in, or at least knew about, Ivar's escape plan? That might explain Bökman's odd behavior during the afternoon of March 12, and shortly thereafter. The police and journalists investigating Ivar's death initially received their information primarily from her. Bökman insisted on being the first one to tell investigators that Ivar had committed suicide. She and Krister Littorin were eager to be the first people to find the body. Why was it so important to be there first, except to set the story? Why did they wait so long before telling the police?

During Bökman's first visit with investigators, when the body was still warm, she did not tell anyone that her bag contained a bulky envelope filled with Swedish kronor that Ivar had given her just two hours earlier. Investigators discovered that later. Nor did Bökman initially tell the French police about the three sealed suitcases. Or that Ivar's last words to her had been that he would see her soon in Stockholm. The police did not even know whether she and Ivar had been having an affair.

For anyone attracted to the escape theory, the key evidence came from lands far away. Various reports found Ivar abroad later during 1932, in Moscow helping Stalin build the Soviet match industry, or in Sumatra simply relaxing. Some journalists reported on a large order from Sumatra for the unique type of custom-made Havana cigars Ivar had favored. Many people, particularly in Sweden, thought Ivar was using this order to confirm, in code, that his escape plan had worked.[12]

If Ivar really had planned to commit suicide, wouldn't he have chosen a more private time than just before a crucial meeting when his whereabouts were known and he was at risk of being interrupted or discovered? Would he have used a new weapon purchased at the last minute, given that he had many guns in Stockholm?

Would he have set up such a seemingly posed bedroom scene, complete with an obscure suicide note? Ivar typically was precise in his choice of language, and the note to Littorin, his closest friend, seems deliberately vague: "I have made such a mess of things that I believe this to be the most satisfactory solution for everybody concerned." What is "this"? Perhaps the word "this" was meant to lay a trail, so that a clever person – perhaps Littorin – would eventually figure it all out. And then there was the form of his signature on the suicide note, which Littorin had never seen: "I.K." What did he mean by that? Why the fat dots?

If Ivar got away, it appears that he never contacted any of his friends. If he promised Karin Bökman he would meet her in Stockholm, he broke the promise. He never told his brother Torsten, who continued to claim Ivar had been murdered. If Ivar contacted Krister Littorin or Anders Jordahl, both men remained silent. Nor did Ivar see Greta Garbo, whose fame surged after the reports of his death, unless they met later in Sumatra, or at the island she had purchased from Ivar's estate.

Perhaps Ivar's closest devotees believed they would help him execute an elaborate escape plan, and then see him again, only to have Ivar betray them, too. Perhaps Ivar understood that the only way for him to ensure he truly could disappear was to mislead his friends, as well as his enemies. Perhaps Ivar had become paranoid, and believed he couldn't rely on even his inner circle. Or perhaps he just wanted to spend his last time on Earth as he had spent his first: alone.

What if Ivar's bipolar displays for Donald Durant, George Murnane, Isaac Marcosson, and others were merely a ruse, a show of manufactured emotions designed to throw everyone off the scent as Ivar flew from his crumpling empire? If Sherlock Holmes really had been on the case, he would have focused on the gaps in the other theories, and asked: If neither suicide nor murder, what else remains? Could that possibility, no matter how improbable, be true?

Doesn't a Hollywood life deserve a Hollywood ending?

Probably not, if facts matter. Yet the fanciful escape theory is not the only one belied by the evidence. None of the most commonly held views of Ivar – as crook, murder victim, or escape artist – reflects the textured and complex reality about his life and death. Ivar was a student of history, a wayward genius with an extraordinary mind who sought, not merely wealth, but greatness. History should regard him as studiously as he regarded history.

As a boy, Ivar had imagined building a life as formidable as the twelfth-century turrets of Kalmar Slott. At first, Ivar's businesses were strong and sturdy: construction projects, real estate, and matches. But the foundation of his empire cracked in October 1929. Just as the shifting of the Swedish–Danish border decimated Kalmar Slott's utility, the market crash wrecked Ivar's companies. He might have responded by downsizing or admitting defeat. But Ivar stubbornly refused to recognize losses or reduce dividends. Instead, he hid his mounting liabilities, and doubled down by lending to Germany. His gamble appeared to work temporarily, but it made his destruction inevitable.

A close analysis of the available evidence suggests that the truth about Ivar Kreuger is somewhere between his stellar reputation before March 12, 1932 and his abysmal reputation after that date. Yes, he committed forgeries and issued false financial statements. Yes, he abused innovative financial techniques to secure control of large publicly traded companies, and then manipulated accounting results so that he would not be beholden to investors he regarded as fickle. But he also legitimately created substantial wealth, revived much of Europe after the war, and generated real profits for investors. He paid out much of those profits as large cash dividends. The bulk of those payments went to Ivar's investors, not to Ivar.

If this revised view is correct, Ivar's role in history is more complicated than previously thought. He was not merely the greatest financial fraudster of the century. He was a builder, as well as a destroyer. He was a victim, as well as a perpetrator. He was a hero, as well as a villain.

His life is like the story of Kalmar Slott, a once-grand fortress that survives even with its core reduced to rubble, a monument to the frailty of any human enterprise in the long run, and a memory of what might have been.

On May 4, 1932, less than two months after Ivar's reported suicide, *The New York Times* featured side-by-side front-page stories on the world's two most infamous criminals.[13] First, the paper reported that, late the previous evening, a police squad car had whisked Alphonse "Scarface" Capone from the Cook County jail to the Dearborn Street station, where he and several government agents had boarded the Dixie Flyer, headed for Atlanta and the federal penitentiary there.

The adjacent story described the first day of hearings before the federal referee overseeing the bankruptcy of International Match – the first witnesses called were Donald Durant and Frederic Allen, from Lee Higginson. "Glad to

Start, He Says" was the tagline for the Capone column; the one about Ivar said "Trusted Him Implicitly."

The implication was that Al Capone and Ivar Kreuger belonged together. When Al Capone's heavy-set, nattily dressed form disappeared into a train in Chicago, people everywhere imagined that Ivar should follow him. That image stuck with Ivar for many years. In these pages I have tried to show that this image is the wrong one. Ivar might have been a crook, at least at the end, but he was a much more attractive one than Capone.

In 1984, Ivar Kreuger made the *Financial Times* list of the top five financial scandals of all time, just behind the South Sea Bubble and the Mississippi Scheme of John Law.[14] In that way, finally, he achieved greatness.

A NOTE ON SOURCES AND ACKNOWLEDGEMENTS

When economist John Kenneth Galbraith reviewed one of the many books on Ivar Kreuger, from 1957, he lamented the absence of source references in that book, and in most of the books that had been written about this remarkable man. He wrote that the "time has come when we must incite readers to violence against all authors – certainly all historians – who do not provide a decent minimum of footnotes. (A place should also be made in the quicklime for the carcasses of publishers who think that footnotes hurt sales.)"[1]

With the hope of avoiding violence, I have included endnotes on pp. 236–62. I have not noted every fact related to Ivar's story, many of which are uncontroversial and were widely reported at the time. In particular, journalists' accounts from 1932 generated much of the material used in later books about Ivar. I have endeavored to set forth sufficient references so that a reader can check the basis for particular facts, or at least see that a reference is there.

With respect to new material not previously cited in other articles and books, I have provided more detailed notes, with the hope that future writers will find it easier to locate sources than I did. In my research, I found that, because of the absence of footnotes in the various articles and books on Ivar, it was difficult to trace numerous secondary references. These difficulties were particularly acute for materials published after 1933, including some of the secondary sources that were the basis of Professor Galbraith's complaints. Therefore, I have tried to refer to primary sources whenever possible in referencing new material.

Most of the primary sources on Ivar are collected in various archives in Sweden and the United States. The largest archives, several miles of documents in aggregate, are in Vadstena, Sweden. Much of the financial information about Ivar's companies, including many of the documents from Anton Wendler, his Swedish accountant, are collected at Riksarkivet, the Swedish National Archive in Arninge, north of Stockholm. Princeton's Mudd Library has a trove of documents from the bankruptcy proceedings of International Match. The Morgan Library & Museum Reading Room includes letters and cables from Jack Morgan about Ivar and some of his dealings, particularly in Germany. The University of Florida Smathers Libraries have an eight-box collection established by Klein, Hinds & Finke, the accounting firm that acted as trustee in bankruptcy for the International Match Corporation. The Match Museum in Jönköping, Sweden, has a fine collection of documents and artifacts, including match machines and a slide show featuring Ivar. I am grateful to the archivists at these places, men and women who carefully watch over the remaining evidence of Ivar's life and death, and particularly to Olle Nordquist and Claes Westling at Vadstena, Nancy Shader at Princeton, and Christine Nelson and Maggie Portis at the Morgan Library.

Although the participants in the saga are not alive, I benefited from numerous discussions and correspondence from several people, some lengthy and others too brief. I am especially grateful to Jonas Ångström, Peter Bevelin, Dale Flesher, Jan Glete, Edward Greenbaum, Axel Hagberg, Maud Hallin, Håkan Lindgren, George Thiel, Henry Tricks, and Ulla Wikander. Laura Adams, Rex Adams, Kent Greenfield, Mark Jackson, Shaun Martin, Christopher McKenna, Larry Mitchell, Michael Pettis, David Skeel, and Adam Winkler gave insightful comments on early drafts.

I also benefited from watching the 1932 film *The Match King* (First National Pictures), which does not refer to Ivar Kreuger by name, but obviously is based on Ivar's life and death. I would caution anyone, though, to take that story with several shovels of salt.

I am grateful to the library staff at the University of San Diego School of Law, and particularly to John Adkins and Sushila Selness. Several students provided invaluable research assistance, especially Kelly Babb and Stefan Cap. I also appreciate the support of Dean Kevin Cole.

Finally, I want to thank Andrew Franklin, who has stood by me faithfully and with good humor, even as I insist on writing about increasingly obscure topics. I am especially grateful to Clive Priddle and Niki Papadopoulos at PublicAffairs for having the courage to embrace Ivar's story and the wisdom to help me tell it. I'm honored to be published by Profile Books and PublicAffairs, and I want to thank everyone at both houses. As always, I appreciate the encouragement, advice, and criticism of Theresa Park, my superstar agent. Thanks to all of you for sticking with this project.

I have included a bibliography of useful sources below. I have relied on many other books and articles, including my own research in other settings. The purpose of this bibliography is not to be comprehensive, but to set forth the most relevant and helpful materials directly related to Ivar's story, and to this book. Minor articles relied on in the book are cited only in the endnotes and are not listed in the bibliography.

BIBLIOGRAPHY

Archives

National Archives of Sweden – Riksarkivet, Arninge, Sweden ("Riksarkivet").
Regional Archives of Sweden – Landsarkivet, Vadstena, Sweden ("Vadstena").
Seeley G. Mudd Manuscript Library, Princeton University, Princeton, New Jersey
   ("Princeton").
The Match Museum, Jönköping, Sweden ("Match Museum").
The Morgan Library & Museum Reading Room, New York, New York ("Morgan
   Library").
The University of Florida George A. Smathers Libraries – Klein, Hinds & Finke
   Records, Gainesville, Florida ("Klein, Hinds & Finke").

Books and book chapters

Adams, Jr, Russell B., *The Boston Money Tree* (Thomas Y. Crowell Company, 1977).
Allen, Frederick Lewis, *Only Yesterday: An Informal History of the 1920s* (Harper
   & Row, 1931).
Allen, Frederick Lewis, *The Great Pierpont Morgan* (Harper & Brothers, 1949).
Allen, Trevor, *Ivar Kreuger, Match King, Croesus and Crook* (John Long, Ltd, 1932).
Anderson, Ingvar, *A History of Sweden* (Weidenfeld & Nicholson, 1955).
Ångström, Lars-Jonas, *Därför Mördades Ivar Kreuger* (Sellin & Blomquist, 1990).
Ångström, Lars-Jonas, *Översättning* (unpublished manuscript).
Berle, Adolf A., Jr & Gardiner C. Means, *The Modern Corporation and Private
   Property* (Macmillan, 1932).
Bernstein, Peter L., *Capital Ideas: The Improbable Origins of Modern Wall Street*
   (John Wiley, 1992).
Bjerre, Poul Carl, *Kreuger* (Natur och Kultur, 1932).

Brooks, John, *Once in Golconda: A True Drama of Wall Street 1920–1938*, at 82 (John Wiley, 1969).

Burk, Kathleen, "The House of Morgan in Financial Diplomacy – 1920–1930," in B. J. McKercher, ed., *The Struggle for Supremacy: Anglo-American Relations in the 1920s* (Macmillan, 1987).

Chernow, Ron, *The House of Morgan: An American Banking Dynasty and the Rise of Modern Finance* (Simon & Schuster, 1990).

Churchill, Allen, *The Incredible Ivar Kreuger* (Rinehart & Company, Inc., 1957).

Deeson, A. F. L., *Great Swindlers: A Fascinating Collection of Some of the World's Most Incredible Frauds*, at 120 (Drake Publishers, 1972).

Drachenfels, Kurt, *The Real Ivar Kreuger* (United Press, 1933).

Edwards, George W., *The Evolution of Finance Capitalism* (Longmans, Green and Co., 1938).

Eichengreen, Barry, *Golden Fetters: The Gold Standard and the Great Depression 1919–1939* (Oxford University Press, 1992).

Galbraith, John Kenneth, *The Great Crash 1929* (Houghton Mifflin, 1954).

Geisst, Charles R., *Wall Street: A History* (Oxford University Press, 1997).

Georg, Manfred, *The Case of Ivar Kreuger* (Jonathan Cape, 1933).

Glete, Jan, *Kreugerkoncerne och Boliden* (LiberFörlag, 1975).

Glete, Jan, *Kreugerkoncernen och Krisen På Svensk Aktiemarknad* (Almqvist & Wiksell, 1981).

Graham, Benjamin and David L. Dodd, *Security Analysis* (Whittlesey House, 1934).

Hassbring, Lars, *The International Development of the Swedish Match Company, 1917–1924* (LiberFörlag, 1979).

Keynes, John Maynard, *The Economic Consequences of the Peace* (Harcourt, Brace & Howe, 1920).

Kindleberger, Charles P., *Manias, Panics and Crashes* (John Wiley, 1978).

Kreuger, Torsten, *The Truth About Ivar Kreuger* (Seewald, 1968).

Lefèvre, Edwin, *Reminiscences of a Stock Operator* (George H. Doran and Company, 1923).

Lindgren, Håkan, *Corporate Growth: The Swedish Match Industry in Its Global Setting* (LiberFörlag, 1979).

Loewe, Walter, Arne Jansson, and Carl Magnus Rosell, *From Swedish Matches to Swedish Match: Sweden's Match Industry 1836–1996* (Wahlström & Widstrand, 1997).

Mackay, Charles, *Extraordinary Delusions and the Madness of Crowds* (Harriman House, 2003).

Marcosson, Isaac Frederick, *Turbulent Years* (Books for Libraries Press, 1938).

Markham, Jerry W., *A Financial History of the United States* (M. E. Sharpe, 2002).

Mitchell, Lawrence E., *The Speculation Economy: How Finance Triumphed Over Industry* (Berrett-Koehler Publishers, Inc., 2007).

Moberg, Vilhelm, *A History of the Swedish People: From Renaissance to Revolution* (Dorset Press, 1971).

Modig, Hans, *Swedish Match Interests in British India During the Interwar Years* (LiberFörlag, 1979).

Partnoy, Frank, *Infectious Greed: How Deceit and Risk Corrupted the Financial Markets* (Profile, 2003).

Rand, Ayn, *Night of January 16th* (Plume, 1971).

Ripley, William Z., *Main Street and Wall Street* (Little Brown & Co., 1927).

Scott, Franklin D., *Sweden: The Nation's History* (Southern Illinois University Press, 1988).

Seligman, Joel, *The Transformation of Wall Street: A History of the Securities and Exchange Commission and Modern Corporate Finance* (Houghton Mifflin, 1982).

Shaplen, Robert, *Kreuger: Genius and Swindler* (Alfred A. Knopf, 1960).

Soloveychik, George, *The Financier: The Life of Ivar Kreuger* (Peter Davies, 1933).

Sparling, Earl, *Kreuger's Billion Dollar Bubble* (Greenberg, 1932).

Stolpe, Sven, *Ivar Kreuger Mördad?* (Médans, 1955).

Stoneman, William H., *The Life and Death of Ivar Kreuger* (The Bobbs-Merrill Company, 1932).

Strouse, Jean, *Morgan: American Financier* (Random House, 1999).

Thunholm, Lars-Erik, trans. George Thiel, *Ivar Kreuger: The Match King* (T. Fischer & Co., 1995).

Train, John, *Famous Financial Fiascos* (Clarkson N. Potter, Inc., 1985).

Wasik, John F., *The Merchant of Power: Sam Insull, Thomas Edison, and the Creation of the Modern Metropolis* (Palgrave Macmillan, 2006).

Wikander, Ulla, *Kreuger's Match Monopolies, 1925–1930: Case Studies in Market Control Through Public Monopolies* (LiberFörlag, 1979).

Wilkins, Mira, *The History of Foreign Investment in the United States, 1914–1945* (Harvard University Press, 2004).

Zuckoff, Mitchell, *Ponzi's Scheme: The True Story of a Financial Legend* (Random House, 2005).

Articles

Austin, K. L., "Ivar Kreuger's Story in Light of Five Years," *The New York Times*, Mar. 7, 1937.

Barman, T. G., "Ivar Kreuger: His Life and Work," *The Atlantic Monthly*, vol. 150, Aug. 1932, at 238–50.

Blystone, Richard, "The Crash Heard 'Round the World,'" The Associated Press, Oct. 29, 1979, AM Cycle.

Cannon, Arthur M., "Kreuger, Genius and Swindler," *Journal of Accountancy*, Sep. 1961, at 94.

Childs, Marquis W., "Sweden: Where Capitalism is Controlled," *Harper's Magazine*, vol. 167, Nov. 1933, at 749.

Citron, Bernhard, "America Sinks; Russia Rises," *Litter's Living Age*, Jun. 1932, at 315.

Crum, W. L. and J. B. Hubbard, "Review of the First Quarter of 1932," *Review of Economic Statistics*, vol. 14, May 15, 1932, at 66–73.

Done, Kevin, "Swedish Match Strikes Back in Royal Style," *Financial Times*, Mar. 31, 1987, at 6.

Fane, Malachy, "The Swedish Juggler," *New Republic*, vol. 71, Jul. 13, 1932, at 239.

"Financial World Not Yet Sure What Kreuger Suicide Means," *Business Week*, Mar. 19, 1932, at 5.

Flesher, Dale L. and Tonya K. Flesher, "Ivar Kreuger's Contribution to Financial Reporting," *Accounting Review*, vol. 61, no. 3, Jul. 1986, at 421–34.

Flynn, John T., "Kreuger: Another Holding Company Debacle," *New Republic*, vol. 71, May 25, 1932.

"Four Masters of Fraud," *Newsweek*, vol. 49, Apr. 11, 1957, at 94.

Galbraith, John Kenneth, "How to Become an International Swindler," *Reporter*, vol. 16, Mar. 21, 1957, at 45.

"German Matches; Strike a Light," *Economist*, Jan. 22, 1983, at 66.

Hertzberg, Sidney, "Aftermath of the Kreuger Crash," *Current History*, vol. 39, Nov. 1933, at 239.

Hertzberg, Sidney, "Ivar Kreuger's Liabilities," *Current History*, vol. 37, Nov. 1932, at 233.

"High Finance: The House of Matches," *Time*, vol. 46, Nov. 5, 1945, at 88.

"Kreuger Finale," *Time*, vol. 28, Jul. 13, 1936, at 66.

Labaton, Stephen, "Archives of Business: A Rogues Gallery; Ivar Kreuger: Sweden's Match King," *The New York Times*, Dec. 7, 1986, sect. 3, at 23.

Lambert, Richard, "Shady Dealings on the Grandest Scale," *Financial Times*, Aug. 15, 1984, at 9.

Lazar, Maria, "Is Kreuger Dead?," *Littell's Living Age*, vol. 344, Mar. 1933.

Lebergott, Stanley, "The Shape of the Income Distribution," *American Economic Review*, vol. 49, Jun. 1959, at 328.

Lewinsohn, Richard, "Second Thoughts on Kreuger," *Littell's Living Age*, Jun. 1932, at 318.

Lundberg, Erik, "The Rise and Fall of the Swedish Model," *Journal of Economic Literature*, vol. 23, Mar. 1985, at 1.

Lyons, Eugene, "Interviewing the Titans," *Saturday Review of Literature*, vol. 18, Oct. 22, 1938, at 6.

Marcosson, Isaac F., "An Interview with Ivar Kreuger," *Saturday Evening Post*, Apr. 2, 1932, at 3–5.

Marcosson, Isaac F., "The Match King," *Saturday Evening Post*, Oct. 12, 1929, at 3–4.

Marcosson, Isaac F., "The Swedish Recovery," *Saturday Evening Post*, Feb. 22, 1936, at 23.

"Matches: Cigarettes Light Way for Continued Diamond Profits," *Newsweek*, vol. 7, Jun. 13, 1936, at 34.

Olson, Alma Luise, "Kreuger is Called Victim of System," *The New York Times*, Mar. 26, 1933, at 2.

Picton, John, "The Death of the World's Greatest Swindler," *Toronto Star*, Aug. 21, 1988, at Ao.

Ross, Nancy L., "Yesterday's Financial Failures, Today's Successful Souvenirs," *Washington Post*, Mar. 1, 1981, at F1.

Rydbeck, Oscar, "Was Kreuger Crazy?," *Littell's Living Age*, Jun. 1932, at 321.

Shaplen, Robert, "Annals of Crime: Kreuger – I," *New Yorker*, vol. 35, Sep. 26, 1959, at 51.

Shaplen, Robert, "Annals of Crime: Kreuger – II," *New Yorker*, vol. 35, Oct. 3, 1959, at 108.

Shaplen, Robert, "Annals of Crime: Kreuger – III," *New Yorker*, vol. 35, Oct. 10, 1959, at 51.

Simons, Rodger L., "The Garden of Sweden," *North American Review*, vol. 238, Nov. 1938, at 414.

Smith, Geoffrey, "The Legacy of Ivar Kreuger," *Forbes*, vol. 136, Dec. 2, 1985, at 143.

Soloveychik, George, "The Tragedy of Ivar Kreuger," *Nineteenth Century*, vol. 111, Apr. 1932, at 421.

"Swedish Stockmarket; Too Hot to Handle," *Economist*, Apr. 30, 1983, at 106.

Taylor, J. R., "Some Antecedents of the Securities and Exchange Commission," *Accounting Review*, vol. 16, Jun. 1941.

"The Diamond Match Co.," *Fortune*, vol. 19, May 1939.

"The Kreuger Case Again," *New Republic*, vol. 73, Jan. 25, 1933, at 284.

"The Kreuger Saga," *Littell's Living Age*, vol. 355, Feb. 1939.

"The Passing of Ivar Kreuger," *Literary Digest*, Mar. 26, 1932, at 56.

"The Week," *New Republic*, Mar. 23, 1932, at 1.

"The World Over," *Littell's Living Age*, vol. 342, May 1932, at 189.

Thompson, Howard and Anita Gates, "Movies: Critics' Choice," *The New York Times*, Dec. 5, 1999, at 6.

Thompson, Ralph, "Sweden's Losses in Kreuger Crash," *Current History*, vol. 36, Jul. 1932, at 501.

Thompson, Ralph, "The Unfolding of the Kreuger Scandal," *Current History*, vol. 36, Jun. 1932, at 361.

Unstad, Lyder L., "Sweden: The Middle Way," *American Economic Review*, vol. 26, Jun. 1936, at 304.

Visser, W. A., "Who was Ivar Kreuger?," *Christian Century*, vol. 49, May 11, 1932, at 617.

Webb, Sara, "Stora Offers 541 M Pounds for Swedish Match," *Financial Times*, Mar. 10, 1988, at 48.

"Why the House of Kreuger Fell," *Literary Digest*, vol. 115, Feb. 4, 1933, at 40.

Whyte, Frederic, "An Interpretation of Ivar Kreuger," *Contemporary Review*, vol. 143, Apr. 1933, at 465.

Winkler, Max, "Playing with Matches," in *Foreign Bonds: An Autopsy*, (Beard Books, 1999), at 93–103.

Winterich, John T., "Swindler Extraordinary," *Saturday Review*, vol. 40, Feb. 2, 1957, at 20.

"World's Greatest Swindler," *Time*, vol. 69, Jan. 28, 1957, at 106.

Wuorinen, John H., "Kreuger's Vanished Millions," *Current History*, vol. 26, May 1932, at 241.

Zeff, Stephen A., "How the US Accounting Profession Got Where It is Today: Part I," *Accounting Horizons*, vol. 17, no. 3, Sep. 2003, at 189–205.

Government publications

Congressional Record, House, Apr. 18, 1932 (US Government Printing Office, 1932).

Congressional Record, House, May 4, 1933 (US Government Printing Office, 1933).

Congressional Record, House, Jul. 13, 1932 (US Government Printing Office, 1932).

Congressional Record, House, May 11, 1933 (US Government Printing Office, 1933).

Stock Exchange Practices, Senate Committee Report (US Government Printing Office, 1933).

Testimony of A.D. Berning, Stock Exchange Practices, Senate Committee Report, at 1249 (US Government Printing Office, 1933).

Testimony of Donald Durant, Stock Exchange Practices, Senate Committee Report, at 1146 (US Government Printing Office, 1933).

Testimony of George O. May, Stock Exchange Practices, Senate Committee Report, at 1260 (US Government Printing Office, 1933).

NOTES

Chapter 1

1. Churchill, at 108–13; Shaplen, at 66–8.
2. Loewe *et al.*, at 238, 241, 247.
3. M. S. Dimand, "Mediaeval Textiles of Sweden," *Art Bulletin*, vol. 6, no. 1 (Sep. 1923), at 11–16.
4. Louis Mancini, *Monsters of the Sea: The Great Ocean Liners of Time, http://www.ocean-liners.com* (2007). RMS *Berengaria* has a celebrated, and somewhat unusual, history. She was launched on May 23, 1912, as SS *Imperator*, and was sold out in all classes for several trips between Cuxhaven and New York. In 1914, officials of the German Imperial Navy stopped the ship from leaving harbor, citing the risk of losing a valuable ship to the enemy. The Germans then hid the ship in a harbor near the Elbe river, where she rusted, stuck in the mud, until 1919, when the US Navy discovered her. The US Navy used the ship to transport troops home to America until 1921, when the Cunard Line bought and remodeled her and rechristened her *Berengaria*.
5. Shaplen, at 59–60 (quoting Carl Bergman).
6. Churchill, at 109.
7. Brooks, at 82.
8. David Cannadine, *Mellon: An American Life* (Alfred A. Knopf, 2006), ch. 10.
9. "About RCA: The Radio Corporation of America," *http://home.rca.com/en-US/PressReleaseDetail.html?Cat=RCAHistory&MN=6* (2007).
10. RCA *v.* MSFT, *http://www.gold-eagle.com* (2007).
11. Loewe *et al.*, at 13–16.
12. Kreuger, at 88b.
13. Stoneman, at 60–68.
14. Thunholm, at 33.

15. Thunholm, at 34.

16. Thunholm, at 34.

17. Barry Paris, *Garbo* (Alfred A. Knopf, 1995), at 43.

18. Thunholm, at 35.

19. Stoneman, at 68.

20. Mackay, at 46–97.

21. US Securities and Exchange Commission, Day Trading, *http://www.sec.gov/answers/daytrading.htm* (2007).

22. Jerry Markham, *The History of Commodity Futures Trading and Its Regulation*, (Praeger, 1987), ch. 1, n. 13.

23. Lefèvre.

24. More recent editions of the book have suggested that Edwin Lefèvre was a pseudonym for Jesse Livermore. Foreword by Jack Schwager, Edwin Lefèvre, *Reminiscences of a Stock Operator* (John Wiley & Sons, Inc., 1994), at 7.

25. Deeson, at 116–25; see also Zuckoff.

26. The idea originated from the Universal Postal Union Congress in Rome in 1906, which sought to resolve the problem of how a person might send a self-addressed stamped envelope abroad. The basic idea survives today, and the postal reply coupon is accepted throughout the world. Indeed, it remains the most viable way to send a self-addressed stamped envelope when foreign stamps are not available in the United States. See http://www.upu.int/irc/en/index.shtml.

27. Churchill, at 112.

Chapter 2

1. "Durant, Financier, Dies on Elevated," *The New York Times*, Aug. 12, 1941, at 20.

2. "Bonds and Bond Men," *Wall Street Journal*, Aug. 15, 1927, at 4.

3. Shaplen, at 69–70.

4. Vadstena, 1921–5, K-004, letter from Anders Jordahl to Ivar Kreuger, Dec. 22, 1922.

5. Vadstena, Amerika 1918–22, K-065, letter from Cary T. Grayson to Ivar Kreuger, Sep. 15, 1922.

6. Adams, at 183.

7. Adams, at 233.

8. Adams, at 233.

9. Adams, at 260.

10. Adams, at 265.

11. "Kreuger's Books," *Time*, Apr. 18, 1932.

12. "Urges Liberal Use of War Savings Stamps," *The New York Times*, Nov. 23, 1917, at 15.

13. Adams, at 260.

14. "Bond Club Elections," *Wall Street Journal*, Jun. 24, 1922.

15. "Bond Club Elections," *Wall Street Journal*, Jun. 24, 1922.

16. "The Bond Club of New York, history," *http://www.thebondclub.com/history.html*.

17. The *Bawl Street Journal* is still published today, in an online version, *http://www.thebondclub.com/bawlstreetjournal.html*. Its 2007 edition included headlines announcing "New Jersey Votes to Go Private," and "Hedge fund managers earning more than $1 billion a year point out that $1 billion is just not what it used to be." *http://www.thebondclub.com/2007BSJ.pdf*.

18. "Durant, Financier, Dies on Elevated," *The New York Times*, Aug. 12, 1941, at 20.

19. Stoneman, at 123; Shaplen, at 58.

20. Princeton, Box 2, Examination of Anders Jordahl, Stenographer's Minutes, In the Matter of International Match Corporation, Bankrupt, United States District Court, Southern District of New York in Bankruptcy, Feb. 1, 1933, at 2–5.

21. Barry Paris, *Garbo* (Alfred A. Knopf, 1995), at 23–4.

22. Vadstena, Amerika 1918–22, letter from Anders Jordahl to Ivar Kreuger, Dec. 11, 1919.

23. Shaplen, at 58.

24. Vadstena, Amerika 1918–22, letter from Anders Jordahl to Ivar Kreuger, Mar. 23, 1921.

25. Vadstena, Amerika 1918–22, cable from Ivar Kreuger to Anders Jordahl, Jul. 7, 1921.

26. *Nosferatu*, "A Symphony of Horror," *http://movies.toptenreviews.com/reviews/mr221868.htm*.

27. Vadstena, Amerika 1918–22, letter from Anders Jordahl to Ivar Kreuger, Dec. 22, 1921.

28. Vadstena, 1921–5, letter from Eric Landgren to Ivar Kreuger, May 28, 1921.

29. Vadstena, Amerika 1918–22, letter from William A. Fairburn to Ivar Kreuger, Dec. 9, 1921.

30. Hollis Alpert, "Saga of Greta Lovisa Gustafson; Saga of Greta Garbo," *The New York Times*, Sep. 5, 1965, at SM26.

31. Barry Paris, *Garbo* (Alfred A. Knopf, 1995), at 241.

32. Vadstena, 1921–5, correspondence and brief of Eric G. Landgren, Aug. 13, 1921.

33. Vadstena, Amerika 1918–22, cable from Froeander to Ivar Kreuger, Mar. 19, 1921.

34. Vadstena, 1921–5, letter from Ivar Kreuger to William A. Fairburn, May 4, 1922.

35. Vadstena, 1921–5, letter from Eric Landgren to Ivar Kreuger, May 21, 1921.
36. Vadstena, 1921–5, letter from W. E. Seatree to Ivar Kreuger, Sep. 13, 1922.
37. Vadstena, 1921–5, letter from W. E. Seatree to Ivar Kreuger, Sep. 13, 1922.
38. Vadstena, Amerika 1922–4, letter from Anders Jordahl to Ivar Kreuger, Jun. 13, 1922.
39. Vadstena, 1921–5, cable from Ivar Kreuger to Anders Jordahl, Sep. 26, 1922.
40. Thunholm, at 78.
41. David W. Dunlap, "Renovation Project Takes New Prep School to the Bank," *The New York Times*, Jun. 21, 2004, at B3. The renovation project was completed shortly after Ivar's initial meeting with Durant.

Chapter 3
1. Adams, at 259.
2. Keynes, at 237.
3. Stoneman, at 47–8.
4. Churchill, at 54–5.
5. Churchill, at 56–7.
6. Churchill, at 53.
7. Churchill, at 58.
8. Stoneman, at 50–51.
9. Stoneman, at 51–2; Soloveychik, at 80–81.
10. Shaplen, at 42.
11. Shaplen, at 41.
12. Thunholm, at 39.
13. Shaplen, at 42.
14. Stoneman, at 58.
15. Thunholm, at 71.
16. Soloveychik, at 6.
17. Adams, at 260.
18. Adams, at 259–60.
19. Stoneman, at 123.
20. Brooks, ch. 1.
21. Chernow, at 213.
22. Allen, at 63.
23. Brooks, at 8–20.
24. Chernow, at 214.
25. Chernow, at 215.
26. Chernow, at 200.
27. Burk, at 4.
28. Chernow, at 210–17.
29. Stoneman, at 139.

30. Stoneman, Table VII (as per prospectus).

31. Vadstena, Amerika 1922–4, letter from T. L. Higginson, Jr to Ivar Kreuger, Oct. 1, 1923; *The New England Historical and Genealogical Register*, vols. 37–52 (1855), at 46.

32. Vadstena, Amerika 1922–4, letter from Oscar Cooper to Ivar Kreuger, Nov. 12, 1923.

33. Vadstena, Amerika 1922–4, letter from J. W. H. Hamilton to Ivar Kreuger, Oct. 23, 1924.

34. Vadstena, Amerika 1922–4, letter from Donald Durant to Ivar Kreuger, Oct. 23, 1924.

35. Vadstena, Amerika 1922–4, letter from Chauncey P. Colwell to Ivar Kreuger, Oct. 20, 1923.

36. Vadstena, Amerika 1922–4, Letter from Edward B. Robinette to Ivar Kreuger, Dec. 24, 1923.

37. "New Issues being Carefully Priced," *Wall Street Journal*, Oct. 26, 1923, at 5.

38. Partnoy; Nelson D. Schwartz, "Inside the Market's Myth Machine," *Fortune*, Oct. 2, 2000, at 114.

39. Kreuger, at 88b–c.

Chapter 4

1. Churchill, at 126.

2. Stoneman, at 124.

3. Churchill, at 125.

4. Vadstena, K. Littorin, 1923, cable from Ivar Kreuger to Krister Littorin, Oct. 28, 1923.

5. Stoneman, at 127.

6. Hassbring, at 177.

7. Hassbring, at 180.

8. Hassbring, at 196.

9. Hassbring at 196–9.

10. Lars Engwall, Staffan Furusten, and Eva Wallerstedt, "The Changing Relationship between Management Consulting and Academia: Evidence from Sweden," in *Management Consulting: Emergence and Dynamics of a Knowledge Industry*, Matthias Kipping and Lars Engwall, eds. (Oxford University Press, 2002), at 38–42; Eva Wallerstedt, *Oskar Sillén: Professor Och Praktiker* (Acta Universitatis Upsaliensis, 1988).

11. Hassbring, at 199.

12. Thunholm, at 62.

13. Hassbring, at 199.

14. Stoneman, at 70.

15. Churchill, at 116.
16. "History: Two Men, One Vision," http://www.big4.com/ErnstYoung/History. aspx.
17. Zeff, at 191.

Chapter 5

1. Vadstena, Berning 1918–31, letter from Ivar Kreuger to A.D. Berning, Jun. 8, 1923.
2. Stoneman, at 125.
3. Stoneman, at 125.
4. Vadstena, Berning 1918–31, letter from A.D. Berning to Ivar Kreuger, Jan. 23, 1924.
5. Vadstena, Berning 1918–31, letter from A.D. Berning to Ivar Kreuger, Nov. 30, 1923.
6. Vadstena, Berning 1918–31, letter from Ivar Kreuger to A.D. Berning, Apr. 28, 1924.
7. Vadstena, Berning 1918–31, letter from Ivar Kreuger to A.D. Berning, Jun. 30, 1924.
8. Vadstena, Berning 1918–31, letter from A.D. Berning to Ivar Kreuger, Apr. 8, 1924.
9. Vadstena, Berning 1918–31, letter from O. Hibma to Lee Higginson, Apr. 15, 1924.
10. Vadstena, Berning 1918–31, letter from Ivar Kreuger to A.D. Berning, Apr. 28, 1924.
11. Vadstena, Berning 1918–31, letter from A.D. Berning to Ivar Kreuger, May 24, 1924.
12. Vadstena, Berning 1918–31, telegram from A.D. Berning to Ivar Kreuger, Jun. 18, 1924.
13. Vadstena, Berning 1918–31, letter from A.D. Berning to Ivar Kreuger, Jul. 19, 1924.
14. Vadstena, Berning 1918–31, letter from A.D. Berning to Ivar Kreuger, Jul. 19, 1924.
15. Vadstena, Berning 1918–31, letter from Ivar Kreuger to A.D. Berning, Jul. 23, 1924.
16. Vadstena, Berning 1918–31, telegram from A.D. Berning to Ivar Kreuger, Jul. 25, 1924.
17. Vadstena, Berning 1918–31, telegram from Ivar Kreuger to A.D. Berning, Aug. 21, 1924.
18. Vadstena, Berning 1918–31, International Match Corporation, Statement of Assets and Liabilities as of Dec. 31, 1924.

19. Vadstena, Berning 1918–31, Consolidated Profit and Loss Account, International Match Corporation and Constituent Companies for the Year Ended Dec. 31, 1924.

20. Vadstena, Berning 1918–31, International Match Corporation, Estimate of Income and Expenses for the Year 1924.

21. Ripley, at 162–88.

22. Vadstena, Berning 1918–31, International Match Corporation, Consolidated Profit and Loss Accounts, 1921–3.

23. Vadstena, Berning 1918–31, International Match Corporation, Consolidated Profit and Loss Account, 1921.

24. Stoneman, at 126.

25. Stoneman, at 127.

Chapter 6

1. Wikander, at 23–5.

2. Wikander, at 22, 24.

3. Wikander, at 155, 161.

4. Wikander, at 25, 289 (citing *Board of Trade Journal*, Sep. 28, 1916, S-157; H-4; K-115).

5. Wikander, at 26.

6. Wikander, at 27.

7. Wikander, at 30.

8. Wikander, at 31.

9. Shaplen, at 81.

10. Stoneman, at 104.

11. "Sweden Bearing Up in Kreuger Crash," *The New York Times*, Apr. 26, 1932, at 29.

12. Thunholm, at 82.

13. Vadstena, Berning 1918–31, telegram from A.D. Berning to Ivar Kreuger, Jan. 6, 1925.

14. Vadstena, Berning 1918–31, telegram from Ivar Kreuger to A.D. Berning, Jan. 7, 1925.

15. Vadstena, Berning 1918–31, telegram from A.D. Berning to Ivar Kreuger, Jan. 15, 1925.

16. Stoneman, at 72.

17. Ripley, at 85.

18. Ripley, at 81.

19. Ripley, at 81–2.

20. Stoneman, at 72.

21. Soloveychik, at 100–101; Stoneman, at 72.

22. Ripley, at 85–90.
23. W. H. Stevens, "Stockholders' Voting Rights and the Centralization of Voting Control," *Quarterly Journal of Economics*, May 1926, at 352–92.
24. Ripley, at 121.
25. Vadstena, Berning 1918–31, letter from A.D. Berning to Ivar Kreuger, Mar. 16, 1925.
26. Vadstena, Berning 1918–31, letter from A.D. Berning to Ivar Kreuger, Jan. 16, 1925.
27. Vadstena, Berning 1918–31, letter from Ivar Kreuger to A.D. Berning, Mar. 16, 1925.
28. Vadstena, Berning 1918–31, letter from A.D. Berning to Ivar Kreuger, May 28, 1925.
29. Vadstena, Berning 1918–31, letter from A.D. Berning to Lee Higginson & Co., Sep. 2, 1925.
30. Vadstena, Berning 1918–31, letter from A.D. Berning to Lee Higginson & Co., Sep. 2, 1925.
31. Stoneman, at 264.
32. Stoneman, at 265, 270.
33. Stoneman, at 266.
34. Stoneman, at 268.
35. Stoneman, at 268.
36. Stoneman, at 269.
37. Shaplen, at 83.
38. Shaplen, at 83.
39. Shaplen, at 84.
40. Shaplen, at 84.
41. Allen, at 27–8.
42. Soloveychik, at 27.
43. Soloveychik, at 27, 29.
44. Soloveychik, at 29.
45. Shaplen, at 84.
46. Shaplen, at 85.
47. "Kreuger was 'Fine,' Says Woman Friend," *The New York Times*, Apr. 24, 1932, at 9.
48. Vadstena, Berning 1918–31, letter from A.D. Berning to Ivar Kreuger, Apr. 7, 1925.
49. http://www.ocean-liners.com/ships/Aquitania.asp.
50. Vadstena, Berning 1918–31, letter from A.D. Berning to Ivar Kreuger, Apr. 15, 1925.
51. Vadstena, Berning 1918–31, letter from Ivar Kreuger to A.D. Berning, May 5, 1925.

52. Vadstena, Berning 1918–31, telegram from Ivar Kreuger to A.D. Berning, Jul. 8, 1925.

53. Vadstena, Berning 1918–31, telegram from Ivar Kreuger, Krister Littorin, and Carl Bergman to A.D. Berning, July 23, 1925.

54. Vadstena, Berning 1918–31, telegram from Ivar Kreuger to A.D. Berning, Jul. 11, 1925.

55. Vadstena, Berning 1918–31, letter from Ivar Kreuger to Ernst & Ernst, Jul. 13, 1925.

56. Vadstena, Berning 1918–31, letter from A.D. Berning to Ivar Kreuger, Aug. 10, 1925.

57. Vadstena, Berning 1918–31, letter from A.D. Berning to Ivar Kreuger, Dec. 7, 1925.

58. Vadstena, Berning 1918–31, letter from A.D. Berning to Ivar Kreuger, Dec. 8, 1925.

59. Vadstena, Berning 1918–31, letter from A.D. Berning to Lee Higginson & Co., Dec. 5, 1925.

60. Vadstena, Berning 1918–31, letter from Ernst & Ernst to Lee Higginson & Co., Dec. 11, 1925.

61. Vadstena, Berning 1918–31, letter from A.D. Berning to Ivar Kreuger, Dec. 11, 1925.

62. Vadstena, Berning 1918–31, letter from A.D. Berning to Ivar Kreuger, Dec. 29, 1925.

Chapter 7

1. Edwards, at 276, 284.
2. Ripley, at 95.
3. Allen, *Only Yesterday*, at 144.
4. Allen, *Only Yesterday*, at 140–41.
5. Allen, *Only Yesterday*, at 141.
6. Allen, *Only Yesterday*, at 109; Gary Alan Fine, "Reputational Entrepreneurs and the Memory of Incompetence: Melting Supporters, Partisan Warriors, and Images of President Harding," *American Journal of Sociology*, vol. 101, no. 5 (Mar. 1996), at 1159–93.
7. Allen, *Only Yesterday*, at 157.
8. Peter Hannaford, *The Quotable Calvin Coolidge* (Images from the Past, 2001), at 169.
9. David Greenberg, *Calvin Coolidge* (Times Books, 2006), at 9.
10. Allen, *Only Yesterday*, at 94.
11. Ripley, at 184.
12. Ripley, at 162.

13. Ripley, at 181.
14. Ripley, at 186–8.
15. Vadstena, Berning 1918–31, letter from Ivar Kreuger to A.D. Berning, Mar. 19, 1926.
16. Vadstena, Berning 1918–31, letter from A.D. Berning to Ivar Kreuger, Apr. 7, 1926.
17. Vadstena, Berning 1918–31, telegram from Ivar Kreuger to Ben Tomlinson, Apr. 21, 1926.
18. Vadstena, Berning 1918–31, letter from A.D. Berning to Ivar Kreuger, May 3, 1926.
19. Vadstena, Berning 1918–31, letter from A.D. Berning to Ivar Kreuger, May 3, 1926.
20. Vadstena, Berning 1918–31, letter from A.D. Berning to Ivar Kreuger, May 10, 1926.
21. Vadstena, Berning 1918–31, letter from A.D. Berning to Ivar Kreuger, Jun. 18, 1926.
22. Vadstena, Berning 1918–31, letter from Ivar Kreuger to A.D. Berning, Jul. 27, 1926.
23. Vadstena, Berning 1918–31, letter from A.D. Berning to Ivar Kreuger, Jul. 14, 1926.
24. Vadstena, Berning 1918–31, letter from A.D. Berning to Ivar Kreuger, Jun. 28, 1926.
25. Vadstena, Berning 1918–31, letter from Ernst August Hoffman to A.D. Berning, Sep. 1, 1926.
26. Vadstena, Berning 1918–31, letter from A.D. Berning to Ivar Kreuger, Sep. 13, 1926.
27. Stoneman, at 128.
28. Stoneman, at 133.
29. Vadstena, Berning 1918–31, letter from Ernst & Ernst to Lee Higginson & Company, Nov. 10, 1927.
30. Vadstena, Berning 1918–31, letter from A.D. Berning to Ivar Kreuger, Jun. 23, 1927.
31. Stoneman, at 61.
32. Vadstena, Berning 1918–31, letter from Ivar Kreuger to A.D. Berning, Feb. 24, 1927.
33. Vadstena, Berning 1918–31, letter from Ivar Kreuger to A.D. Berning, Feb. 15, 1927.
34. Vadstena, Berning 1918–31, letter from Ivar Kreuger to A.D. Berning, Feb. 15, 1927.

35. Vadstena, Berning 1918–31, letter from A.D. Berning to Ivar Kreuger, Mar. 25, 1927.

36. Soloveychik, at 30.

37. Stoneman, at 133.

38. Stoneman, at 94.

39. http://www.grandhotel.se/in_english/about_grand_hotel/history/the_building.asp.

40. Vadstena, Berning 1918–31, letter from A.D. Berning to A. Wendler, May 14, 1927.

41. Vadstena, Berning 1918–31, letter from A.D. Berning to Ivar Kreuger, May 14, 1927.

42. Gerald Leinwand, *1927: High Tide of the 1920s* (Basic Books, 2001), at 1.

43. Wilford J. Eiteman, "The Relation of Call Money Rates to Stock Market Speculation," *Quarterly Journal of Economics*, vol. 47, no. 3 (May 1933), at 449–63.

44. "Stock Market," *Time*, Apr. 18, 1927.

45. Wikander, at 28.

46. Thunholm, at 94.

47. Thunholm, at 95.

48. "World in Grip of Big Match Trust," *Boston Post*, Jan. 16, 1928.

49. Vadstena, Berning 1918–31, letter from A.D. Berning to Ivar Kreuger, Nov. 10, 1927.

50. Soloveychik, at 109.

51. Vadstena, Berning 1918–31, letter from A.D. Berning to Ivar Kreuger, Nov. 10, 1927.

52. Barman, at 242.

53. Marcosson, at 28.

54. Churchill, at 164.

Chapter 8

1. Soloveychik, at 30–36.

2. Soloveychik, at 19.

3. "Ivar Kreuger's Monument," *The New York Times*, Mar. 20, 1932, at 10X; T. Allen, at 55–63.

4. Soloveychik, at 20.

5. Grünewald and his wife, Sigrid Hjertén, were widely credited with bringing modernism to Sweden, along with what were then unfashionably forward-thinking ideas about the role of Jews and women in society.

6. "Monopolist," *Time*, Oct. 28, 1929, at 46.

7. Soloveychik, at 12–13.

8. Churchill, at 218.
9. Soloveychik, at 22.
10. Vadstena, Berning 1918–31, letter from Ivar Kreuger to A.D. Berning, Feb. 20, 1928.
11. Vadstena, Berning 1918–31, letter from A.D. Berning to Ivar Kreuger, Feb. 23, 1928.
12. Vadstena, Berning 1918–31, letter from A.D. Berning to Ivar Kreuger, May 31, 1928.
13. "All the King's Horses and All the King's Men were Still Optimistic," *The New York Times* Think Tank, Apr. 3, 1999.
14. Vadstena, Berning 1918–31, letter from A.D. Berning to Ivar Kreuger, Jul. 2, 1928.
15. Vadstena, Berning 1918–31, telegram from A.D. Berning to Ivar Kreuger, Jun. 30, 1928.
16. Vadstena, Berning 1918–31, letter from A.D. Berning to Ivar Kreuger, May 31, 1928.
17. Vadstena, Bökman, receipt from Restaurant Paillard, Jun. 13, 1928.
18. Vadstena, Berning 1918–31, letter from Ivar Kreuger to A.D. Berning, Jun. 14, 1928.
19. Vadstena, Berning 1918–31, letter from A.D. Berning to Ivar Kreuger, Oct. 3, 1928.
20. Vadstena, Berning 1918–31, letter from Ivar Kreuger to A.D. Berning, Nov. 27, 1928.
21. "Match Trust Wins in Latvia," *The New York Times*, Jan. 13, 1929, 6: 7.
22. "Gets Rumanian Match Monopoly," *The New York Times*, Jan. 31, 1929, 3: 5.
23. "Swedish Match Report for 1928," *The New York Times*, Apr. 11, 1929, 42: 2.
24. Shaplen, at 128.
25. Thunholm, at 107.
26. Vadstena, Dondurant I, 1929, telegram from Ivar Kreuger to Donald Durant, Feb. 13, 1929.
27. "Gets Rumanian Match Monopoly," *The New York Times*, Jan. 31, 1929, 3: 5.
28. "Brazil Pays More for Food in Flood," *The New York Times*, Feb. 21, 1929, 8: 7.
29. Vadstena, Berning 1918–31, telegram from A.D. Berning to Ivar Kreuger, Feb. 22, 1929.
30. Vadstena, Berning 1918–31, telegram from A.D. Berning to Ivar Kreuger, Mar. 3, 1929.
31. Vadstena, Berning 1918–31, telegram from Ivar Kreuger to A.D. Berning, Mar. 4, 1929.
32. Princeton, Box 2, Kreuger & Toll Syndicate Letter, Lee Higginson & Co.,

Guaranty Company of New York, The National City Company, Brown Brothers & Co., Dillon, Read & Co., Clark, Dodge & Co., and The Union Trust Company of Pittsburgh, Mar. 6, 1929, at 1–3.

33. Vadstena, Berning 1918–31, letter from A.D. Berning to Ivar Kreuger, May 8, 1929.

34. Vadstena, Berning 1918–31, letter from A.D. Berning to Ivar Kreuger, May 8, 1929.

35. Vadstena, Berning 1918–31, letter from A.D. Berning to Ivar Kreuger, May 8, 1929.

36. Vadstena, Berning 1918–31, letter from A.D. Berning to Ivar Kreuger, May 8, 1929.

37. Vadstena, Berning 1918–31, letter from A.D. Berning to Ivar Kreuger, Jul. 23, 1929.

38. "Albert Berning, Accountant, 84," *The New York Times*, Oct. 20, 1970.

39. Riksarkivet, Kreuger & Toll, vol. 0131, ser. F II a/b 1, Consolidated Balance Sheets and Income Accounts, Continental Investment Aktiengesellschaft and Certain of International Match Corporation's Subsidiaries, Dec. 31, 1928.

40. "Donald Durant Elected," *The New York Times*, May 2, 1929, 46: 1.

41. Vadstena, Berning 1918–31, memorandum from A.D. Berning to Donald Durant, undated.

42. Vadstena, Berning 1918–31, memorandum from A.D. Berning to Donald Durant, undated.

43. Vadstena, Berning 1918–31, memorandum from A.D. Berning to Donald Durant, undated.

44. Vadstena, Berning 1918–31, memorandum from A.D. Berning to Donald Durant, undated.

45. Vadstena, Berning 1918–31, letter from A.D. Berning to Ivar Kreuger, undated.

46. Vadstena, Berning 1918–31, letter from Ivar Kreuger to A.D. Berning, Aug. 16, 1929.

47. Vadstena, Berning 1918–31, letter from Ivar Kreuger to A.D. Berning, Aug. 16, 1929.

48. Vadstena, Berning 1918–31, letter from Ernst & Ernst to Brown, Fleming & Murray, Aug. 28, 1929.

49. Vadstena, Berning 1918–31, letter from Ivar Kreuger to A.D. Berning, Sep. 6, 1929.

50. Vadstena, vol. E XXV g: 23, letter from Isaac Marcosson to Ivar Kreuger, Apr. 15, 1929.

51. Vadstena, vol. E XXV g: 23, letter from Isaac Marcosson to Ivar Kreuger, Jun. 17, 1929.

52. Vadstena, vol. E XXV g: 23, letter from Isaac Marcosson to Ivar Kreuger, Aug. 23, 1929.

53. Galbraith, at 45.

54. Galbraith, at 59.

55. Galbraith, at 92.

56. Galbraith, at 66.

57. Galbraith, at 70.

58. Marcosson, at 29.

59. "Monopolist," *Time*, Oct. 28, 1929, at 46.

Chapter 9

1. Wikander, at 167.

2. "German Press Halts Match Monopoly," *The New York Times*, Sep. 29, 1929, 7: 1.

3. Wikander, at 172.

4. Thunholm, at 115.

5. "Match Monopoly Near in Germany," *The New York Times*, Oct. 11, 1929, 8: 1.

6. "Germans Hear Terms of Match Monopoly," *The New York Times*, Oct. 13, 1929, II, 1: 3.

7. Wikander, at 190.

8. Thunholm, at 118.

9. Soloveychik, at 22.

10. The Morgan Library, J. P. Morgan, Jr, papers, Box 38, cable from Jack Morgan to J. P. Morgan, Jr, Aug. 30, 1929.

11. The Morgan Library, J. P. Morgan, Jr, papers, Box 37, cable from Jack Morgan to Schacht, Oct. 16, 1929.

12. The Morgan Library, J. P. Morgan, Jr, papers, Box 38A, cable from Jack Morgan to J. S. Morgan, Jr, Oct. 17, 1929.

13. The Morgan Library, J. P. Morgan, Jr, papers, Box 38A, cable from J. S. Morgan, Jr, to Jack Morgan, Oct. 17, 1929.

14. The Morgan Library, J. P. Morgan, Jr, papers, Box 38A, cable from T. W. Lamont to Jack Morgan (London), Oct. 22, 1929.

15. Galbraith, at 97.

16. Galbraith, at 98–101.

17. Galbraith, at 102.

18. The Morgan Library, Morgan Bank European and Argentinean Records, Series 4, J. P. Morgan, Jr, Personal Cable File, Box 23, cable from Denkstein to Jack Morgan, Oct. 24, 1929.

19. Thunholm, at 122.

20. Thunholm, at 122.

21. Princeton, Box 9, letter from Donald Durant to Mr Quier, May 1, 1930.

22. Princeton, Box 9, cable from Donald Durant to Joseph R. Swan, Oct. 25, 1929 (enclosing cable from Ivar Kreuger).

23. Galbraith, at 94.

24. Princeton, Box 9, cable from Joseph R. Swan to Donald Durant, Oct. 25, 1929.

25. Princeton, Box 8, German 6% External Loan, cable from Donald Durant to Ivar Kreuger, Oct. 22, 1929.

26. Princeton, Box 8, cable from G. Bergenstrable to Lee Higginson & Co., Nov. 18, 1929 (calculating total commissions to Lee Higginson of $1,383,802.87).

27. Princeton, Box 8, German 6% External Loan, cable from Ivar Kreuger to Donald Durant, Oct. 25, 1929.

28. Thunholm, at 123.

29. Shaplen, at 137.

30. The Morgan Library, J. P. Morgan, Jr, papers, Box 37, cable from 29/2523 for Jack Morgan, Oct. 24, 1929 (sent at 10 a.m.).

31. The Morgan Library, J. P. Morgan, Jr, papers, Box 37, cable from 29/5049 for J. P. Morgan, Oct. 24, 1929 (sent at 3.15 p.m.).

32. The Morgan Library, J. P. Morgan, Jr, papers, Box 37, cable from Jack Morgan to 29/5056, Oct. 25, 1929.

33. The Morgan Library, J. P. Morgan, Jr, papers, Box 37, cable from Jack Morgan to 29/5058, Oct. 26, 1929.

34. The Morgan Library, J. P. Morgan, Jr, papers, Box 37, cable from Jack Morgan to N. Dean Jay, Oct. 24, 1929.

35. The Morgan Library, J. P. Morgan, Jr, papers, Box 38A, cable from Jack Morgan (London) to Junius Morgan, Oct. 26, 1929.

36. Galbraith, at 94.

37. Galbraith, at 109–12.

38. The Morgan Library, Morgan Bank European and Argentinean Records, Series 4, J. P. Morgan, Jr, Box 23, cable from Jack Morgan to Denkstein, Oct. 30, 1929.

39. "Reich Match Loan Brings $125,000,000," *The New York Times*, Oct. 22, 1929, at 10: 4.

40. Soloveychik, at 111–12.

41. The Morgan Library, Morgan Bank European and Argentinean Records, Series 4, J. P. Morgan, Jr, Box 23, cable from J. P. Morgan to Denkstein, Oct. 31, 1929.

42. Vadstena, Dondurant II nov–dec 1929, dondurant 1930, cable from Ivar Kreuger to Donald Durant, Nov. 5, 1929.

43. "Granesberg Back to 17%," *The New York Times*, Nov. 30, 1929, 32: 5.

44. Vadstena, Bökman, letter from E. C. Oakley, Whinney, Murray, Baguley & Co., Chartered Accountants (Berlin) to Karin Bökman, Nov. 1, 1929.

45. Vadstena, vol. E XXV g: 23, letter from Isaac F. Marcosson to Ivar Kreuger, Nov. 22, 1929.

46. Vadstena, vol. E XXV g: 23, letter from Ivar Kreuger to Isaac F. Marcosson, Nov. 5, 1929.

47. "A Storm Unforeseen, Always About to Pass," *The New York Times*, Week in Review, Oct. 12, 2008, at 5.

48. Barry Paris, *Garbo* (Alfred A. Knopf, 1995), at 171.

49. Barry Paris, *Garbo* (Alfred A. Knopf, 1995), at 169.

50. Wikander, at 209–10.

51. "Greeter," *Time*, May 26, 1930; Soloveychik, at 24.

52. Soloveychik, at 23.

53. Vadstena, Bökman, letter from Svenska Tändsticks Aktiebolaget to the Consulate General of the United States, Apr. 14, 1930.

54. Vadstena, vol. E XXV g: 23, letter from Katharine von Rosenberg to Ivar Kreuger, Dec. 12, 1929.

55. Soloveychik, at 25.

56. Vadstena, vol. E XXV g: 23, letter from Ivar Kreuger to Wilma Waite, Dec. 21, 1929.

57. Vadstena, Dondurant II nov–dec 1929, dondurant 1930, cable from Ivar Kreuger to Donald Durant, Mar. 1, 1930.

58. Vadstena, Dondurant II nov–dec 1929, dondurant 1930, cable from Donald Durant to Ivar Kreuger, Apr. 5, 1930.

59. Vadstena, Dondurant II nov–dec 1929, dondurant 1930, letter from Ivar Kreuger to Donald Durant, Aug. 29, 1930.

60. Princeton, Box 9, cable from Donald Durant to John D. Harrison, Guaranty Company of New York, Mar. 21, 1930.

61. Vadstena, Berning 1918–31, cable from Ivar Kreuger to A.D. Berning, Jan. 25, 1930.

62. Vadstena, Berning 1918–31, draft memorandum of A.D. Berning, Dec. 23, 1929.

63. Vadstena, Berning 1918–31, letter from Ivar Kreuger to A.D. Berning, Feb. 1, 1930.

64. Vadstena, Berning 1918–31, telegram from A.D. Berning to Ivar Kreuger, Mar. 1, 1930.

65. Vadstena, Berning 1918–31, memorandum from A.D. Berning to J. I. Spens, Jun. 7, 1930.

66. Stoneman, at 73.

67. Stoneman, at 74.

Chapter 10

1. Stoneman, at 203.
2. "Glorified I.O.U.s," *Time*, Apr. 28, 1930.
3. Wikander, at 33, 35, 39.
4. Princeton, Box 6, Special Investment Analysis, Confidential Bulletin AB-8-16, McNeel's Financial Service, Apr. 21, 1930.
5. Wikander, at 28.
6. Stanley Jackson, *J. P. Morgan: The Rise and Fall of a Banker* (William Heinemann, 1983).
7. Thunholm, at 187.
8. Shaplen, at 147.
9. Wikander, at 28.
10. Shaplen, at 147.
11. Shaplen, at 145.
12. "Kreuger was 'Fine,' Says Woman Friend," *The New York Times*, Apr. 24, 1932, at 9.
13. Vadstena, Berning 1918–31, letter from A.D. Berning to Karin Bökman, Nov. 10, 1930.
14. Vadstena, Berning 1918–31, telegram from Ivar Kreuger to A.D. Berning, Nov. 29, 1930.
15. Vadstena, Berning 1918–31, telegram from Ivar Kreuger to A.D. Berning, Dec. 2, 1930.
16. Shaplen, at 146.
17. Princeton, Box 8, German 6% External Loan, cable from Lee Higginson to Kreuger & Toll Syndicate, Mar. 21, 1930.
18. Princeton, Box 8, German 6% External Loan, cable from Ivar Kreuger to Donald Durant, Dec. 29, 1930.
19. Princeton, Box 8, Examination of Donald Durant, In the Matter of Aktiebolaget Kreuger & Toll, Feb. 14, 1935, at 51.
20. Princeton, Box 8, Examination of Donald Durant, In the Matter of Aktiebolaget Kreuger & Toll, Feb. 14, 1935, at 53.
21. Princeton, Box 8, German 6% External Loan, cable from Skandinaviska Kreditaktiebolaget to Lee Higginson & Co., Dec. 29, 1930.
22. Vadstena, Berning 1918–31, letter from A.D. Berning to Ivar Kreuger, Dec. 8, 1930.
23. Vadstena, Berning 1918–31, letter from A.D. Berning to Ivar Kreuger, Dec. 8, 1930.
24. Vadstena, Berning 1918–31, letter from Ivar Kreuger to A.D. Berning, Feb. 11, 1931.

25. Vadstena, Berning 1918–31, memorandum from A.D. Berning to Ivar Kreuger, Dec. 6, 1930.

26. Stoneman, at 128.

27. Shaplen, at 149.

28. Shaplen, at 150.

29. Thunholm, at 195.

30. Vadstena, Berning 1918–31, telegram from A.D. Berning to Ivar Kreuger, Mar. 25, 1931.

31. Vadstena, Berning 1918–31, memorandum from A.D. Berning to Ivar Kreuger, Jan. 30, 1931; Vadstena, Berning 1918–31, letter from Ivar Kreuger to A.D. Berning, Feb. 11, 1931.

32. Thunholm, at 197.

33. Vadstena, Berning 1918–31, letter from A.D. Berning to Ivar Kreuger, Mar. 12, 1928.

34. Shaplen, at 126.

35. Vadstena, Berning 1918–31, telegram from Ivar Kreuger to A.D. Berning, Jul. 23, 1931.

36. Shaplen, at 152.

37. Vadstena, Berning 1918–31, telegram from Ivar Kreuger to A.D. Berning, May 13, 1931.

38. Shaplen, at 154.

39. Princeton, Box 6, Report of Edward S. Greenbaum, In the Matter of Aktiebolaget Kreuger & Toll, Mar. 5, 1934.

40. Shaplen, at 155.

41. Shaplen, at 156.

42. Riksarkivet, vol. 304, letter from Kreuger & Toll to Colonel Sosthenes Behn (IT&T), Apr. 6, 1932.

43. Riksarkivet, vol. 304, cable from American Kreuger & Toll to Lee Higginson, Jun. 18, 1931.

44. Vadstena, Berning 1918–31, letter from Donald Durant to Ivar Kreuger, Apr. 23, 1931.

45. Vadstena, Berning 1918–31, letter from Donald Durant to Ivar Kreuger, Apr. 23, 1931.

46. Vadstena, Berning 1918–31, letter from Donald Durant to Ivar Kreuger, Apr. 23, 1931.

47. Vadstena, Higginson: New York (Dondurant), 1931, cable from Ivar Kreuger to Donald Durant, Apr. 4, 1931.

48. Vadstena, Higginson: New York (Dondurant), 1931, letter from Donald Durant to Ivar Kreuger, May 30, 1931.

49. Vadstena, Higginson: New York (Dondurant), 1931, letter from Donald Durant to Ivar Kreuger, Jul. 1, 1931.

50. Stoneman, at 129.

51. Stoneman, at 130–31.

52. Princeton, Box 3, memorandum to S. A. Russell, Lee Higginson, Jul. 3, 1931.

53. Princeton, Box 3, letter from Donald Durant to Ivar Kreuger, Aug. 5, 1931, at 2.

54. Princeton, Box 3, letter from Ivar Kreuger to Donald Durant, Oct. 12, 1931, at 2.

55. Stoneman, at 130.

56. Princeton, Box 3, letter from Donald Durant to Ivar Kreuger, Nov. 1, 1931, at 1.

57. Princeton, Box 6, Summary of Testimony, In the Matter of Aktiebolaget Kreuger & Toll, US District Court, Southern District of New York, Feb. 6, 1933, at 4–5.

58. Vadstena, Berning 1918–31, letter from A.D. Berning to Ivar Kreuger, Oct. 30, 1931.

59. Vadstena, Berning 1918–31, telegram from Ivar Kreuger to A.D. Berning, Nov. 12, 1931.

60. Riksarkivet, vol. 0131, ser. F II a/b 1, Consolidated Balance Sheet, International Match Corporation and Constituent Companies, Dec. 31, 1930, at 2.

61. Vadstena, Berning 1918–31, letter from A.D. Berning to Ivar Kreuger, May 7, 1931.

62. Vadstena, Berning 1918–31, cable from A.D. Berning to Ivar Kreuger, May. 12, 1931.

63. Thunholm, at 202.

64. Thunholm, at 202–3.

65. Thunholm, at 206.

66. Thunholm, at 208.

67. "Exploring the Kreuger Legend," *The New York Times* magazine, Jul. 24, 1932, at 1.

68. Shaplen, at 167.

69. Vadstena, K. Littorin 1931–2, cable from Krister Littorin to Ivar Kreuger, Nov. 24, 1931.

70. Shaplen, at 166.

71. Vadstena, vol. E XXV g: 62, cable from Krister Littorin to Ivar Kreuger, Sep. 19, 1931.

72. Vadstena, K. Littorin 1931–2, cable from Krister Littorin to Ivar Kreuger, Feb. 27, 1931.

73. Vadstena, K. Littorin 1931–2, cable from Krister Littorin to Ivar Kreuger, Apr. 13, 1931.

74. Vadstena, vol. E XXV g: 62, cable from Krister Littorin to Ivar Kreuger, Oct. 27, 1931.

75. Vadstena, vol. E XXV g: 62, cable from Krister Littorin to Ivar Kreuger, Oct. 28, 1931.

76. Vadstena, vol. E XXV g: 62, cable from Krister Littorin to Ivar Kreuger, Nov. 24, 1931.

77. Vadstena, K. Littorin 1931–2, cable from Krister Littorin to Ivar Kreuger, Nov. 26, 1931.

78. Vadstena, K. Littorin 1931–2, cable from Krister Littorin to Ivar Kreuger, Nov. 26, 1931.

79. Vadstena, K. Littorin 1931–2, cable from Krister Littorin to Ivar Kreuger, Nov. 30, 1931.

80. Vadstena, K. Littorin 1931–2, cable from Krister Littorin to Ivar Kreuger, Nov. 30, 1931.

81. Shaplen, at 163.

82. Vadstena, Higginson: New York (Dondurant), 1931, cable from Donald Durant to Ivar Kreuger, Oct. 1931.

83. Vadstena, Higginson: New York (Dondurant), 1931, numerous cables.

84. Vadstena, Higginson: New York (Dondurant), 1931, cable from Ivar Kreuger to George Murnane, Aug. 14, 1931.

85. Vadstena, Higginson: New York (Dondurant), 1931, cable from Ivar Kreuger to George Murnane, Aug. 14, 1931.

86. Shaplen, at 169–70.

87. "Kreuger Forgeries Laid to Loan Deal," *The New York Times*, Apr. 27, 1932, at 5.

88. "Untermyer to Sift Kreuger Concerns," *The New York Times*, Apr. 23, 1932, at 23.

89. "Kreuger was 'Fine,' Says Woman Friend," *The New York Times*, Apr. 24, 1932, at 9.

90. Shaplen, at 172.

91. Vadstena, K. Littorin 1931–2, cable from Krister Littorin to Ivar Kreuger, Nov. 30, 1931.

92. Vadstena, vol. E XXV g: 62, cable from Krister Littorin to Ivar Kreuger, Dec. 19, 1931.

93. "Coincidence," *New York Herald Tribune*, December 23, 1931.

Chapter 11

1. "Kreuger Reassured Americans After Talk with Hoover Jan. 7," *The New York Times*, Mar. 13, 1932, at 1.

2. Thunholm, at 217.

3. Thunholm, at 215.

4. Shaplen, at 181.

5. Vadstena, K. Littorin 1931–2, cable from Ivar Kreuger to Krister Littorin, Dec. 26, 1931.

6. Shaplen, at 181.

7. Vadstena, K. Littorin 1931–2, cable from Ivar Kreuger to Krister Littorin, Feb. 16, 1932.

8. Soloveychik, at 143.

9. Vadstena, K. Littorin 1931–2, cable from Ivar Kreuger to Krister Littorin, Feb. 16, 1932.

10. Shaplen, at 192–3.

11. Thunholm, at 220.

12. Edna Ferber, *A Kind of Magic* (Doubleday, 1963).

13. Soloveychik, at 33–4.

14. Shaplen, at 194.

15. Vadstena, K. Littorin 1931–2, cable from Ivar Kreuger to Krister Littorin, Feb. 16, 1932.

16. Edna Ferber, *A Peculiar Treasure* (Doubleday, 1938).

17. Shaplen, at 194–5.

18. Thunholm, at 219.

19. Vadstena, vol. E XXV g: 23, cable from Krister Littorin to Ivar Kreuger, Feb. 27, 1932.

20. Vadstena, K. Littorin 1931–2, cable from Krister Littorin to Ivar Kreuger, Feb. 23, 1932.

21. Princeton, Box 3, letter from International Match Corporation to Lee Higginson, Feb. 27, 1932; Minutes of Special Meeting of Executive Committee, International Match Corporation, Feb. 27, 1932.

22. Princeton, Price Waterhouse & Co., reported dated August 26, 1932, on German Reich 50 Year 6% External Gold Loan 1930 being Annex "B" to the Main Report, at 13.

23. Princeton, Box 8, letter from A.D. Berning to Ivar Kreuger, Jan. 6, 1932.

24. Princeton, Edward S. Greenbaum Interview Notes, vol. 2, at 25.

25. Vadstena, K. Littorin 1931–2, cable from Krister Littorin to Ivar Kreuger, Feb. 28, 1932.

26. Vadstena, vol. E XXV g: 62, cable from Krister Littorin to Ivar Kreuger, Mar. 2, 1932.

27. Marcosson, at 26–9.

28. Princeton, Box 8, letter from Sherwin C. Badger to Alexis Aminoff, Jan. 19, 1932.

29. Princeton, Box 8, letter from Karl A. Bickel to Ivar Kreuger, Feb. 11, 1932.

30. Marcosson, ch. 2.

31. Marcosson, at 26.

32. "Marcosson Tells of Kreuger's Aims," *The New York Times*, Mar. 13, 1932, at 1.

33. Princeton, Box 14, translation of statement by A.B. Kreuger & Toll, Oct. 2, 1934, at 118.

34. Marcosson, at 27.

35. Marcosson, "An Interview with Ivar Kreuger," at 86.

36. Vadstena, vol. E XXV g: 62, cable from Krister Littorin to Ivar Kreuger ("passenger ss Iledefrance Lehavreradio"), Mar. 8, 1932; "Kreuger Withdrew $60,000 on Last Visit," *The New York Times*, Jul. 1, 1932, at 33.

37. Riksarkivet, vol. 805, Alexis Aminoff Special Accounts.

38. Barry Paris, *Garbo* (Alfred A. Knopf, 1995), at 84.

39. Soloveychik, at 148.

40. Soloveychik, at 149.

41. Thunholm, at 288.

42. Stoneman, at 236.

43. Soloveychik, at 150.

44. Soloveychik, at 151–3; Stoneman, at 233–4.

45. "Sweden Plans to Save Kreuger Business," *The New York Times*, Mar. 13, 1932, at 2.

46. Soloveychik, at 152–3.

Chapter 12

1. Stoneman, at 236–7.

2. Stoneman, at 234–8; Soloveychik, at 153–5; Shaplen, at 218–22; Churchill, at 255–9.

3. Shaplen, at 220–21.

4. R. Blake Stevens, *The Browning High Power Automatic Pistol* (Collector Grade Publications, 1990).

5. Thunholm, at 227.

6. Soloveychik, at 156.

7. Soloveychik, at 31–2.

8. "Trustee Satisfied Kreuger is Dead," *The New York Times*, Jan. 26, 1933, at 6.

9. "Sleeping," *Time*, Mar. 21, 1932.

10. Stoneman, at 238.

11. Adams, at 264.

12. Testimony of Donald Durant, at 1208.

13. "Poor Kreuger," *Time*, Mar. 21, 1932.

14. Shaplen, at 227.

15. Shaplen, at 228.

16. Stoneman, at 240–42; Churchill, at 267–9.

17. "Market Sags Here on Kreuger Selling," *The New York Times*, Mar. 15, 1932, at 15.

Chapter 13

1. "Sweden Plans to Save Kreuger Business," *The New York Times*, Mar. 14, 1932, at 2.
2. "King of Sweden to End Holiday Because of Kreuger's Suicide," *The New York Times*, Mar. 15, 1932, at 15; Soloveychik, at 164.
3. "Woman Seeks Cash Kreuger Promised Her; His Final Gift of $65,000 Stock is Worthless," *The New York Times*, Apr. 25, 1932, at 6.
4. "Untermyer to Sift Kreuger Concerns," *The New York Times*, Apr. 23, 1932, at 23.
5. "Kreuger Was 'Fine,' Says Woman Friend," *The New York Times*, Apr. 24, 1932, at 9.
6. "Markets in London, Paris and Berlin," *The New York Times*, Mar. 17, 1932, at 33.
7. "Find Kreuger Books are 'Grossly Wrong,' Some Assets False," *The New York Times*, Apr. 6, 1932, at 1.
8. Stoneman, at 244.
9. "Secret X-Y-Z Grants Claimed by Kreuger," *The New York Times*, May 5, 1932, at 28.
10. "Ivar Kreuger's 'Waste Paper' Helping to Reveal Secrets," *The New York Times*, Jun. 13, 1932, at 7.
11. Flesher & Flesher, at 426–30.
12. "600 Dealers Here Sold Kreuger Issue," *The New York Times*, Jun. 21, 1932, at 33.
13. Testimony of Donald Durant, at 1155.
14. "Why the House of Kreuger Fell," at 40.
15. "Man Who Trapped Kreuger Describes Deals to Senators," *The New York Times*, Jan. 12, 1933, at 1.
16. Stock Exchange Practices, at 1255.
17. "Whitney Says Short Sales Saved Market Last Fall," *The New York Times*, Apr. 19, 1932, at 1.
18. Stock Exchange Practices, at 1357.
19. Stock Exchange Practices, at 1271.
20. Congressional Record, Jul. 13, 1932, at 15201.
21. Taylor, at 194.
22. Stock Exchange Practices, at 1355.
23. Austin, at 6.
24. Princeton, Box 1, Report of Gordon Auchincloss, Esq., Trustee in Bankruptcy,

In the Matter of Aktiebolaget Kreuger & Toll, US District Court, Southern District of New York, Feb. 6, 1933, at 7.

25. Princeton, Box 1, Fifth Intermediate Report and Account of Edward S. Greenbaum, Esq., Trustee in Bankruptcy, In the Matter of Aktiebolaget Kreuger & Toll, US District Court, Southern District of New York, Oct. 24, 1936, at 3.

26. "Why the House of Kreuger Fell," at 40.

27. Riksarkivet, vol. 434, cable from Lee Higginson to American Kreuger & Toll, Mar. 16, 1932.

28. "Moratorium Urged for Kreuger & Toll," *The New York Times*, Mar. 26, 1932, at 21; "Attach Funds Here of Kreuger & Toll," *The New York Times*, Mar. 30, 1932, at 25.

29. Princeton, Box 8, letter from Lee Higginson to the holders of securities of Kreuger & Toll Company and International Match Corporation, Mar. 17, 1932, at 1.

30. Princeton, Box 8, letter from Lee Higginson to the holders of securities of Kreuger & Toll Company and International Match Corporation, Mar. 17, 1932, at 2–3.

31. Princeton, Box 8, letter from Lee Higginson to the holders of securities of Kreuger & Toll Company and International Match Corporation, Mar. 17, 1932, at 2.

32. Princeton, Box 14, translation of statement by A.B. Kreuger & Toll, Oct. 2, 1934, at 113; "Kreuger's Juggling of Millions: An Amazing Story Now Unfolds," *The New York Times*, May 22, 1932, at 3.

33. "New Kreuger Deal by Swedish Match," *The New York Times*, Apr. 23, 1936, at 33.

34. Princeton, Box 7, Stab *v.* Kreuger & Toll, In the Matter of Aktiebolaget Kreuger & Toll, No. 54418, Feb. 4, 1933.

35. Lindgren, at 311.

36. http://www.swedishmatch.com/en/Our-company/Company-history/Svenska-Tandsticks-AB/.

37. http://www.swedishmatch.com/cn/Our-company/Our-company-in-brief/.

38. Princeton, Box 14, translation of statement by A.B. Kreuger & Toll, Oct. 2, 1934, at 87.

39. "Poor Kreuger," *Time*, Mar. 21, 1932.

40. Princeton, Box 8, letter from Edmund J. Port, Worthing Whitehouse Company to Kreuger & Toll, Apr. 20, 1932.

41. Princeton, Box 8, German 6% External Loan, cable from Reichsschuldenverwaltung, Berlin to Aktiebolaget Kreuger & Toll, Jan. 19, 1932.

42. Wikander, at 215.
43. "Ivar Kreuger's Monument," *The New York Times*, Mar. 20, 1932, at 10X.
44. "Kreuger's Home is Sold," *The New York Times*, Aug. 21, 1932, at 4F.
45. "Fantastically High Prices Paid for Kreuger Effects at Sale," *The New York Times*, Sep. 10, at 17.
46. "Move to Protect Kreuger Holdings," *The New York Times*, May 7, 1932, at 23.
47. Stoneman, at 247.
48. Stoneman, at 247.
49. "Trustee of International Match Reports Income Exceeds Expenses by $1,315,000," *The New York Times*, Apr. 2, 1934, at 25.
50. "International Match Gets Refund of Taxes Paid on Fictitious Earnings Under Kreuger," *The New York Times*, May 5, 1939, at 35.
51. "15,000 Checks to Go Out for International Match," *The New York Times*, Oct. 20, 1936, at 37.
52. "Kreuger's Trail," *Time*, Sep. 5, 1932.
53. Stoneman, at 137.
54. Princeton, Box 1, Fifth Intermediate Report and Account of Edward S. Greenbaum, Esq., Trustee in Bankruptcy, In the Matter of Aktiebolaget Kreuger & Toll, US District Court, Southern District of New York, Oct. 24, 1936, at 25–7.
55. "Kreuger's 'Empire' Reviewed by Bank," *The New York Times*, Oct. 24, 1945, at 29.
56. "Bankers at Work," *Time*, May 23, 1932.
57. "High Finance: The House of Matches," *Time*, Nov. 5, 1945, at 89.
58. "Match Creditors Realize 51.5%," *The New York Times*, Nov. 16, 1937, at 37.
59. "Kreuger Creditors to Get 23% Dividend," *The New York Times*, Mar. 2, 1937, at 36.
60. Princeton, Box 1, Fifth Intermediate Report and Account of Edward S. Greenbaum, Esq., Trustee in Bankruptcy, In the Matter of Aktiebolaget Kreuger & Toll, US District Court, Southern District of New York, Oct. 24, 1936, at 55, Exhibit 1.
61. Princeton, Box 1, Fifth Intermediate Report and Account of Edward S. Greenbaum, Esq., Trustee in Bankruptcy, In the Matter of Aktiebolaget Kreuger & Toll, US District Court, Southern District of New York, Oct. 24, 1936, at 51; "Untermyer to Sift Kreuger Concerns," *The New York Times*, Apr. 23, 1932, at 23.
62. "Bankers at Work," *Time*, May 23, 1932.
63. "Bankers at Work," *Time*, May 23, 1932.

64. "Many Banks Hold Kreuger Securities," *The New York Times*, Aug. 13, 1932, at 19.

65. "Kreuger's Brother Sentenced to 3 ½ Years at Hard Labor," *The New York Times*, Dec. 18, 1932, at 1.

66. "Acquitted in Kreuger Case," *The New York Times*, Jan. 28, 1933, at 7.

67. "Says Power Sapped Reason of Kreuger," *The New York Times*, Apr. 22, 1932, at 5.

68. "Albert Berning, Accountant, 84," *The New York Times*, Oct. 20, 1970.

69. Princeton, Box 2, Anders Jordahl and Mary D. Jordahl *v*. Irving Trust Company, *et al.*, United States Circuit Court of Appeals for the Third Circuit Dec. 19, 1933, at 2–3

70. Princeton, Box 2, safe deposit box records, undated.

71. Princeton, Box 2, transcript of telephone conversation between Anders Jordahl and Edward Greenbaum, Mar. 15, 1935, at 1.

72. "The Real Estate Field," *The New York Times*, Mar. 17, 1915, at 18.

73. "Durant, Financier, Dies on Elevated," *The New York Times*, Aug. 12, 1941, at 20.

74. "Three are Arrested in Kreuger Inquiry," *The New York Times*, Apr. 16, 1932, at 2.

75. Princeton, Box 14, translation of statement by A.B. Kreuger & Toll, Oct. 2, 1934, at 39.

76. Princeton, Box 14, translation of statement by A.B. Kreuger & Toll, Oct. 2, 1934, at 4–6, 18–24, 35, 41, 104–10; "Kreuger's Board Sued in Sweden," *The New York Times*, Oct. 16, 1932, at 26.

77. Rydbeck, at 322.

78. "Kreuger's Board Sued in Sweden," *The New York Times*, Oct. 16, 1932, at 26.

79. Whyte, at 466.

80. Allen, at 89.

81. "Alfonso Denies Deal," *The New York Times*, Apr. 20, 1932, at 5.

82. "Stockholm Suspects Kreuger Blackmail," *The New York Times*, Apr. 18, 1932, at 8.

83. "Kreuger Gift Ousts Premier of Sweden," *The New York Times*, Aug. 7, 1932, at 3.

84. "600 Dealers Here Sold Kreuger Issue," *The New York Times*, Jun. 21, 1932, at 33.

85. Riksarkivet, vol. 806, Alexis Aminoff Office Accounts.

86. Riksarkivet, vol. 805, Alexis Aminoff Special Accounts.

87. Riksarkivet, vol. 805, Alexis Aminoff Special Accounts.

88. Flynn, at 37.

89. "How Kreuger Myth Swayed Banks Told," *The New York Times*, May 12, 1932, at 5.

90. Stoneman, at 139.

91. "The Diamond Match Co.," at 170.

92. "Lee Higginson Men Quit Kreuger Group," *The New York Times*, May 20, 1932, at 42.

93. Sven-Hugo Borg, "The Only True Story of Greta Garbo's Private Life," http://www.greta-garbo.de/private-life-of-greta-garbo-by-sven-hugo-borg/22-greta-garbo-and-the-match-king.htm.

94. Barry Paris, *Garbo* (Alfred A. Knopf, 1995), at 179.

95. Barry Paris, *Garbo* (Alfred A. Knopf, 1995), at 283.

96. Barry Paris, *Garbo* (Alfred A. Knopf, 1995), at 285.

97. Barry Paris, *Garbo* (Alfred A. Knopf, 1995), at 286.

98. "Paris Denies Hoax in Kreuger Suicide," *The New York Times*, Apr. 19, at 5.

99. "People," *Time*, Jun. 17, 1935.

100. Thompson and Gates, at 6.

Chapter 14

1. Stoneman, at 45.

2. Soloveychik, at 65.

3. Churchill, at 29.

4. "The Kreuger Saga," at 564.

5. Stolpe; Ångström.

6. Thunholm, at 231.

7. See "Ivar Kreuger: The Prince of the First Global Finance State," http://www.qikrux.com/kreuger/.

8. Shaplen, at 229.

9. "Kreuger Truly Dead, Say French Police," *The New York Times*, Mar. 19, 1933, at 31.

10. Lazar, at 46.

11. Lazar, at 46.

12. Soloveychik, at 47.

13. "Al Capone Bound for Atlanta Prison," *The New York Times*, May 4, 1932, at 1.

14. Lambert.

A note on sources and acknowledgements

1. Galbraith, "How to Become an International Swindler."

INDEX

FERGUS GREER

Frank Partnoy is the author of *F.I.A.S.C.O.: Blood in the Water on Wall Street* and *Infectious Greed: How Deceit and Risk Corrupted the Financial Markets.* He has worked as an investment banker at Morgan Stanley and as a corporate lawyer, and he has testified as an expert before both the United States Senate and House of Representatives. A graduate of Yale Law School, he is the George E. Barrett Professor of Law and Finance at the University of San Diego.

PublicAffairs is a publishing house founded in 1997. It is a tribute to the standards, values, and flair of three persons who have served as mentors to countless reporters, writers, editors, and book people of all kinds, including me.

I. F. STONE, proprietor of *I. F. Stone's Weekly*, combined a commitment to the First Amendment with entrepreneurial zeal and reporting skill and became one of the great independent journalists in American history. At the age of eighty, Izzy published *The Trial of Socrates*, which was a national bestseller. He wrote the book after he taught himself ancient Greek.

BENJAMIN C. BRADLEE was for nearly thirty years the charismatic editorial leader of *The Washington Post*. It was Ben who gave the *Post* the range and courage to pursue such historic issues as Watergate. He supported his reporters with a tenacity that made them fearless and it is no accident that so many became authors of influential, best-selling books.

ROBERT L. BERNSTEIN, the chief executive of Random House for more than a quarter century, guided one of the nation's premier publishing houses. Bob was personally responsible for many books of political dissent and argument that challenged tyranny around the globe. He is also the founder and longtime chair of Human Rights Watch, one of the most respected human rights organizations in the world.

•   •   •

For fifty years, the banner of Public Affairs Press was carried by its owner Morris B. Schnapper, who published Gandhi, Nasser, Toynbee, Truman, and about 1,500 other authors. In 1983, Schnapper was described by *The Washington Post* as "a redoubtable gadfly." His legacy will endure in the books to come.

Peter Osnos, *Founder and Editor-at-Large*